YOU ARE NOT

'I Am' is the source of all that 'You' imagine that 'You Are'.
What happens when you look beyond, peeling back,
before and beyond the veils of consciousness or as
Ramana Maharishi says 'go back the way you came'?
Explore 'what is like' when the veil parts and 'you'
'see' with the implicit understanding of
I Am That - You Are Not.

D0862671

YOU ARE NOT

*Beyond the Three Veils
of Consciousness*

STEPHEN H. WOLINSKY

New Age Books

ISBN: 81-7822-261-2

First Indian Edition: Delhi, 2006
(First Published 2002 by Stephen Wolinsky, Quantum Institute Press.)

© 2002 by Stephen H. Wolinsky

All rights reserved: No part of this publication may be reproduced
or transmitted in any form or by any means, electronic or mechanical,
including photocopying, recording, or by any information storage and
retrieval system, without permission in writing from the publishers.

Published by
NEW AGE BOOKS
A-44 Naraina Phase-I
New Delhi-110 028 (INDIA)
Email: nab@vsnl.in
Website: www.newagebooksindia.com

Printed in India
at Shri Jainendra Press
A-45 Naraina Phase-I, New Delhi-110 028

AVADHUT NITYANANDA

DEDICATION

To the memory of Sri Nisargadatta Maharaj, the ultimate
teacher and Guru who demonstrated and taught the
unspoken side of **I AM THAT—YOU ARE NOT.**

To the memory of Avadhut Nityananda, whose initiation
changed the course of "my life."

To the memory of Shirdi Sai Baba;
who "died" in 1918.

To the (Sakyamuni) Buddha,
who was the vehicle for the purest teachings
the world has ever known.

To the memory of Alfred Korzybski,
the father of the Structural Differential.

To the memory of Ramana Maharishi;
"Go back the way you came."

ACKNOWLEDGEMENTS

Gregory Sawin
(for his monograph on the Structural Differential,
and for his editorial support in this massive project)

Bryn Samuels
(word processing)

Ruth Weilert
(word processing)

To my divine Leani;
for everything!!

To Sri Nisargadatta Maharaj
"YOU ARE NOT"

Photos of Ramana Maharishi from
*The Essential Teachings of Ramana Maharshi:
A Visual Journey.*
Reprinted by arrangement with Inner Directions
Publishing, Carlsbad, California. www.InnerDirections.org.
Copyright, Sri Ramanasramam, Tiruvannamalai,
Tamil Nadu, India.

Dingeman Boot, Meinhard Van de Reep
and Alexander Smit for providing me
with photos of Nisargadatta Maharaj.

TABLE OF CONTENTS

PART III
The Veil of Enlightenment:
Beyond the Awarer   **261**

PROLOGUE

"I" remember once being with Nisargadatta Maharaj; and he pointed at people and said, **"YOU ARE NOT."** To understand this phrase, we can begin with the Sanskrit word, **Darshan.** The literal meaning of **Darshan** is a "look," a "view"; and generally refers to the process of going up to a "sage," teacher, guru, etc., to receive a blessing as a way to pierce through this illusion, which is made of **consciousness.** To have a "look" (**Darshan**) behind or beyond this **consciousness,** is what *You Are Not* hopes to "give." The "realization," I AM THAT is the spoken *Darshan.* YOU ARE NOT is the unspoken *Darshan. Darshan* is often associated with an "outer" teacher or guru. However, "inner" *Darshan* is when I AM THAT—YOU ARE NOT is "realized." "I" once heard Baba Muktananda say, "When you discover who you are there will be no reason to get up out of your seat for *Darshan*; you will already have *Darshan.*"

A metaphor to describe this process could be like unraveling gauze (veils). As in H. G. Wells's book, *The Invisible Man,* who takes off the gauze (veils) around his head to find nothing there, is to unwrap the veils of **consciousness** and *apperceive* THAT SUBSTANCE. "There" I AM THAT—YOU ARE NOT "is," as the ultimate *Darshan,* and this is what "we" will attempt to convey. "I" also should include in this prologue the difficulty, if not the impossibility, of language. Language is, by its nature, binary and descriptive; hence, in all language and descriptions, particularly in what we are embarking on, it is important to take note of this: All language, all thoughts, all experiences, descriptions of experiences, including the "I" "you" call "you," are representations. In this way, all language, thoughts, experiences, descriptions of experiences, and the "I" "you" call "you," are stuck in language; hence they can be only metaphors, by their very nature.

In this book, we hope to provide "you" with **Darshan**— a "look" beyond the veils of **consciousness** and enable "you" to *apperceive* the implicit understanding of **I AM THAT**— **YOU ARE NOT** as the "final" *Darshan*.

In India, Lord Siva is depicted as a yogi sitting, with his eyes closed in meditation. But what is the significance of this archetypical metaphor? One can say only that when the eye(s) of Siva are closed, solidified **consciousness** and the illusion of the world **appears**. When the eye(s) of Siva are open, the world, like a **mirage**, vanishes and "the apperception of" the "GREAT VOID" "behind" and "beyond" **consciousness** from which the dream world "*seems to appear*," and upon awakening from a dream this world disappears. William Shakespeare, in *The Tempest*, said it this way: "**We are such stuff as dreams are made of.**"

Another important "understanding" that we will attempt to translate is the often misunderstood word **Nirvana**. Often, people think of **Nirvana** as a heaven or another world where we will go to "get" something—a state, an everlasting experience of bliss, etc. However, *Nirvana means extinction*, and the metaphor of a lit candle which is extinguished can be used to describe **Nirvana**.

This book is not yet another book about *how* to open the "eye(s) of Siva." Rather, it is merely an attempt to explain verbally what happens "when" the veil of this illusion parts (like the Red Sea [Sea or Ocean often is used as a metaphor for the mind]), and **THAT SUBSTANCE** is *apperceived*. This is *Darshan*: The peeling back before, and beyond, the veils of **consciousness**, which is Ramana Maharishi's "**go back the way**

you came" (to be discussed in detail throughout the text).

This book does not attempt to suggest that the world is bad, or made of a different SUBSTANCE than THAT SUBSTANCE. Rather, it is a discussion of "what is" *apperceived* ("looks") like, when the veil parts and "you" "see," (*apperceive*) into the vastness of THAT SUBSTANCE from which the world is made, arises, with its pleasure and pain, and—like a puff of smoke—vanishes, "when" THAT is *realized*.

Beginning a book on the salient understanding of I AM THAT—YOU ARE NOT seemed like the last thing "I" would embark upon. However, whether "I" like it or not, "it" or "THAT," as "I," will continue as "long" as it "does." And "I" as just a shadowy reflection of THAT, a mere particle of cosmic dust, a **mirage**, which did not know it was a **mirage**, a child of a barren woman lets it happen. Often, however, it is asked, "But still even after 'realization' the body **appears** to act and react. How can this be?" The *Bhagavad Gita* explains it this way:

> "Even after the wind has ceased blowing, trees may continue to sway; the fragrance of camphor may remain in a casket even after the camphor has been used up, even when a pattering for a song is over, its moving effect remains; moisture lies on the ground long after water has been poured on it. Even after an arrow is shot, it continues its flight until its momentum is lost. When a potter removes from his wheel the vessel which he has made, the wheel keeps revolving with the force of its spinning... even when the sense of individuality comes to an end, its activity continues." (Jnaneshwar, *Jnaneshwari, a Song-Sermon on the Bhagavad Gita*, p. 259)

This is what "I" attempted to describe to workshop participants several years ago when "I" said that "I" would stop teaching Quantum Psychology. "I" would say "I" feel like "I" am on a freeway going 60 miles per hour, and the car was put in neutral—"I" am just gliding; soon it will stop on its own.

This embarkation, however, is different from the other books in that the premise is YOU ARE NOT, and as such, the only real question is, *what makes "one" imagine that they are?* After investigation, it becomes clear that the root problem "you" have is that "you" imagine that YOU ARE. Why? Because I AM is the "source" (source, not as creator, but where the "I" first shows or posits itself) of all that "you" imagine yourself to be. In this way, to select such a word to describe this, veils or illusions of **consciousness** seemed appropriate. For as THAT ONE SUBSTANCE contracts or condenses, it forms the I AM and all illusions both perceivable or conceivable, which includes not only work, relationships, and, dare "I" say it, the concept of God, spirituality, psychological health, growth, spiritual paths, and even knowingness itself.

However, what must be borne in "mind" is THAT SUBSTANCE of which everything is made, never loses its true nature, but only **appears** as something other than itself. It is as if we used 100 pounds of gold to make a watch, a ring, or a bracelet—still, the underlying SUBSTANCE remains gold.

It is only through the "awar_er_'s" **appearance**, which makes it seem that all of this world is made of different substances, and like a spider (**consciousness**) weaving a web (the world), we **appear** TO BE "as if," WE ARE. It is the **appearance** of condensed **consciousness** (which is THAT SUBSTANCE) that gives the illusion of being made of something other than **consciousness** itself, and gives the illusion that there are many different substances; this is the veil or illusion **made of consciousness**. It seems that each culture has its own concepts or veils or illusions of "I" and "it" which vanish like a **mirage** in the desert as we move closer to investigate it. Soon "we" discover that even the "awar_er_" or awareness has a location in space-time, and hence, as the root of experience, vanishes upon investigation.

The problem of "I" arises because the underpinnings of the "awar*er*" and I AM go unquestioned and uninvestigated, and hence we assume not only that I AM and YOU ARE, but that IT IS; hence, there is "no way out."

What, then, is this book really about? It is about clarifying the underpinnings, understructures—veils—which go unquestioned, and hence, hold **consciousness** solid. In order to do this, the following set of major understandings is where we depart from.

"YOU ARE NOT" MADE SIMPLE

1) There is only ONE SUBSTANCE, call it what "you" will.

2) THE SUBSTANCE contracts or thins out, thus dissolving or appearing, as I AM, YOU ARE, which leads it (the I AM) to imagine that it (the outer world and itself) **are** and **is**.

3) There is a pulsation of appearing and disappearing (in Sanskrit called *spanda*) that underlies and describes this throb, or appearance-disappearance, also called a pulsation.

4) In the contracting of THAT SUBSTANCE, it **appears** to become condensed **consciousness**, of which everything arises, including the "awar*er*"; experiences; the physics dimensions; the earth, sun, moon; stars and galaxies; the body; spiritual paths and spirituality along with the concept of God.

5) When **consciousness** thins out and there is only THAT ONE SUBSTANCE, and hence YOU ARE NOT.

6) There is no **consciousness**.

7) There is no expansion or contraction.

8) There is no underlying principle called *spanda*.
9) There is No thing.
10) **YOU ARE NOT.**

With love
Your **mirage** brother,
Stephen
May 30, 2000
Heading to Amsterdam

INTRODUCTION

Overview of the Three Parts

PART I:
THE BODY AND ITS
ABSTRACTED PSYCHOLOGY

In this section, "I" will begin by isolating the body as an object in space-time, and how it organizes an "I," which "you" call "you." This will lead us to *question* not only the western veils of **consciousness** of both the physics dimensions and the world of psychology, but hopefully, it also will lead us to *dispel* not only the illusion of a solid, stable universe, but also the veils of the psychological world, whose mythology, for many people, has become *the religion of psychology*.

THE VEIL OF THE BODY

We begin by isolating the body as compacted **consciousness**, which forms its condensation, i.e., the nervous system; hence, we explore and demonstrate that the pre-supposed body, pre-ceiver, "I," and "self," imagines *it is*, and has pre-ceptions that arise after the "experience" has already occurred. Moreover, this "I" **appears** through a chemical reaction; and that *before* the I AM, which "you" call "yourself," there is a more fundamental level or microscopic level "where" YOU ARE NOT.

Without prejudice, we will take off the veils of "personal" psychology, which represents the seductive premises, which keep us bound, or better said, keeps the "I" in its belief *it is*.

Finally, with no pre-ceiver, the concepts of even the physics dimensions vanish as the western blindfolds disappear and even YOU ARE NOT or YOU ARE THAT is seen only as a description of "what is"—which is **not** "what is"—or as Korzybski said, "Whatever one might *say* something *"is,"* *it is not*. . . . [because] a word *is not* the object it represents . . ." Illustratively, when Nisargadatta Maharaj was asked, "Who are you?" He replied, "**Nothing perceivable or conceivable.**"

PART II:
THE EASTERN VEILS
OF CONSCIOUSNESS

In this section, exploration into the Eastern veils of consciousness, namely the **forces that organize the world**, which are called *gunas*; and the Buddhist aspects of personality, which are called the *skandas*, will be dismantled **prior to** the moving into, beyond, and through the spiritual veils of **consciousness**.

THE VEIL OF SPIRITUALITY

Within the context of Eastern religions, too, lies the promise of some "realization." A liberation which, when "realized," liberates "one" from the cycle of birth and death; pain and suffering, etc. However, built upon the presupposition of birth and death, all cosmologies, which are *assumptions*, seductively entrap the seeker who believes in the assumption. He or she imagines that somehow "they" or "I" will become liberated and find out WHO I AM. All of these imaginings are based on the existence of a separate "awar_er_," or I AM, which is a fantasy, a chemical reaction caused by electromagnetism moving neurotransmitters. In this way these chemical reactions of Section I will demonstrate that the I AM and the sense of "I" is only a result of chemical reactions, a "coming together of fluids." And with this, how can an "I," merely an outcome of chemical reactions, imagine that it has a purpose, a mission, that it is bound, is spiritual, and can attain something or become liberated. To paraphrase Nisargadatta Maharaj, **it is through fluids and chemicals coming together that the I AM appears; hence, all the troubles.**

PART III:
BEYOND THE "AWAR_ER_"
AND THE ILLUSION OF ENLIGHTENMENT

In this section, we shatter the illusions of the "awar_er_," including ONE SUBSTANCE, veils of **consciousness**, expansion-contraction, the *spanda*, and even the concept of "beyond."

THE VEIL OF ENLIGHTENMENT

In this section, we explore the most implicit subtle and ultimately "realizable" outcome of Advaita Vedanta, Kashmir Shaivism, the *Spanda Karikas*, the Buddhist *Heart Sutra*, the *Yoga Sutras*, and the Buddhist *Diamond Sutra*. Moreover, it reveals the unspoken side of I AM THAT—YOU ARE NOT, and, like a candle being extinguished, the "true" meaning of **Nirvana**.

Without hesitation, therefore, "I" suggest that the reader use prior books, along with the recommended books at the back of *I Am That I Am: A Tribute to Sri Nisargadatta Maharaj*, as a context for this enquiry into the salient side of the "realization," I AM THAT—YOU ARE NOT.

With love, again,
Your **mirage** brother,
Stephen

CHAPTER 1

Why? You Are Not

The first question that arises around a book with a title like *You Are Not: Beyond the Three Veils of Consciousness* is why choose this title? The answer is contained within the thread that will carry us throughout the book: **YOU ARE NOT**.

Before we focus on the term, **YOU ARE NOT**, let's start with the subtitle, *Beyond the Three Veils of Consciousness*. What exactly do we mean by "veils of consciousness"? To best appreciate this, recall the famous Sufi story of the three blind men who are asked to describe what an elephant looks like. The first blind man feeling its trunk says, "An elephant is like a snake." The second blind man feeling its leg proclaims, "An elephant is like a tree trunk." The third blind man feeling its ear asserts, "An elephant is like a big thin plate." Now, obviously, for someone who can "see," all of these are untrue descriptions of what an elephant looks like, because once we "look," we can "see" the whole elephant (underlying unity). Using this story, with only a slight addition, explains why "I" chose *Beyond the Three Veils of Consciousness* as the subtitle.

Now let us imagine our three "blind" men. However, rather than each being blind, imagine that each wears many blindfolds or veils made of thin cloth or gauze covering their eyes. As in the story of the blind men, the *veiled* men cannot see "what is" (the elephant) instead, they conclude, select-out and abstract from "what is" because the veils over their eyes prevent them from seeing "what is." However, if we were to unwrap each veil one by one, eventually, the elephant, ("what is") would become clearer and clearer until it was eventually "seen." The word "seen" is an interesting word in itself, because "sages" of the ancient past often were called "seers," in that they could "see" (*apperceive*) the underlying whole (the elephant); as they no longer were blindfolded by the *veils of consciousness.*

In this way, it is the *veils of "our" concepts*, which are made of "condensed" **consciousness**, which must be discarded in order for "those" who are blind(folded) to see the *underlying unity* (elephant).

Why do we use the word **consciousness** to describe these veils? Because whether we could call this underlying SUBSTANCE, the NOTHINGNESS, or the UNDERLYING SUBSTANCE, *the veils, also, are made of THAT same ONE SUBSTANCE condensed*, which for the present we will call **consciousness**. In this way, we begin to unwrap the veils of **consciousness**, until the unwrapper, and the "seer" too, is "seen" as THE SAME SUBSTANCE as everything else. What, then, are these veils [unquestioned] concepts made of—condensed **consciousness**? The *Yoga Sutras* say it this way:

> "Knowledge [concepts] is produced by imposition of mental limitations on *pure* consciousness. When all these limitations are removed, the Yogi passes into the realm of *pure* consciousness [THE SUBSTANCE]. It is not possible to solve any real problem of Life as long as our consciousness is confined within the realm of the unreal." (Taimini, *The Science of Yoga*, p. 436)

In this, just the "understanding," YOU ARE NOT—or better said, **prior to** the emergence of the "awar*er*," ARE YOU?— all the imagined Veils of Consciousness begin to dissolve.

CHAPTER 2

What is Consciousness?

The next question that must be asked when embarking on a book such as, *You Are Not: Beyond the Three Veils of Consciousness*, is the question, "what is **consciousness?**"

Let me first suggest, for ease of reading, that the words *UNDIFFERENTIATED CONSCIOUSNESS* or *THE SUBSTANCE* are interchangeable; hence, we will use bold capital letters, and when **THE SUBSTANCE** "condenses," we will use no bold caps, we will just use **consciousness** in lowercase bold type.

Consciousness is that **SUBSTANCE** which somehow "tells" us that **I AM** and that this **I AM** is made of a different **SUBSTANCE** than other **I AM**s and objects. "Our" **consciousness** makes us imagine that this is "my" arm, that is "your" leg, etc. Yet this describes only **differentiated consciousness**, or what could be called "my" **consciousness**. But **THE SUBSTANCE** condensed, which we call **differentiated consciousness**, and which proclaims this is "my" **consciousness** and mistakenly distinguishes a "you" from a "me," still is only *THAT SUBSTANCE*, of which and by which the **differentiated consciousness** is made of, and condenses from. To make this clear throughout, we will call UNDIFFERENTIATED CONSCIOUSNESS "THAT SUBSTANCE," and upon its *imagined* differentiation, we will call it **consciousness**.

There is only THAT SUBSTANCE; however, upon its contraction or condensing, the illusion of differentiation occurs and, hence, we get what we could call **consciousness**. It is this contraction of THAT SUBSTANCE, which forms **consciousness** and which gives the illusory **appearance** of separation, and that there are two or more substances of which this alleged universe is made of. However, there is only THAT UNDERLYING SAME SUBSTANCE.

THAT SUBSTANCE **appears** to become **differentiated consciousness** and weaves a web of separation called "I" and a world. And it is out of this spider's web and the power of condensation (in Sanskrit, called **Maya**), which forms the great illusion. And it is this "power" of illusion, which, like a spider, weaves a web out of itself (its urine). The power of condensation (which is still THE SUBSTANCE), weaves a web made from THE SUBTANCE that forms the concept called **consciousness** from within itself. And it is this web of **consciousness** that makes us believe in a "my" **consciousness**, a "your" consciousness, and in separation, war, peace, and divisions— when, in reality, it is only THE SAME SUBSTANCE. Simply put, ultimately, there is ONLY THAT UNDERLYING ONE SUBSTANCE.

Thus **consciousness**, and even the concept called "my" **consciousness**, is formed and is still made of THE SUBSTANCE and as such, it forms I AM and the veils of **consciousness**, thus solidifying the illusion of two or more substances, even though it is still made of THAT ONE SAME SUBSTANCE.

This, in archetypal terms, is often depicted as Siva, an archetypal yogi sitting on Mount Kailas meditating (the spider), **consciousness** (the web), and **Maya** the power of condensation that holds the web together. "I" spent much time with a teacher, Baba Prakashananda, who once said to me, "**Consciousness, Shakti** is Maya." In other words, **consciousness** is condensed "from" THE SUBSTANCE; but in its condensation, the illusion of a separate world and "I," "you," etc., seem to **appear**; this is an illusion.

To apperceive visually, and *metaphorically*, the Eyes of Siva, the world can be pictured[1] as **A VAST EMPTINESS**, and, like a grain of sand floating in this vast **emptiness** is "our universe." It is a universe that could be likened to cosmic dust made of **consciousness** (**THAT SUBSTANCE** condensed), and it is the web of **consciousness** that arises, which is this world.

Recently, within "me," out of the vastness of **VOID**, arose an image of Shirdi Sai Baba. And, as he appeared to "me," he was holding a grain of sand, which was what we call "our" or "this" universe.

In this way, *metaphorically speaking*, we are dream characters, an **appearance** of cosmic dust within the great **VOID**.

> "Being awaked from the sleep and the illusion of his cosmic dream he becomes conscious of the union with Brahma [**THE SUBSTANCE**]" (Taimini, *The Science of Yoga*, p. 436)

In this way, *You Are Not: Beyond the Three Veils of Consciousness* takes "us" "beyond" the **mirage** world of cosmic dust that we call "I" and this universe, which ultimately is made of **THAT SUBSTANCE**, which, when it **appears** to condense, forms Veils that intermittently **appear** to be made of **consciousness**, but which are still only **THAT ONE SUBSTANCE**, and **ARE NOT**.

This book attempts to demonstrate that, **prior to consciousness, prior to** the "emergence" of the **I AM** or the "awar<u>er</u>," beyond awareness itself, beyond the cosmic dust, the cloud **mirage** world bubble we call this universe, which Nisargadatta Maharaj called a *pin prick*, is an **appearance** within the **VASTNESS OF EMPTINESS**, and yet made of the **SAME SUBSTANCE** as the **VASTNESS OF EMPTINESS**.

---

[1]Please note that this is only a pictorial representation, and *is not It!!!*

May this book give the understanding that might take us
BEYOND THE VEILS OF CONSCIOUSNESS "to" THAT.

With love
Your **mirage** brother, Stephen
May 15, 2000

CHAPTER 3

Why?

How does one approach and discuss a topic such as YOU ARE NOT, when within it there could be so many classic objections. For example, are we talking about copping out from the complexities, responsibilities, and problems of life? Is it not dissociation in the sense of avoiding, numbing out or even denying that we are in the world? After all, we are reading this book. Is this just another philosophical, cerebral discussion centered on our existence? Is this not a reinforcement of a False Core, particularly "I do not exist," or *so what*, what would or does this understanding really mean to all of us?

These questions will be both explored and examined so that there is no confusion as to the "purpose" of *this understanding*, which when held and when all else is discarded, *might* pierce layer upon layer of ideas, concepts, and, in a word, missunderstandings, which have arisen and have been re-enforced over the years because the very purpose of a society (which is a by-product of the nervous system) is to re-enforce YOU ARE.

It is for this reason and this reason alone, that the use of "*this understanding*" is explored to discover *who "you" are*. For, as "my" teacher Nisargadatta Maharaj said, "*All you can really teach is understanding, the rest comes on its own.*"

So, as "*his understanding*" is adopted, all else is removed until NOTHING remains. Why is this important? Because THAT NOTHINGNESS is the UNDERLYING SUBSTANCE that everything is made of, or to use the words of noted physicist, John Wheeler, "NOTHINGNESS is the building block of the universe."

It is at this juncture that "I" wish to caution the reader about where this book leads. "You" *will never discover who "you" are.* "Who Am I" and "Who You Are" is not a technique to find out WHO YOU ARE, it is merely a technique that dissolves the concept of "I" in its entirety because "*there is no I that you are,*" so "You" will never discover who "you" are— "you" will discover only that YOU ARE NOT. It is with this "understanding" that all else is removed.

So, to approach such a task, it seems imperative to first focus on the human body as a vehicle in space-time, and then to consider the nervous system independently, "as if" it is separate from THE SUBSTANCE so that, for the doubters, YOU ARE NOT can be viewed from a neuroscience level. In this way and *at this level only*, the body can be seen as the "source" of all "you" think or imagine yourself to be.

This will require the reader to "hang in there" for the next section. "I" will attempt to provide the easiest and simplest explanation of the organization of the "I" "you" call "yourself" that "I" have seen. To do this, the work of the Father of General Semantics[1], Alfred Korzybski, will be explored to demonstrate the organization of experience through the senses, brain, nervous system, and language.

In the mid-1980s, "I" was introduced to *Science and Sanity,* Alfred Korzybski's 896-page classic. For ten years "I" read, absorbed, and tried to "get" the meaning of Korzybski's revo-

---

[1]General Semantics has been defined as "the study of relationships between nervous systems and symbol systems as expressed in behavior." (Pula, *General Semantics Seminar,* Tape 106-B)

lutionary theory of human behavior. Through that struggle, its importance was "gotten"—it was Korzybski's most famous statement, "*the map is not the territory*." "I" will use "*the idea is not the thing it is referring to*" as a jumping-off point.

At that time, "I" "imagined" that "I" might have to spend years creating a summary of Korzybski's *Science and Sanity* and synthesizing it with other fields. Fortunately for "me," "I" then remembered a wonderful man, Gregory Sawin. In his early years as a student of General Semantics in the mid-1980s, he wrote an 80-page monograph, *The Structural Differential: Alfred Korzybski's General Semantics Diagram*, which summarized Korzybski. With Greg's permission, excerpts from his paper will appear in this book to represent Korzybski's essence, the Structural Differential Diagram.

Since "I" am no longer a part of Quantum Psychology, "I" called Greg and he agreed to let me use his remarkably clear and straightforward explanation of the diagram. For this, "I" can say "Thank you, Greg" for your contribution, and for saving me the time and energy so that "I" did not have to "reinvent the wheel." In short, this is "*time-binding*" (to be discussed later).

Please, as "you" read this, apply it to everything—because if "you" do, "you" will be doing "yourself" a real favor and taking a giant step toward "getting" that *there is no "I that you are.*"

"I" added commentaries to the excerpts from Greg's paper (with his permission) in the hope of focusing on the direction this book takes us, and how cultivating a Korzybskian orientation can give us a neurophysiological understanding of the biological piece of *Buddhism, Yoga, Tantric Yoga, Kashmir Shavism,* and *Advaita-Vedanta.*

I therefore implore the reader to stay with it; this is not an easy read, but a deep exploration into and confrontation with all that "you" know and hold near and dear. Simply stated; understanding is often only "gotten" through struggle.

With love,
Your **mirage** brother,
Stephen

PART I

The Veil of the Body

CHAPTER 4

The Physiology of I AM

KORZYBSKI MADE SIMPLE

To read, understand, digest, imbibe, and integrate Korzybski's theory took me 10 years of study. Certainly the English of this Polish social scientist writing a book (in 1933) on neurology and the brain made it no simple task. However, the genius of Korzybski and the reader's integration of his understanding of how the nervous system works is so paramount that "I" say, without reservation, that this understanding is a must for anyone in the field of psychology who wishes to understand the physiology from which psychology arises. Moreover, if "you" do not "*intuitively*" understand the organization of the nervous system, it will become difficult to "*grasp*" and "*understand*" the process of the **appearance** of the "I."

I dare to say this, not because everyone must understand the organization of the nervous system, but because "*understanding*" it, or "*intuitive recognition*" of how it works, is helpful in explaining clearly and precisely how and why "*spiritual*" and "*psychological*" theories, assumptions, beliefs, and rituals form major obstacles that are a hindrance—not a help—in unraveling the *Who Am I?* puzzle.

"I," of course, *must admit up front* that how "I" use Korzybski's Structural Differential in "my" explanations is very different from the way that Korzybski would have intended. Moreover, "I" have made additions to the understanding, which will be clearly noted so that there is *no confusion* between what Korzybski proposed and the additions to his understanding that "I" have proposed. However, perhaps Korzybski would have considered my work in 2000, which draws on his work in 1933, as an example of "*time-binding,*"— his term for the uniquely human ability to create and use written and spoken languages to record, preserve, accumulate, develop, synthesize, and transmit information from older generations to younger generations. For example, we write books, create libraries, schools, etc. Our language skills enable us to bind time: In the *present*, we learn from the *past* to prepare for the *future* (Korzybski, *Manhood of Humanity*). Korzybski believed that this human time-binding behavior was distinctively different from animal behavior. Sir Isaac Newton said it this way:

"If I have seen further than other men, it is only because I have stood on the shoulders of giants."

Therefore, it is not "my" intention to hang on to Korzybski's coattails. But, rather to stand on his shoulders and take a view *quite different* from Korzybski (1933)—namely, understanding that the organization of the "I" "you" call "yourself" is a by-product of the functioning nervous system, produced in the body by the electrochemical reactions of neurotransmitters. This is certainly not new, and it is not anti-Korzybskian. However, here we will utilize his Structural Differential, not as a means to *enhance survival and self-preservation as Korzybski's system directs us,* but rather to *demonstrate that the "I" which "you" imagine that "you are" appears after an experience has already occurred. Hence, before the "I" appears, YOU ARE NOT. This represents a major deviation from Korzybski's work.* He was interested in time-binding and enhancing survival; "I" am interested in only I AM THAT—YOU ARE NOT, or *the discovery of who you are, by discovering WHO YOU ARE NOT* and the realization of THAT ONE SUBSTANCE.

In short, and daring to move 100 pages ahead of "myself," the "I" "you" call "yourself" and the idea that I AM—"I am a person"; "I am here right now"; "I have a past, present and future"; "I have a purpose and mission"; "I makes choices"— is a fantasy, an illusion that is a representation created by the nervous system and represents the first veil of **consciousness**. The "I" "you" call "yourself" **appears** because chemicals called neurotransmitters have come together to form I AM and what "you" call "you"; and being a person, and more importantly, the "I" that imagines **it is** and claims **doership** for "what is," **appears** *after* the action has already taken place. Moreover, without this chemical reaction, which produces I AM and the idea of being a person, this "you" and all "you" imagine "yourself" to be; would **not** be. Possibly, it is for this reason that A. R. Orage, a student of G. I. Gurdjieff, suggested that when "you" look at a person, "you" should see them as a mass of chemicals (Orage, *On Love*).

The "I Am" is a by-product of the nervous system

EXERCISE
_____

(From Orage)
Chemicals

1) Look at someone.
2) See them as just chemicals.
3) "Look" at the "you" that "you" call "you," and "realize" that the perceiver ("I") occurs only through a chemical reaction.

4) "Wonder," **prior to** this chemical reaction that produces a perceiver ("I"), what or who am "I"?

So, now that the direction of **YOU ARE NOT**, at a physiological level, has been presented in Section I, we can take this as our point of departure for a summary of the Structural Differential, which we will use as a description of how the nervous system is organized to produce the **I AM** concept, and all that follows from it.

YOU ARE NOT A PERSON . . . THE PERSON IS NOT, YOU ARE NOT.
—*Nisargadatta Maharaj*

In Nisargadatta Maharaj's statement above, we again "feel" the understanding that **prior to I AM . . . YOU ARE NOT.** In fact, even more profoundly, we understand that **I AM appears** only as the nervous system becomes solidified (to be discussed later). Moreover, fluids (neurotransmitters) come together, driven by electromagnetism, which forms the **appearance** of the concept of **I AM** and the delusional psychology (mythology) that follows. **Prior to** this **I AM,** however, **YOU ARE NOT.** **ENQUIRE:** *Prior to the appearance of I AM, are you?*

SUMMARY OF THE STRUCTURAL DIFFERENTIAL

The purpose of this summary is to give a *very brief* explanation of two major functions. First, how both physics and yoga support what we call the universe as a condensation or contraction of **THAT SUBSTANCE**—call it **Nothingness** or **UNDIFFERENTIATED CONSCIOUSNESS**—which "later" forms **consciousness.** The *Yoga Sutras* say it this way:

"The manifested universe is an emanation of the ultimate reality . . . and may be considered to be funneled by a progressive condensation or involution of consciousness." (Taimini, *The Science of Yoga*, p. 34)

We begin by starting out with "my" version of the Structural Differential, which we can call *The Substance Diagram*. The reader can turn to page 30 for this diagram. First we begin with **THAT ONE SUBSTANCE**, which contracts to form **consciousness**, which contains the **VOID prior to** movement.

It is clear that before contraction or condensation, there is no level, and **YOU ARE NOT**. There is **NO-I**; however, as **THE SUBSTANCE** condenses we get the concept of **consciousness**. It is from the further condensation or contraction of **consciousness** that we get what Korzybski called the *process level*, where the concept of "some **SUBSTANCE**," which "I" call **consciousness**, begins to move. As the process-movement level further contracts we get the physics or quantum level, another add-on to the Structural Differential, which contains the primary dimensions and forces of physics, such as energy, space, mass, time, gravity, radiation, electromagnetism, light, sound, and dark matter superceded by superstrings[1]. As the physics level further contracts we get what Korzybski called the submicroscopic level of atoms, electrons, protons, etc. Please "consider" that at all of these "levels," **YOU ARE NOT**.

Now to qualify, **prior to** the process level is **consciousness**, and **prior to consciousness** is **THE SUBSTANCE**; in all of these "phases" **YOU ARE NOT**. At the next level, which is the quantum physics level of energy, space, mass, etc.—**YOU ARE NOT**. Furthermore, as the "contraction" continues and the microscopic level of atoms, electrons, protons, etc., **appears**, again **YOU ARE NOT**. To illustrate how still **YOU ARE NOT** at the physics or microscopic level, imagine that "you" could see the world only through an electron microscope. Now,

---

[1]See *The Way of the Human, Volume III*.

obviously, using this microscope to look at things on the microscopic level, "you" would see no "boundaries." On this level, two apples on a table, for example, would not be seen as separate objects. The apples and the table would appear as one mass of the same stuff—protons, electrons, etc.—just particles in emptiness. *Now, if we turned the electron microscope around and looked at "you," we would see that* **YOU ARE NOT**. We would see only the "movement of atoms," etc., in emptiness with no boundaries, no "I," no "you," no "self," no "other"—and no separate, individual, independent "you."

As the condensation proceeds, we get what Korzybski calls the *object level, condensations that we perceive as objects—pencils, people, etc.* This is a pivotal level because as **THE SUBSTANCE**, and at the consciousness level, the process level, the quantum physics level, and the microscopic levels, there is **NO-I; YOU ARE NOT**. However, as the *condensing-abstracting* process continues, the I AM, a body and a nervous system, **appears**. The **I AM** is the point of contact where the *abstracting-condensing* process yields the **I AM**, an "I," which is a representation that is later assumed to be the "you" that "you" call "you." Here again, we will add something to Korzybski; namely, at the object level, six things appear:

1) The body and nervous system **appear**.
2) The **I AM** is formed.
3) An "awar*er*," which is part of the **I AM**, is formed.
4) There is a sensation level.
5) The perceiver **appears**.
6) There is the **appearance** of the "my" or "self"-**consciousness** as an independent, separate, individual, entity.

Before this contraction, however, **YOU ARE NOT**. Next as the *abstracting-condensing* process continues, the nervous system creates[2] a label, "this is a car," then through further contracting, creates a description, "My neighbor's car door is smashed in." Further abstracting-condensing can lead to Inference-1, such as "The owner had an accident." This statement is a guess that goes beyond the observable facts. Still more abstracting-condensing can lead to a "higher" level Inference-2, "The owner had an accident because he is a reckless driver." This inference is even more removed from the facts the observer had about the condition of the car. This abstracting-condensing process on successively "higher" levels can result in a conclusion such as, "I will never let my neighbor drive me anywhere because we would have an accident." What needs to be emphasized again and again is that as we move from level to level, much of the prior level is omitted and only a small fraction selected out. This process of omitting and selecting out is what Korzybski called "abstracting." Abstracting is defined, as the act of taking away; forming an idea apart from concrete things, situations, events, etc. (*American College Dictionary*, p. 4). To best appreciate this term, imagine a scientific article of 75 pages. Now, imagine an abstract of 2 paragraphs that describes the 75 pages. This condensation or super-Cliff Notes is called an abstract. And, as we will discuss later, the devil is in the details that are omitted, or in our case, **Nirvana** or **YOU ARE NOT** is in the pre-abstracted whole (elephant) which is unseen; this pre-**consciousness** "state" Nisargadatta Maharaj pointed us to when he asked: **"Eight days prior to conception who were you?"**

Now, as is abundantly clear, Inference-3 is "farther" from THE SUBSTANCE than Inference-2, and Inference-2 is "far-

---

[2]Please note, the nervous system automatically produces an "I" and all that is to follow, the illusion or veil is the "I" believing that *it does*, when the "I" and doership or beliefs, perceptions, actions, etc., have already taken place. Nisargadatta Maharaj put it this way: "A stage is reached where one feels deeply that whatever is being done is happening and one ("I") has not got anything to do with it." (Powell, *The Ultimate Medicine*, p. 101)

ther" from THE SUBSTANCE than Description. In this way, with each *abstraction-condensation*, we move farther away from "*what is*" and the fundamental I AM, and the realization: I AM THAT—YOU ARE NOT.

SRI RAMANA MAHARISHI
"Go back the way you came"

CHAPTER 5

The Structural Differential Diagram

The Organization of the Nervous System
and the Appearance of "I"
"Go Back The Way You Came"

—Ramana Maharishi

The story of the great Sage Ramana Maharishi might be a good place to begin and illustrate the physiological *understanding* of YOU ARE NOT.

A student journeyed from Europe to Ramana's Ashram in the 1940s. Suffering from the pain of not knowing who he was, he arrived after many months at the feet of this revered sage. Bowing down and touching his feet he begged Maharishi, "Show me who I am!" to which Maharishi proclaimed "*Go back the way you came.*" Ramana's disciples were angry at such a response because they imagined he was treating this seeker so badly by telling him to go. Maharishi explained, "No, "I" told him to go back the way he came." Translated, trace the "I" thought or "I" back to before it arose. This is the same as Nisargadatta Maharaj saying to a student, **"Prior to your last thought – stay there."** Below we will try this as an experiment.

GO BACK THE WAY YOU CAME

Pick an object in the room. Withdraw your attention backward **prior to** any knowledge or information or impressions "you" have about the object. So "you" are looking from back "there." Look at a person; withdraw your attention backward **prior to** any thoughts, impressions, knowledge, or information that "you" have about the person. Look at any person in the room and withdraw your attention backward **prior to** any thoughts, any ideas, any knowledge, any information or impressions "you" have of that person. "Look" eyes open, "look." Oftentimes, people found that when they looked at someone from "back there," the person began to look less formed, lost their boundaries. It is because your ideas about them are not them. When "you" "look" through ideas, "you" are not seeing them; "you" are seeing your ideas about them; your information, your impressions about them. When "I" am not seeing "you," "I" am seeing "my" ideas about "you," and "I" don't even know that "I" am seeing "my" ideas about "you," and not "you." Moreover, "I" see only my ideas and representations of this "I" or "me," which means "I" don't see "you" and "I" don't see "me." It relates to abstracting, which is automatic. **Going back the way you came** is going the other way, so everything just "becomes" the way it is.

If anything were to typify, even on a physiological level, the *understanding* of this statement, it is Korzybski's Structural Differential. For as we will see, to *go back the way you came*, on a physiological level means moving from the inference level back "down" to the descriptive level, to the label level, to the object level (**I AM**), to the microscopic level, to the quantum physics level, to the process-movement level, to the **consciousness** level, and ultimately to **THE SUBSTANCE**. The *Yoga Sutras* say it this way:

"As the progressive involution of consciousness in matter . . . imposes increasing limitation is the reverse process of evolution progressively releases *consciousness* from its limitation. The different stages of Samadhi[1] represent the progressive release of consciousness from limitations." (Taimini, *The Science of Yoga*, p. 33)

It's during the process of expansion or thinning-out of **consciousness** that there is a withdrawal of the external, thinking, emotional and even body consciousness.

"Each vehicle has its own function. . . . The progressive withdrawal of consciousness into increasingly subtler vehicles. The recession of consciousness is not steady and uninterrupted sinking into greater and greater depths, but consists in this alternate out and inward movement of consciousness." (Taimini, *The Science of Yoga*, pp. 33-36)

The body is made of **THE SUBSTANCE**. However, in order to understand the body and the concept of **consciousness** (which is **THAT SUBSTANCE** condensed), we must first understand how **consciousness** animates the body through what we call the nervous system.

To best appreciate how the *veils of consciousness* **appear** through the body's nervous system we will start with Alfred Korzybski.

After 12 years of research, Korzybski, a Polish-American social scientist, published his monumental work, *Science and Sanity*, which introduced his non-Aristotelian system, a synthesis of intellectual trends in the Western world that evolved during 20th century and earlier. A fundamental part of this system is to recognize that people make sense of the world through a process of abstracting—from our limited sense perceptions to our use of language to describe some aspects of what we perceived, we then make inferences and draw con-

---

[1]Samadhi at the "I AM" phase in most forms of yoga and will be discussed in great detail in Part II: The Veil of Spirituality.

clusions about our experience. Whatever knowledge, opin-
ions, or beliefs people acquire about themselves and the world
around them always results from abstracting—there is no way
to get around it. What "you" know or believe is the product
of your functioning nervous system. The findings of modern
science support this theory of abstracting.

The essence of Korzybski's theory of abstracting is represented as a diagram called the Structural Differential (page
41). For our purposes of understanding the "Who AM I?"
puzzle, it stands at the forefront for helping us understand
how the nervous system and brain organize and form the representation called "I" by forming a veil that is made of **consciousness**, which made the "I" believe *It Is*, but which ultimately *IS NOT*.

THE STRUCTURAL DIFFERENTIAL

"Korzybski created the Structural Differential to explain (from a scientific point of view) some aspects of
how a human nervous system perceives 'reality' and how
a person deals with 'reality' through the use of language."
(Sawin, *The Structural Differential*)

It should be noted here that the body is a perception made
by a perceiver, an abstraction that **appears** to be, is made
intermittently of **consciousness**, but ultimately is **THE SUB-
STANCE**. In this text, we will come from a yoga perspective,
and hence, formulate and use the Structural Differential in
that context.

In another version of the Structural Differential, which I
call *The Substance Diagram*, we will *add on* the "**THAT ONE
SUBSTANCE**" (Level A) and the **consciousness** (Level B),
which are **prior to** Korzybski's process-movement level. (See
The Substance Diagram on page 30.)

THAT ONE SUBSTANCE we will use as our point of departure followed by the **consciousness**; and it is from **con-**

sciousness that the "movement" **appears** to arise, although it "originates"² in THE SUBSTANCE. Please note that although Korzybski refers below to "energies," the concepts of energy and atoms are not formed yet. Thus, it is for the sake of clarity that we will "go **prior to**" "energies" and movement to and even **prior to consciousness** itself as THE SUBSTANCE. (See page 30 for diagram.)

Let us begin, with the process-movement event (Level C) in The Substance Diagram, which is Korzybski's departure point:

"Think of everything in the universe as some sort of energy, which involves constant movement of matter. At this point I am not referring to objects in the universe such as people, apples, etc. I mean all the basic materials of the universe on the subatomic level (on a scale smaller than the level of atoms). So do not think of this level in terms of atoms—think of the universe in more indefinite terms: constant movement of extremely small subatomic energies." (Sawin)   •

For us, the physics dimension is "after" the process-movement level, hence **consciousness** (B), begins to "move" forming the process level (C), which is "some unnamed SUBSTANCE," However, "it" does not **appear** as energy until the quantum physics level (D) and it does not **appear** as electrons until the microscopic level (E).

MOREOVER, OBJECTS AND THE "I" PEOPLE DO NOT APPEAR UNTIL "LATER."

---

²Please note that we do not mean "originate" in its classic definition, "to come from." Here we are stuck in language. Again, if all the world was the ocean and *only* the ocean, we could not say that a wave *originated* from the ocean because it's all ocean. Hence, there is no point or source or location of origination nor an origina*tor*.

THE SUBSTANCE DIAGRAM

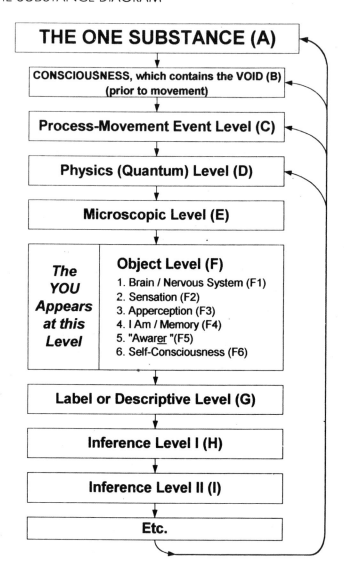

Please Note:

The diagram implies a Source or Origin called the **SUBSTANCE**. There is no Source or Origin; there is only the **SUBSTANCE**. If everything were the ocean, could we say the ocean was the Source of a drop of water? To have a Source or Origin implies two or more substances, which is Not.

"If we take something, anything, let us say the object
...called pencil, and inquire what it represents, according to science 1933, we find that the scientific object represents an event, a mad dance of electrons, which is different every instant, which never repeats itself, which is known to consist of extremely complex dynamic processes of very fine structure, acted upon by, and reacting upon, the rest of the universe, inextricably connected with everything else and dependent upon everything else." (Korzybski, *Science and Sanity*, p. 387)

This constant movement of "energy" now becomes subatomic 'energies' of the universe, which we will represent as the physics level (D) and the microscopic level (E) in the **ONE SUBSTANCE** Diagram.

"We do not know how big the universe is; we only can say that it appears to be indefinitely large, extending very far but we do not know how far." (Pula, *General Semantics Seminar*, Tape 103-A)

"The universe [at this level] consists of indefinitely many subatomic energies, which we can represent as dots in the parabola (see Structural Differential Diagram pg. 41)— each dot representing some sort of subatomic energy particle ... Korzybski called this part of the diagram the event or process level (Korzybski, *Science and Sanity*, p. 387). I will use the term process level to remind us of the dynamic quality of the universe [which for Korzybski begins at the process or quantum level]." (Sawin)

This place is critical to note. **THAT SUBSTANCE** contracts forming **consciousness**, when in movement Korzybski calls it

---

Please note, that Korzybski via Sawin does not begin with **THAT ONE SUBSTANCE**. Before the concept of large or small, infinite or large, etc., is **THAT ONE SUBSTANCE**, all else follows.

the process or event level, **prior to**, there be no movement, place, thing or size. THAT SUBSTANCE is the "origin."[3]

Now, at the "level" of THAT SUBSTANCE, YOU ARE NOT; at the level of **consciousness**, YOU ARE NOT. At the process level, YOU ARE NOT; at the quantum level of atoms, etc., YOU ARE NOT; and through further contraction at the microscopic level, YOU ARE NOT. However, at the next level, the object level, the body and nervous system are formed and I AM. Please note again that "at" THE SUBSTANCE, **consciousness**, process, physics, or microscopic levels, there is *no you*, and (as will be discussed in depth) the "time" when this "you" **appears** is much later and only **appears** as an "event" (but after the event level), which still is made of THE SUBSTANCE. Hence, THERE IS NO PERSONAL CHOICE OR FREE WILL (to be discussed throughout).

The "purpose" of the nervous system is two-fold; 1) to organize chaos and 2) to survive.
A nervous system responds to both external and internal processes to promote survival of the person.

"[In the Structural Differential Diagram (p. 41)] the dots in the parabola, in the object level disk, and in the tags, unfortunately all look alike, which might lead one to assume that the dots at these different levels represent the same thing. They do not. The dots in the parabola represent something completely different from the dots in the object level disks: The dots in the parabola represent inferred energies of the basic material of the universe; and the dots in the disk represent sensations of some energies of reality, which are really abstractions, translations, and interpretations of those energies. The dots in the tags represent the features of qualities of an

---

[3]Please note, words are difficult here because "origin" implies a location. However, since there is only one SUBSTANCE, there can be no origin, source, or location.

object, which are understood to be part of the definition of the label for the object.

Now, I will attach a string to each dot in the parabola. In a moment it will be apparent why this is done. A human nervous system, through the various sense organs, cannot perceive individual subatomic energies (now represented by the hanging strings). It takes enormous amounts of these energies to make up something substantial enough to be seen, felt, smelled, etc. (Korzybski, *Science and Sanity*, pp. 375-389, ff.) Think of the billions of energies that make up a grain of sand. Out of all the subatomic energies in the universe, a person's nervous system can detect only some of them: most will be too far away to sense; many may be of a character that we cannot sense under any conditions; some we cannot sense directly, but can sense only indirectly by using scientific instruments. (Bois, *The Art of Awareness*, p. 79) Remember that our eyes cannot detect all types of light waves, our ears cannot detect all frequencies of sound, etc. (Mueller, *Sensory Psychology*, pp. 8, 49) Korzybski put it this way: '... we are immersed in a world full of energy manifestations, out of which we [the nervous system][4] abstract directly only a very small portion, these abstractions being already colored by the specific functioning and structure of the nervous system . . .' (Korzybski, *Science and Sanity*, p. 238)

So, a person's nervous system is limited in its ability to perceive reality. Korzybski called this limited ability,

---

[4]"I" added the term "the nervous system" in brackets because there is no-I that abstracts. The "I" is an abstraction of the nervous system, which already arose. Hence, it is ludicrous to take personal responsibility for what has already taken place before "you" even **appeared**. This, is true ego-taking personal responsibility for something that "you" did not do, (**You Are Not the Doer**) will be discussed in greater detail to follow.

'. . . abstracting [which] implies selecting, picking out, separating, summarizing, . . . removing, omitting. . . .'
(Korzybski, *Science and Sanity*, p. 379)" (Sawin)

At the object level the body, nervous system and I AM are formed. However, even the I AM is an inference, an assumption. Nisargadatta Maharaj called it the "*Seed of Consciousness*," because it was from or through the I AM that all other assumptions **appear**: The *Yoga Sutras* say it this way:

". . . self discipline is to hold onto the "I AM." (Mishra, *The textbook of yoga psychology*, p. 414) "Egoism or personal "I Amness" is the False Identification of the "I AM" with mental faculty which is when the I AM gets identified with the . . . thinking mind. . . . The principle "I AM" (as THE SUBSTANCE) is beyond time and space. . . . The individual I am is part of ignorance." (*Ibid.*, p. 402)

Here it is important to both differentiate and add to the standard "spiritual" definition of identification. Identification in Eastern traditions is—"I" I-dentify myself as something, like a thought. For example, if a thought goes by, which says, "I am bad," it pre-supposes that I AM has this thought.

Korzybski defined "identification" as confusing the orders of abstraction. To illustrate, the I AM has no thoughts, memory, emotions, associations, or perceptions. The "I" (nervous system) then *labels* itself as peaceful, then *describes* peaceful as an absence of conflict, then abstracts-condenses further to Inference-1: "Being peaceful is good and spiritual; anger is not spiritual," then abstracts-condenses still further to Inference-2: "I want to be spiritual, so I must become more peaceful by getting rid of my anger." This "spiritual" idea is not true; it is not a statement of fact, it is an inference and has nothing to do with the personal I AM, let alone THE SUBSTANCE. Simply stated, what Korzybski referred to as Identification (confusing, one level with another), in this case, is the confusion of "I AM peaceful" as a spiritual quality of THE SUBSTANCE with THE SUBSTANCE, which is qualityless and is *not*. This is a confusing of levels of abstraction.

To summarize: I AM→Label→Description→ Inference-1→ Inference-2→Inference-3→etc. ("→" = abstracts).

"Everything a person senses about reality is the result of some energies of the universe being selected by that person's nervous system through the sense organs. These external energies of reality activate internal energy processes in the sense organs, such '. . . chains of electrical [nerve] impulses . . . ' (Gregory, *The Intelligent Eye*, p. 9) and these processes are themselves converted to other sorts of impulses when they are received by the brain. (Mueller, *Sensory Psychology*, Ch. 2). The brain takes these impulses and tries to make sense of them by comparing them to its memories of similar impulses. (Gregory, *Eye and Brain*, p. 13) When it finds a fit, that is when a person can understand what he is perceiving—I see a chair, I hear a train, etc. (Pula, *General Semantics Seminar*, Tape 102-B) Hayakawa made a good point concerning this process when he wrote, '[A new] experience does not tell us what it is we are experiencing. *Things simply happen*.' (Hayakawa, *Language in Thought and Action*, p. 291) The main point I want to emphasize here is this: Anything a person senses about reality in terms of lights, colors, sounds, shapes, temperatures, etc., is not a direct recording of absolute reality. *It is the nervous system's interpretation* of a very limited sample of the energies of reality. For example, the eye does not simply record reality. Professor of Bionics, R.L. Gregory, put it this way: 'The retina [in the eye] is not merely a layer of light-sensitive cells, it is also a 'satellite computer' in which visual information is pre-processed for the brain.' (Gregory, *The Intelligent Eye*, p. 24) The eye takes in a little of the energies of reality, translates that sample and the brain interprets the translation. What a person sees is based on this *interpretation* of light patterns *that were perceived a split second ago*. So, when we think we are reacting to what is happening in reality, we are really reacting to an interpretation of some translated energies of reality. To live is to abstract—everything we do involves abstracting (Bois, *The Art of Awareness*, p. 105). Johnson put it this way: 'Abstracting, like digestion, is a natural bodily function (as a matter of fact, digestion too is a variety of abstracting process) . . .' (Johnson, *People in Quandaries*, p. 155)." (Sawin)

This is the crucial part of *The Substance Diagram*, because from **THAT ONE SUBSTANCE**, comes the condensation or contraction of **THE SUBSTANCE** thus **appearing** as **consciousness**. Then comes Korzybski's process-movement event, ("here," still **YOU ARE NOT**). At the next condensation, the physics level, "there" **YOU ARE NOT**, and then at the microscopic level there too—**YOU ARE NOT**. During the next condensation a nervous system **appears**. **Prior to** the object level we can call the condensed "space" of the body, the object level, which is where the **I AM appears**, as well as the objects the **I AM** views through perception. However, the **I AM** views without thoughts, memory, emotions or associations and is **prior to** the label or descriptive levels of abstraction.

This is in the *Yoga Sutras*:
"Nirvikalpa Samadhi is experienced when memory is purified and the mind is able to see the true nature of gross objects of the universe as they are directly, without distortion, without the mixture of words and meaning." (Mishra, *The Textbook of Yoga Psychology*, pg. 398)

We call this NO FRAMES OF REFERENCE—
NO REFERENCES TO FRAME

"The free-hanging strings represent energies of reality by a nervous system; they get left out. In general, any human experience is represented by strings in the object level disk. Korzybski wrote, '. . . our actual lives are lived entirely on objective, unspeakable levels. ' (Korzybski, *Science and Sanity*, p. 477) A living person, who is constantly sensing some energies of reality, is represented by the object level disk." (Sawin)

Please not that what Korzybski says is that we live on the nonverbal (**I AM**) level. This occurs **prior to** the Object Level Sensation (F2 in The Substance Diagram on page 30). Unfortunately, as we will come to see as the abstracting process continues, so does the place we imagine we live at and on.

"For the sake of clarity, let's simplify the Structural Differential Diagram (page 41); but remember that to be more accurate, there would be many billions of dots in the process level parabola, each one with a string attached. The disk would actually hold many thousands of dots, which would represent thousands of strings connecting the parabola with the disk.

It also should be pointed out that although the process level is supposed to represent all the material of the universe and, strictly speaking, a person is part of that material; we show the person as the object level disk 'outside' the parabola[5]. The person is separated from the process level only to illustrate how a person should not confuse her experiences with the process level itself[6].

---

[5]The "person" has not appeared yet; hence; "it," the concept of a person **appears** much later, after "doing" has occurred.
[6]Why? Because the person has not yet appeared.

(Pula, *General Semantics Seminar*, Tape 103-B) Whatever a person's nervous system makes out of some process level energies of reality is not the process level itself. It might be useful to point out that although the 'open curve' of the parabola represents indefinitely many subatomic energies of the universe, the 'close curve' (circle) of the object levels disk suggests that a limited number of energies are abstracted by a person's nervous system. (Chisholm, *Introductory Lectures on General Semantics*, p. 104) A sensation results from a nervous system responding to billions and billions of subatomic energies of reality. This point is illustrated in the diagram as several strings from the process level parabola meeting at the same spot in the object level disk. These last remarks lead to making a distinction between the dots in the process level parabola and the dots in the object level disk. The dots in the parabola represent subatomic energies of reality, but the dots in the disk represent sensations, which result from a person's nervous system transacting with energies of reality.[7] For example, you cannot see the individual subatomic energies that make up a wooden table, but you can get visual sensations of some details in the wood of the table." (Sawin)

Here we see a major difference between the Structural Differential Diagram and *The Substance Diagram* because it indicates that the person cannot react to any "energies" separate from reality. The body and later the idea of I AM and I AM a person are part of THE ONE SUBSTANCE'S condensation, which is **consciousness**. Therefore it is the illusion or veil of

---

[7]Here we contend that there is no person who reacts to "energies," rather these "energies" are what the person is made of. There is no person separate from these "energies." In this way, it is not the person who reacts, because there is no person, just at least a movement of **consciousness**, and, at most, not even that.

consciousness at the object level after the formation of **I AM**, which gives the illusion that "you" actually **ARE** when, that idea is an abstraction-condensation of **THE SUBSTANCE**, and the "you" or "I" is only an **appearance** of **THE SUBSTANCE**.

"All that we have dealt with so far, concerning the process level parabola and the object level disk, is on the non-verbal level. I have described the subatomic process level of reality and the object level of reality, but not yet the level of words, ideas and statements. Korzybski warned us against confusing these two levels when he wrote: 'Whatever we may say or feel, the objects and events remain on the unspeakable levels and cannot be reached by words[8] . . . we can only reach the objective [sense] level by seeing, handling, actually feeling, etc., . . . all of which cannot be conveyed by words alone.' (Korzybski, *Science and Sanity*, p. 420) By using language, a person can assign symbols, in the form of words, to his sensations and describe to himself and others what he experienced. I like Hayakawa's description of this process: 'Human beings use extremely complicated systems of . . . noises called language, with which they express and report what goes on in the nervous systems.' (Hayakawa, *Language in Thought and Action*, p. 9)" (Sawin)

"NOBODY HAS EVER SEEN MATTER."
Bishop George Berkeley

---

[8]Moreover, as noted philosopher David Hume said, "You cannot have direct experiences." All that you call experiences are *mediated* by the brain and nervous system. Furthermore, we would say *prior to the "I" experience*, YOU ARE NOT; so who but an "I" fabricated by the nervous system through a chemical reaction is having an experience?

It is imperative to understand that as THE SUBSTANCE, consciousness, the process-event[9], at the physics level, or at the microscopic level, the "I" has not appeared yet: YOU ARE NOT. To best illustrate this, consider that if "we" were to look at the "world" through an electron microscope, we would not see solid objects. All people, objects, and events would have no boundaries and would not be determinable as separate, with their own self nature. If we turn the electron microscope toward "the perceiver" there is no perceiver. All perceiving perception and what is perceived appears later.

Once the condensing continues we move from the non-verbal silent level of I AM to the descriptive level; now we are at the level of words, and we can represent this on the Structural Differential as a tag attached by strings to the object level disk. Korzybski called this the "label" level. (Korzybski, *Science and Sanity*, p. 392)[10].

"Notice that in going from the process level to the physics level to the microscopic level to the object level, there are many subatomic energies that are *not* abstracted by the nervous system and these are represented by the free hanging strings in the parabola. There are also free-hanging strings attached to the object level disk, indicating that in going from the object level to the label level,

---

[9]Please note that the "event" (like the perception of a chair) is only recorded and perceived *after* the event (level) has already occurred.

[10]Regarding abstracting as leaving out or omitting, the "I," as perceiver is still made of THE SUBSTANCE. It is just that the condensation leaves "I" with an *abstracted perception* of reality. "I" always remain as THE SUBSTANCE. The "I'"s perception however, does not "realize" this. Imagine the ocean (THE SUBSTANCE). The ocean does not know separate droplets of water. Through movement, waves appear, and through further movements, droplets of water appear. "I," as a droplet of water, is still made of the ocean; but the droplet cannot perceive this. Instead, the droplet perceives as the droplet; and from the point of view of a droplet, the droplet has lost its knowingness of THE SUBSTANCE that it appeared from, will subside into and is made of.

THE STRUCTURAL DIFFERENTIAL DIAGRAM

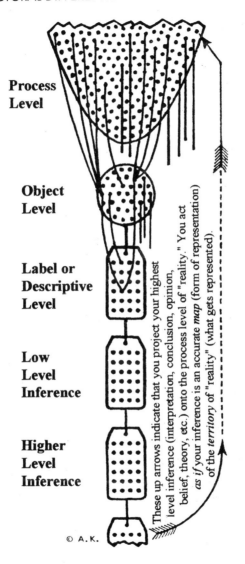

Process Level

Object Level

Label or Descriptive Level

Low Level Inference

Higher Level Inference

These up arrows indicate that you project your highest level inference (interpretation, conclusion, opinion, belief, theory, etc.) onto the process level of "reality." You act *as if* your inference is an accurate *map* (form of representation) of the *territory* of "reality" (what gets represented).

© A.K.

The Structural differential diagram is reproduced by permission of the Literary Exector of the Alfred Korzybski Estate. The Structural Differential appears on page 398 of *Science and Sanity: Introduction to Non-Aristotelian Systems and General Semantics* (5th edition, 1993), by Alfred Korzybski. This book is published by the Institute of General Semantics in Brooklyn, NY.

some sensations (or perceived aspects) of something in reality are left out of the meaning of the label for that thing. Any word or description can represent only some aspects of something in reality. As Korzybski put it: 'The object has more characteristics [such as its features or qualities] than we can include in the . . . definition of the label for the object.' (Korzybski, *Science and Sanity*, p. 414)" (Sawin)

"Korzybski often used the terms map and territory to help explain the difference between the non-verbal levels of reality (territory) and the verbal levels (maps), consisting of words, descriptions, beliefs, theories, etc. (Korzybski, *Science and Sanity*, p. 58) With language we create map-like descriptions of the territory of reality. The map is not the territory and the word is not the thing, and there is '. . . no connection between the symbol and that which is symbolized.' (Hayakawa, *Language in Thought and Action*, p. 22) Among other things, this last quote means that just because there is a word for something that does not mean that the something actually exists. For example, as far as scientists know, there is no thing or process in the real world which corresponds to the word 'luck.'" (Sawin)

This becomes a major departure point in both appreciating and understanding the problem with modern-day psychology. First let us begin by understanding that the description or symbol of the thing *is not* the thing. In this way characterizing, diagnosing, or typing people in some way can only describe behavior, but *the description is not the thing it is describing*. Moreover, "there is no connection between the symbol, (diagnosis character type, etc.) and the symbolized (the person to whom it is referring). Furthermore, just because the nervous system symbolizes something or someone, this does not mean that the someone or something exists. Because with each abstraction-symbol, that which the person abstracted or symbolized is assumed to be when the concept of *being* is only a representation and an abstraction of "what is"—the abstraction is not *it*. Each time we condense-abstract down to another level, we lose more and more information. So, as we will come to see, the inferences made about the symbol have not only nothing to do with the symbolized, they have nothing to do with "what is."

Words are static in the sense that they have relatively unchanging and general meanings that are supposed to represent ever-changing, unique objects, situations, etc.

Weinberg wrote:

"The words are maps, and the map is not the territory. The map is static; the territory [or process level] constantly flows [THE SUBSTANCE is **prior to** flowing]. Words are always about the past or the unborn future, never about the living present. The present is ever too quick for them; by the time the words are out, it is gone." (Weinberg, *Levels of Knowing and Existence*, p. 35)

**WORDS, THOUGHTS, EXPERIENCES,
AND EVEN THE "I"
ARE
SYMBOLIC REPRESENTATIONS,
OR METAPHORS
OF "WHAT IS"
AND
HAVE NOTHING TO
DO WITH
"WHAT IS."**

—*Stephen H. Wolinsky*

THERE IS NO CHOICE: WE SEE ONLY THE PAST

Once we understand the nature of the abstracting process, ultimately what is grasped is that since the perceiver of "reality" **appears** at the object level, all the perceiver's descriptions and interpretations **appear** further along in time. In this way, all the perceiver can perceive is the past—something that has already occurred. Therefore, to believe in choice would require a NOW. But since all the perceiver can perceive is what has already occurred, by the time it occurs to the perceiver to do or choose this or that, and the "I" imagines it chooses and does something, the something has already occurred. *Even at a physiological level there is no doer, you are not the doer,* or better said, *"there is no "I" which does".*

To understand that the perceiver, and hence, its perception, **appear** only after the experience has already occurred, not only boggles the mind, but also changes our entire understanding of choice and free will. Let us explain it this way: First we have **NOTHING-EVERYTHING (THE SUBSTANCE)**, which contracts or condenses to form **consciousness.** Then the process-event (movement) level forms the physics level of energy, space, mass, time, gravity, light, sound—in short, the physics dimensions and forces. Further condensation forms the microscopic level of atoms, electrons, etc. Through this condensation we get the body and chemicals (which have *no I*), but produces the fluids, the concept of I AM (first at a non-verbal level, then later at verbal levels). From there, the *label level,* for example, there is a "book"; the *descriptive level,* "I am reading the book"; then Inference-1: "I am choosing to read the book"; then Inference-2: "I am choosing to read the book to get understanding." With each abstraction the illusion of choice **appears.** However, the *"I" that views the world is produced by the nervous system after the experience and action have already occurred, then the "I" declares doership, choosership, ownership, and volition, imagining that* *it is, was, will be, has a purpose, mission, etc.* In this way, not only is all perception and what is perceived in the past, but so all experiences and concepts of choice have already occurred by the time the nervous system produces, perceives, thinks, posits, experiences, or, in a word, appears an "I," which formulates "I chose this."

"For all these reasons and more, we have strings in the object level disk, which do not connect with the label level tag. Any description of something is always going to leave out some aspects or features of the thing described—a map is not *all* of the territory. Each point on the label level tag where strings from the object level disk connect represents a perceived feature of the unique object, which is a part of the definition of the word for that object. The feature, which is left out of the label apple, is represented as one of the free-hanging strings in the object level disk.

When people do not know that there is much more to something than the meaning of a *word* for it can cover, they are in danger of allowing the word to determine their attitude toward that something, rather than finding out for themselves through experience what their attitude should be. (Johnson, *People in Quandaries*, p. 261) This problem is especially serious when a person prejudges a stranger on the basis of how *he* labels the stranger. (Weinberg, *Levels of Knowing and Existence*, p. 56) Labeling a person does not define what a person is. Labels do not necessarily represent accurate or true definitions of people. To a great extent, labels reflect the assumptions and points of view of the person who does this labeling.".

Getting back to the object level, and label level, each represent different levels of abstraction in the label level tag actually represents an abstraction of an abstraction. I find it amazing that when I label something I see as apple, something as simple and obvious as that, I am already at the second level of abstraction. (Korzybski, *Science and Sanity*; p.389) (Sawin)

This becomes one of the most extraordinary things. *WHAT "YOU" SEE HAS ALREADY OCCURRED*, and, the idea of "I" chose this or that or "I" created this or that **appears** after the experience has already taken place. In other words, the condensation or water droplet ("I") that is part of the wave in the ocean has already hit the beach, when an "I" is formed, which says "I chose to go to the beach." In this way, not only is the past, or what has occurred, the only thing seen by a nervous system, but also *the idea of "I chose this," "There are lessons to learn," "I must have needed this," etc., etc., appears with the "I" after the experience has already passed. The illusion is that the nervous system makes it seem that "you" have choice and what "you" see is now, when by the time this "you" is produced and sees—the new is gone and the representation called "I" sees only what has already happened. In other words, the produced "I" sees only the past.*

Concerning the dots in the label level tag, Korzybski wrote: We ascribe . . . characteristics to the labels, and we indicate these characteristics by the little . . . [dots]. The number of characteristics which we ascribe by definition to the label, is still smaller than the number of characteristics the object has. (Korzybski, *Science and Sanity*, p. 387)

As a practical example, imagine that the first tag represents the label, "depressed," then the second tag can represent a statement like, "depression is bad."

This is critical to dissecting the lack of "progress" made in both developing spiritual as well as psychological insight or

understanding. To review; the symbol or description is a con-
densation-abstraction of the microscopic level, hence it leaves
out much more information than it includes. Moreover, the
label level does the same. The problem soon lies with the
inferential level. To illustrate, if we were to start with **I AM**—
the object level—with sensations, then at the next level **appears** a label of behavior, then a descriptive level statement:
"I like sugar," "I like to talk," etc., "I don't like studying," "I
don't want a relationship." Let us take the last example to illustrate a point. The description "I don't want a relationship,"
moves to Inference-1 (diagnosis) "this is bad (not normal) in
some way," which then moves to an Inference-2 "we should
want to have a relationship."

"This is an inference, a guess (Bois, *The Art of Awareness*, p. 87), a statement that is not based [even] on sense
perception. Hayakawa warns that . . . the making of inferences is a quick, almost automatic process. (Hayakawa,
Language in Thought and Action, p. 36) Many people are
so quick in jumping to conclusions (inferences) that it
seems they are unaware of the difference between a
descriptive and an inferential statement. Referring to the
quickness that Hayakawa mentioned, I would guess that
if you could time the abstracting process of people, you
would find that they shift from the object level through
the label level and the descriptive level to the inferential
level in less than a second. More tags could be added to
the diagram, which represent more general statements,
with the last tag representing . . . [the belief, everyone
should want a relationship]. In general, additional tags
at successively higher levels of abstraction can represent
more general or more interrelated descriptions or inferences about something.

You might ask at this point, aren't you just playing
with words to claim that different kinds of statements

belong to different levels of abstraction? I would say no, you couldn't make an inference about something without first having a description of that something. There is a structural character to the successive levels of abstraction [condensation], represented by tags linked to tags in the diagram, just as there is a structural character to a ten-story building. You do not construct the frame for the second floor until you have built the frame for the first floor. So it is in making statements: we build descriptions on labels, we build inferences on descriptions, we build conclusions on inferences, etc. This is how we use language to deal with reality. This process of making statement about statements potentially can go on indefinitely in humans. (Korzybski, *Science and Sanity*, p. 392) It is always possible to make a new statement about a previous statement. For example, the new statement can be a criticism or further development of a previous statement.

Eventually, this chain of tags, representing higher and higher levels of abstraction [condensation], lead back to the process level [**consciousness** or **SUBSTANCE**]. This takes the form of a projection onto reality of a person's belief (map) about what reality (territory) is. A person's maps of reality can be called "as if" formulations. (Chisholm, *Introductory Lectures on General Semantics*, pp. 105-106)

As if formulations are the mental maps that people have which they believe corresponds to the territory of reality. These formulations can be theories or just beliefs about the nature of reality. " (Sawin)

This is particularly critical when looking at "spiritual" or "religious" understanding. This projection of belief by a nervous system is described in the following example.

To illustrate, a nervous system will project onto the process level or **consciousness** level or THE SUBSTANCE (called God, which is already at Inference-1) that being "good" or "forgiving" is "spiritual," could be followed by Inference-2 that GOD (**consciousness-SUBSTANCE**) likes forgiving people and to enter THE SUBSTANCE (now inferred to be some "heaven"), which has no-I, and is described in Sanskrit as Neti-Neti (Not this–Not this) or (Not this–Not that), and hence cannot have preferences, ideas, wants, etc. This anthropomorphic reasoning explains the Zen Patriarch saying, "The Great Way is easy, except for those who have preferences."

"The Structural Differential (page 41) shows three and a third tags connected to the object level disk, with an arrow leading from the last tag (broken off to indicate that the tags could go on and on) back up to the process level parabola. The arrow leading back to the process level parabola indicates that whatever a person's highest level abstractions ("as if" formulations) are at a given date, a person projects these onto reality and the person acts as if reality conforms to those formulations. (2) Sometimes, this takes the form of people noticing and accepting aspects of reality which support their beliefs and ignoring or denying aspects of reality, which contradict their beliefs. (Weiss et al., *Education for Adaptation and Survival*, pp. 50, 78, 65)" (Sawin)

This is where THE SUBSTANCE understanding can come to bear, if THE SUBSTANCE is taken in at an earlier level or lower level of abstraction.

For example, let us imagine a "spiritual" student who infers that THE SUBSTANCE is a God who is wrathful if you're angry and loving if you're good. Now, if, somehow an "enlightened" "ONE SUBSTANCE" understanding could creep in at the I AM level or at an earlier level, suddenly the student realizes that these beliefs about God are nonsense, just "spiritual" concepts that have nothing to do with anything. To clarify, a concept is just a word, which is infused with meaning. Once this is "taken in," the earlier beliefs are "seen through," and become absolutely meaningless.

To illustrate, picture a spiritual student who believes that being loving is a way to God, and not being loving takes one away from God; that "path" (concept) disappears when it is "seen through." Unfortunately, however, the spiritual groups might imagine that seeing through concepts and not "acting them out" anymore is a form of resistance.

The *Substance Diagram* can also be used to illustrate the relative importance of the various levels of abstraction. In life, the process level is "closer" to **THE SUBSTANCE** than the object level; the object level is "closer" than the label level, etc. We orient ourselves, in many instances, by the label instead of realizing the object level (silent level) **prior to** the label. (Korzybski, *Historical Note on the Structural Differential*)

On this topic, Weinberg wrote:

> "The verbal level, with its plotting, planning, theorizing, predicting, operates in the final analysis for the sake of the non-verbal [object level] and not vice versa. This is one reason that the general semanticist assigns more value to this level than to the verbal level. (Weinberg, *Levels of Knowing and Existence*, pp. 58-59)

At this point, it can be understood that as the abstractions move farther and farther away from the **THE SUBSTANCE**, the farther they move away from "what is."

CONCLUSION

> "To avoid being misled, we must make a very fine distinction: There is a difference between saying what the process level [or **THE SUBSTANCE**] *is* and saying what the process level [**THE SUBSTANCE**] of reality *acts like*

according to the latest physics theories. (Johnson, *People in Quandaries*, p. 71) We know that we are abstracting organisms we cannot know reality directly or in an absolutely objective way without using our nervous systems. So, we cannot say what anything *is*. We are left with using *as if* formulations such as, 'Matter in the universe acts *as if* it has a physical structure we can describe as atoms, electrons, neutrons, protons, etc.' If we try to say that the process level represents the structure of reality beyond what physics theories currently suggest, we would be implying that structure exists independently from someone perceiving and theorizing about it." (Sawin)

Here, we recall the noted philosopher, George Berkeley's statement, "Nobody has ever seen matter." A nervous system, which occurs after the fact, responds to imagined external and internal processes to promote survival of the imagined person.

This is an excellent point of departure. For what Einstein calls "a condensation of Emptiness," or what Buddha says, "Form is none other than Emptiness; Emptiness is none other than Form" (*Heart Sutra*), or what the *Yoga Sutras* call a contraction of **consciousness**—all of these are abstractions from **THE SUBSTANCE** to **consciousness** on "downward." Hence, there is **NO-I prior to**, and moreover, at the object level, what we call an object or "I" is merely an abstraction, a representation of the nervous system on one level, a coming together of **emptiness** on one level, and a coming together of atoms on another.

This is critical to "gaining understanding," *we cannot say what anything is or why it acts the way it acts!!!!*

Why? Because we do not experience things as they "are," but rather, experiences are *mediated* by the nervous system— they are representational. *Even the "I" is a representation, and what the "I" experiences within itself on a psychological level is a representation of a representation!!!* In this way, we can say only what is NOT (Neti-Neti).

This is critical to understanding the nature of the nervous system. The nervous system perceives and determines (after the fact) an object or event and then justifies what has already occurred—NOT it is there and then "I" see it. Everything is there because the nervous system produces a perceiver that sees its own abstractions and then believes they are real.

The Buddha said:

"All these molecules are not really such; they are called 'molecules.' futhermore . . . a world is not really a world; it is called 'a world.'" (Buddha, *The Diamond Sutra*, p. 41)

Because we see and experience only the past, our perceptions and justifications are more in the past and more abstracted than the object level of sensation, since it is farther away from "what is."

We used the Structural Differential as the basis for creating *The Substance Diagram*, which shows that even at the physiological level, **YOU ARE NOT.**

Both diagrams also help us avoid confusing one level of condensation abstraction with another. This informs us that the inference level *is not* the descriptive level, the descriptive level *is not* the label level, the label level *is not* the object (I AM) level, the object (I AM) level *is not* the microscopic level, the microscopic level *is not*, the physics level, the physics level *is not* the process level, the process level *is not* the **consciousness** level, and when all is THE SUBSTANCE—then there are no levels and **YOU ARE NOT.**

In this way, the following suggestion of Ramana Maharishi holds true even on a physiological level:

GO BACK THE WAY YOU CAME.

RAMANA MAHARISHI

CHAPTER 6

Questions & Answers and Exercises

Question: When the nervous system organizes to defend or organizes around the wound, by just allowing the experience does it disappear?

Wolinsky: Anything can trigger separation. If there is Identification and "you" could stop, and just be in or with it, as energy, and notice what occurs.

Neurophysiologically, if "I" move from sensations to cortical pictures and focus our attention on the story, then it never gets resolved. If I turn my attention the other way, and **go back the way we came** to sensation, or if "you" sit in the **I AM** of sensation and then to the Life Force **prior to** sensation, there can be a shift. Sensation is **prior to** belief (and belief is condensed sensation).

Question: As "you" "go back the way you came," is there a reorganization of the nervous system?

Wolinsky: Over time, yes; but if "I" *go cortical* into story it is impossible to work it out with yourself or another, because it reinforces abstractions, which have nothing to do with anything, and are condensed sensations intermediately and ultimately the condensed **SUBSTANCE**.

If we *go back the way we came*, then I'm going back without the intention of getting rid of it or changing it.

It takes a long time for changes to occur from belief (top) to (sensation) down because the neurological connections are 5 times greater from the brain stem (lower brain) to the cortex (top) than from the cortex (top) to the brain stem (down). There has to be a neurological shift and unwinding for the "realization" to remain stable.

If that be true, then the more "you" move from higher (cortex or cortical level) to lower abstractions back to sensation (brain stem or thalamic level) and ultimately into energy, then "you" will be "closer" to "what is" (**THE SUBSTANCE** level), provided that later "you" don't move back the other way (cortical level) and draw conclusions about "what is."

Question: As soon as "you" draw conclusions, you're back in your story?

Wolinsky: This is why in neuroscience it is suggested that each time there is a movement toward cortical, millions of stimuli are omitted and just a fraction of them are selected.

Each time "I" move from lower to higher (from brainstem to cortical level), I get "farther" away from **THAT**.

This is a neurological picture of "**go back the way you came.**" That's why "you" should take the labels off, have it as energy, then take the label off of energy, and dive into the **NOTHINGNESS.**

I can stay in the land of psychological abstractions or the spiritual story and game, but then I am stuck in abstractions.

Question: It seems that when "you" hit sensations, then people systematically go into stories and that's where the resistance hits?

Wolinsky: That's because it's hard-wired into the nervous system, fight-flight-freeze. To organize chaos, the nervous system automatically shifts sensations to thoughts, etc. For its survival, in other words, the chaos must come up with a reason, a story, a false cause. To organize, the nervous system goes cortical. When it goes cortical, the nervous system gets into the cause-effect.

The nervous system has a searching-seeking mechanism, which, for survival, keeps it going, and it will get into anything to avoid the chaos of not knowing

Question: "You" said in Volume III of *The Way of the Human* that thoughts come out of the personal level.

Wolinsky: Let's not jump levels. There is no personal thought. The illusion is that if a thought goes by, such as "I love myself" or "I hate myself," the "I" Stephen is having that thought.

At a physiological level, my nervous system is producing this thought, this representation of the idea of Stephen and "I." But, ultimately, that is not occurring. Ultimately, "I's" are coming and going all the time. They are not personal to a "you" or the "I" "you" call yourself. Stay with I AM; discard all else.

Question: What about patterns?

Wolinsky: There are no such things as patterns. There is an "I" thought, which believes in patterns and sees patterns as a way to imagine that it can secure survival. Seeing and believing that the future mimics the past is a trick of the mind a habit that the noted philosphers David Hume, and later John Stuart Mill, call a "habit of mind," to paraphrase: "The mind [nervous system] will create the illusion and make it appear as though the future mimics the past, and will take whatever measure it must to make it appear so." Why? Because it aids in the illusion of control and better future survival, if I imagine that the past mimics the future, then "I" (imagine) by knowing the past (as in psychotherapy) "I" can control the future (relationships, money, etc.) and survive better.

There is no pattern that independently exists separate from the perceiver or observer of the pattern.

"YOU NEVER PUT YOUR FOOT IN THE SAME RIVER TWICE."

—Heraclitus

Your mind (nervous system) makes "you" think it's the same river; it's not the same river.

This is the reason psychology has such a problem. Freud was accurate on a physiological level that the nervous system will "organize trauma into chains of earlier similar events," so that "You" survive better, but *it is not an accurate organization.*

EACH MOMENT IS A NEW MOMENT OF SPACE-TIME

The illusion that "I" have a problem in 2000 because "my" mother didn't love me in 1950 is nonsense.

THE PERCEIVER OF THE PATTERN IS PART OF THE PATTERN.

There are no patterns, the perceiver of the pattern is part of the pattern, and the perceiver of the pattern perceives a pattern where there is none.

When we understand that the perceiver of the pattern, the pattern, and the "awar__er__" of a pattern are all made of the same UNDERLYING SUBSTANCE then (puff) it all disappears. "Patterns" and "the body" are inferences that **appear** *after the fact* and they function only as a reinforcement of survival, or to make "one" mistakenly believe that they WERE, ARE and WILL BE.

Descartes Catastrophe

Descartes famous statement; "I think therefore **I AM**" has impacted the western world, more than this book could even say.

However, in the light of 2001 neuroscience, it is a totally inaccurate statement.

The "I" that the nervous system produces after the experience has already occurred is a representation, which imagines *it was, is,* and *will be,* but; the "I," which was produced by the nervous system, is merely a representation, a chemical reaction. It could be said that "I AM" **appears** and imagines it is, and that it thinks; however, it is just an **appearance,** *it is not*. Metaphorically, consider H_2O (water). If we were to add hydrogen (2 parts) to oxygen (1 part), the water **appears**. In the same way, chemicals mix together and the "I" **appears**.

"You" could ask, "*Who were you prior to the appearance of the "I"? Who were you prior to emergence of the I AM"? Who were you prior to emergence of the "awarer"?*

To paraphrase Nisargadatta Maharaj, "They ask me who my successor will be, my successor will come from my body, my sperm, and what is the body—the body is made of food and "you" (the "I") are made of food since the "I" comes from the body. And what is the essence of food? *Sperm* (sexual fluid). So you are all a bunch of sperm; what do you have to be proud of?"

The Designer Impulse

So powerful is this cause-effect habit that people see the world and its design and then they reason backward and conclude that there must be a *designer* who caused this. At the object level, the body formation, the nervous system, and the I AM appear. The nonverbal I AM appears; it is a most primitive part of the nervous system. In a way, the object level appears with the formation of the nervous system. The I AM of no thoughts, memory, emotions, associations, perceptions, attention, or intentions is the touchstone between this perceived (imaginary) world that occurs through perception and the nervous system (not an "I" perceiving) and THAT SUBSTANCE. The *Yoga Sutras* say it this way:

The principle of "I AM," is the witness of the body and mind in the form of awareness, pure consciousness alone. It is pure awareness, pure consciousness, still it sees through the coloring of the perceptual mechanism, that is to say, through the spectacles of the mind and senses in the relative universe. By practicing the different steps of Yoga for the destruction of impurity (thought constructs), there arises spiritual illumination . . . awareness of the universal "I AM" beyond the individual or personal "I am." (Mishra, *Textbook of Yoga Psychology*, p. 406)

EXERCISE #3

Look at an object in the room; then withdraw your attention from it, **prior to** any thoughts, ideas, knowledge, information you have about the object. (Singh, *Vijnanabhairava*)

(Notice the Non-verbal I AM prior to Inferences)

EXERCISE #4

Notice a sensation, withdraw your attention from it, **prior to** the sensation any thoughts, ideas, knowledge or, information "you" have about the sensation.

(Notice the Non-verbal I AM prior to any thoughts, memory, emotions, association, perceptions, attention or intentions.)

WHEN THE MIND TURNS ON ITSELF (UPON ITSELF), YOU GO BACK THE WAY YOU CAME.

Question: What about the techniques of diagnosis in the *Diagnostic and Statistical Manual of Mental Disorders* (DSM-IV), the enneagram, etc?

Wolinsky: All of this only reinforces the abstracting process, basically categorization represents an undifferentiated nervous system. Psychology begins with a client who has an undifferentiated nervous system. They see all men as Dad, all women as Mom, etc. Now a differentiated nervous system sees differences, not only similarities. Diagnoses and enneagram typing sees mostly, if not only, similarities, which represents an undifferentiated nervous system, which means greater and greater abstractions and farther away from "what is."

So, on a neurological level and psychological level we could say, "The greater the degree of differentiation the greater the health." Why? Because no labels, descriptions, or inferences are "NOW" in this moment of space-time, and "closer" to "what is."

The less the differentiation of the nervous system, the more it gets into categories, frames, lenses, boxes, and, in short, the nervous system trying to make everyone the same as everyone else, thus the further away from "what is."

Student: Where does intention come in?

· Wolinsky: I do not trust what people declare their intentions or motivations to be because they are always honorable. There is a therapy, which says that all thoughts, etc., have a positive intention or useful purpose.

That's bullshit. The thoughts at a physiological level are survival driven because they are manufactured by the body and nervous system to survive, including the concept that all thoughts have a positive intention or useful purpose.

If we slowed down the process, we would discover that all verbalization is cortical and it **appears** after the fact, only to justify and explain.

Student: But in my experience by asking, "what is the positive intention or useful purpose of a thought or action," it *always* has a positive intention.

Wolinsky: Of course it does, for two reasons: First, the question pre-supposes and elicits that positive answer. Second, "you" are asking a person, after the fact, to justify a positive reason for their actions. This *infers* that there is one. Moreover, intentions are part of the pulsation that arises **prior to** the action and the "I" realizing the action occurring. Intentions are **prior to** the "*I*"'s appearance. Some have even said that if "you" want to know what was "intended" (not by an "I," since an "I" appears later), just notice what occurred. That is the non-verbal, pre-"I" intention **prior to** the **appearance**—"I" which justifies and infers *why* this or that occurred.

              Let's take an example.

Wolinsky: Hitler wanted to kill Jews. What was his positive intention?

Student: In his mind, to purify the world.

Wolinsky: What was his negative intention?

Student: To get their money and property.

Wolinsky: What was his positive intention?

Student: To make Germany more Aryan and better, more space.

Wolinsky: What was his negative intention?

Student: To destroy what he saw as enemies and use a scapegoat to unite people behind him.

Wolinsky: The point is that the question provides the context for the answer, and brings out an answer that matches the question, and secondly, the question pre-supposes the **appearance**—"I"'s inferences are real.

Student: Let's say "I" want to go someplace, don't "I" have an intention to go before "I" go?

Wolinsky: EACH MOMENT APPEARS AS A NEW MOMENT OF NO-TIME NOW. The **appearance**—"I" **appears** after the action has already been put in motion. The "I" has no say. It appears as part of the intention wave and then the "I" says "I" intended or created that. Metaphorically, if we· first have the ocean, then through movement, the wave (intention), then through wave intention, a water droplet ("I" **appears**) and says, "I" am now deciding to go to the beach. Well, the wave (intention) pre-appearance—"I" is already going to the beach. The **appearance**—"I" did nothing; the **appearance**—"I" assumes doership when it's already happening. That is the illusion. It's already happening and then an "I" **appears** and declares its intention. One student said that when they were in "no time now," he would be at the door opening it and walking outside, and all of a sudden, a thought would say, "I need to go outside now."

Pure intention is pre-verbal and is a movement that cannot be known until an "I" **appears**. Therefore, it cannot be an "I"'s intention. The intention, like a wave, arose before the "I" (water droplet) even knew of the wave, the movement, or that it was.

THE KNOWER

"Find the knower." Nisargadatta Maharaj said to me, "Who is the knower of the knowledge of your birth?" Find that out. "I" thought that there was a knower of the knowledge of "my" birth. But when "you" look for it, *it is not.* Upon investigation, everything disappears like a **mirage** in the desert, and *"go back the way you came."*

Each knower has limited knowing. When "you" look for the knower, it evaporates. And "you" are getting "closer" to **THE SUBSTANCE**. Once "you" go beyond the knower-known, there is an appreciation that if there is no knower, there is no known.

Student: What about judgment or values?

Wolinsky: It's the nature of the cerebral cortex to judge. Many existential philosophers believe that judging is part of the human condition, and is normal. If I try to change the judgment or judger, "you" get further away from "WHAT IS" and the "REAL." The more into abstractions we get, the more into the **mirage** we find ourselves. We are trying to go *back the way the "I" came.*

Student: It seems like it's easier to go up into abstraction than down or *back the way we came.*

Wolinsky: Yes, because there are many more neurological connections from down (brain stem) to up (cerebral cortex) than from up (cerebral cortex) to down (brain stem).

Student: How do I get behind or *back the way we came?* I seem to get more and more I-dentities and thoughts.

Wolinsky: Notice the knower of the I-dentities and thoughts, and ask what knower is knowing them.

Student: The mind.

Wolinsky: And if the knower of the mind and the mind were made of THE SAME SUBSTANCE?

Student: _____Blank_____(Silence)_____

Wolinsky: That blank is **prior to** inferences and is the non-verbal I AM. The illusion is that the "I" which knows the mind is made of a different **consciousness** than the concept called MIND. The H. H. Dalai Lama said, "The mind is devoid of mind."

When "you" realize they are the same, "you" realize "The mind is devoid of mind."

When Nisargadatta Maharaj said, "Who is the knower? Find out." "I" thought there was one who was the knower, but actually upon investigation, the knower-known and the process of knowing, all disappeared; they are one unit.

Student: I am here now, "I" can see and feel that, how can "you" say "I" am not or that I am an illusion?

Wolinsky: Let's begin by trying to just give the understanding that YOU ARE NOT. First, "you" get that the nervous system abstracts and selects out so that what "your" eyes see is an abstraction of THAT ONE SUBSTANCE.

Student: Yes "I" can understand that intellectually.

Wolinsky: Good place to start Now, the perceiver of, let's say, what "you" call your hand is also an abstraction of the microscopic level, and the image of the hand is an abstraction of the perceiver.

Student: Yes.

Wolinsky: Now if we start from THE SUBSTANCE and go through all the levels **prior to I AM**, there still is **No-I** or **No-You**.

Student: Yes.

Wolinsky: If we define a **mirage** as an illusion, whereby the perceiver's nervous system (at one level), THE SUBSTANCE at another makes something **appear** like water in the desert, out of NOTHING (since it is not there), is not that a mirage—an optical illusion?!!

Student: Yes, so "I" am here, and the **I AM** and the body only **appear** to exist to the **I AM**, or the perceiver?

Wolinsky: Yes. In this way, the story is told of a Zen Master who upon "realization" proclaimed "Where is my body?"

IF A TREE FALLS IN THE FOREST AND NOBODY IS THERE . . . DOES IT MAKE A SOUND?

Answer: No, no perceiver of the sound, no nervous system to record the event and say "This is a sound"—no sound.

The great illusion is that the perceiver of the body or even the "awarer" of the body is separate from the body. *Both* are by-products of the nervous system and they occur only as the neurotransmitters (fluids, to use Nisargadatta's terminology) come together and form I AM.

THE NERVOUS SYSTEM CLEANS ITSELF

The nervous system, through periodicity, blanks or cleans itself many times per second. Niruddha Samadhi (see Section III: The Spanda) is realizing this gap. Then "you" ultimately *apperceive* that there is a gap-thought-gap-thought, then "you" become aware that the "I" "you" think "you" are also disappears in the gap. "Normally," "you" do not realize this, because in the gap, YOU ARE NOT. This could explain why, when Korzybski was asked a question, he pointed to where "you" were (object level, inference level, etc.) on the Structural Differential, thus, keeping it as non-verbal as possible.

Student: It seems like we are going into destruction and creation.

Wolinsky: There is no destruction-creation, there is just a flashing-forth, called nimesa-unmesa in Sanskrit, but we do not recognize the disappearance because we are not there. (See Section II and Section III: The Spanda.)

"BELIEVE ME, THERE CANNOT BE ENOUGH DESTRUCTION."

—*Nisargadatta Maharaj*

GO BACK THE WAY YOU CAME

EXERCISE #5

1) Recall a time you felt sad.
2) Take the label off of sadness.
3) Then allow the label called energy to dissolve.
4) Notice the NOTHING, under the energy label.

IF EVERYTHING IS CONSCIOUSNESS, ALL THE SAME SUBSTANCE "YOU" GO INTO NO-ME SAMADHI.

Student: What about imaging and changing beliefs?

Wolinsky: Don't try to change the abstraction. Imaging is an abstraction. The nervous system makes things **appear** solid which are not solid. It does this by omitting millions of stimuli and selecting only a small fraction. Hence it **appears** solid to the perceiver; but the perceiver is part of the nervous system, which perceives itself.

If "you" look at your body or anyone's body, my hand, for example, to the looker, perceiver, it looks solid. But the perceiver is part of the nervous system perceiving itself as solid. To the perceiver, it is solid.

Is your body there? **No.** There is no body there unless a perceiver is there, which is the nervous system perceiving itself. No nervous system, no body.

"LIBERATION" IS NOT GETTING THAT YOU ARE NOT THE BODY. "LIBERATION" IS GETTING THAT THERE IS NO BODY.

Question: What is sleep?

Wolinsky: There are two parts to this. The first is that the body is not solid and the perceiver of the body is not solid. And second that the body-mind/perceiver/nervous system, "I" is a lens, and it is through this lens that the **mirage appears** to itself, which is condensed **consciousness.** The **mirage** is made of **consciousness.** The I AM which is nervous system produced is the first lens of condensed **consciousness.** No I AM, no **mirage.** The force or vital force just underneath the sensation is the mover of the sensation one step **prior to I AM.** When "you" sleep, the **I AM** is not. During sleep the **consciousness** thins-out. The body is compacted **consciousness.** When the **consciousness** *is not* body-identified, the body goes to sleep. The body sleeps when "you" wake up it is because **consciousness** is now body identified. "You" assume "you" were when "you" were asleep—but *"you" were not.*

Ramana Maharishi suggested "noticing" the NOT-I AM to I AM space between deep sleep to waking sleep. And then notice, as Nisargadatta Maharaj said, "Find out how this **I AM** came on "you," first "I" *wasn't,* now I **AM.**

Dreaming is less-solidified **consciousness** then sleep. Dreams are a **mirage** within a **mirage.**

Some people try to think that the dream **mirage** is or has meaning for the waking **mirage.**

There is the story in the Astravaka Gita where King Janaka realizes that dream and waking state are the same.

Student: I oftentimes feel disoriented.

Wolinsky: When the **appearance**—"I" loses its point of reference or structure in space-time, it feels disoriented, or not oriented in space-time. It seems to happen in layers.

As "you" *go back to the way you came* there is disorientation. This is part of the deconstruction process.

Student: I realized that as a child, "I" was told "I" *was too much.*

Wolinsky: In the book, *Murder of Christ*, Wilhelm Reich likens the Life Force to Christ. He described what he called the Emotional plague. It is, basically, "Why do people try to kill others who have a BIG Life Force." "You do unto others that which was done unto you." "I" must kill their Life Force, to the degree that mine was killed (repressed) by others.

There was a movie about a horse, *Phar Lap.* In this true story, Phar Lap, who was the greatest racehorse, had a life force so big that he was murdered. The mantra of the movie was; "*You can be good—but not too good.*"

Student: Too much Life Force is dangerous?

Wolinsky: Yes, people will try to kill your life force to the degree that theirs was killed. *Just be the Life Force.* Let go of everything else. Life Force is **prior to** sensation. Suppression of Life Force in homeopathy causes disease. When "you" are *going back the way you came,* there is no living, living occurs with No-I.

Student: What about the development of awareness?

Wolinsky: Developing awareness *can be a trap* when trying to find out who you are because awareness, which is produced by an "awar<u>er</u>," implicitly "believes" that if it becomes more aware, it will survive better.

The "awar*er*" is a very subtle structure.

Ask the question: What psychotherapy or spiritual paths (games) could not be played if "you" did have the concept of awareness?

All psycho-spirituality depends on the concept of awareness. The psychospiritual games (paths) usually emphasize awareness, which implies an "awar*er*."

Beyond the last step of Eight-Limbed Yoga, beyond even Samadhi, there is no more awareness.

EXERCISE #6

The thinker, hearer, sensor is contained within and is part of the experience itself.

1) What hearer is hearing these words? Notice the hearer is part of the hearing and heard.
2) What sensor is sensing these words? Notice the sensor is part of the sensing and sensed.
3) What thinker is thinking this? Notice the thinker is part of the thinking and thought.
4) What "awar*er*" is awaring this? Notice the awarer is part of the awaring or awareness and the awared.

CONTEMPLATION: If the nonverbal I AM is made of THE SAME SUBSTANCE as the experience, thought, sensation, or awareness itself, then what occurs?

THE "I" APPEARS—AFTER THE FACT OR AFTER THE HAPPENING HAS ALREADY HAPPENED, AND THEN THE APPEARANCE—"I" DECLARES IT DOES, DID, CREATED, OR INTENDED THIS OR THAT TO HAPPEN.

Student: Why can "I" not see THE SUBSTANCE that the I AM is made of?

Wolinsky: A sculpture is, at first, only clay. Someone, looking at a block of clay, asked Michelangelo, "Where's the statue?" He replied, "It's already in there, all I have to do is remove the clay that is not the statue." In the same way, "you," as THE SUBSTANCE, are there. "You" cannot see it because "you" think "you" are the clay. The master sees "you" beyond the clay while "you" cannot.

Moreover, since "you" within the clay are created by the nervous system, as the clay gets taken away, the nervous system goes into fight-flight-freeze.

The abstracting process is so great that, metaphorically, to make a coffee cup, "you" would have to remove so much clay that it would equal the size of the earth.

Student: What about the observer?

Wolinsky: The observer, too, is part of the nervous system and hence, because the nervous system organizes through abstraction, the "I" and the observer see patterns both internally and externally, a solid world, etc., because it is a vehicle or filter of the nervous system.

THE WORD PROCESS

The question often arises, "Why are words, ideas, theories—in short, abstractions— created on a physiological level? The answer is **survival**. But why would this increase the chance of survival? My answer is that if "an experience" is viewed as a threat to the survival of the nervous system the animal or person takes action with the result that the experience is not digested. In other words, the unwanted experience is viewed as a predator. This threat to the nervous system includes a physical threat as well as a conjured up belief system. This is why theories, inferences, and other abstractions are produced automatically by the nervous system to explain the alleged chaos or threat or false causes that are created so that the nervous system imagines that it can control, prevent, or stop something that might threaten its survival. In this way, concepts, which are words infused with meanings, get charged with energy. To dis-charge these words, do the exercises below:

Defusing letters from words. Going beyond the meaning of words.

EXERCISE #7

1) Take a charged word.
2) Make associations based on each letter.
3) Notice what occurred.

Example

Student: I freak out that people are a-n-g-r-y at me.

Wolinsky: Tell me an association about the letter 'a.'

Student: Anxiety, alone, angst, annoying, animosity, anonymous, preposterous, fanomomus.

Wolinsky:	Tell me an association about the letter 'n.'
Student:	Nasty, negative, now, noun, nuts, never, nerd, knuckle-head.
Wolinsky:	Tell me an association about the letter 'g.'
Student:	Girl, girly, gorilla, gridlock, girdle, gorgeous.
Wolinsky:	Tell me an association about the letter 'r.'
Student:	Riddle, ridiculous, ridicule, rhyme, wire, time, fine, climb.
Wolinsky:	Tell me an association around the letter 'y.'
Student:	You, Fuck you, yodel, yucker, finger pointing, hey you.
Wolinsky:	How are you doing?
Student:	Calm, more peaceful.

EXERCISE #8

Looking from back there.

1) Now notice the "charged" word.
2) Pull your attention back **prior to** any thought, impression, knowledge, or ideas "you" have about the changed word.
3) From "back there," how does the word seem to "you"?

**THE NERVOUS SYSTEM GIVES THE ILLUSION
THAT THERE IS A CONTINUAL UNINTERRUPTED
CONTINUITY OF "YOU."
ACTUALLY THIS "YOU" OR "I"
APPEARS-DISAPPEARS-APPEARS-DISAPPEARS.
THE "I" OR "YOU," BEING AN APPEARANCE
AND A BY-PRODUCT OF THE NERVOUS SYSTEM.
THE "I" OR "YOU" DOES NOT KNOW
WHEN "YOU" ARE NOT.
WHY? BECAUSE THERE IS
NO "YOU" IN THE GAPS.**

THE BODY CONCEPT

The perceiver, through inference, develops an image of "her/his" body, which is then seen by the perceiver. It is important, therefore, to enquire into the nature of the perceiver's inference in order to *GO BACK THE WAY WE CAME*

ENQUIRY INTO THE NATURE OF THE BODY CONCEPT

Wolinsky: Where is the concept called "my" consciousness that believes in the concept of the body?

Note:

The concept called "my" **consciousness** is a pivotal abstraction because it presupposes more than one SUBSTANCE and separation.

Bill: My head.

Wolinsky: How would the concept called "my" **consciousness** and the concept called I AM define the body?

Note:
We always try to phrase the question so as to "distance" the "my" consciousness as a structure, which I AM NOT.

Bill: The body is a vehicle of the **consciousness.**

Wolinsky: What assumptions has this concept called "my" **consciousness** and the concept **I AM** made about the body?

Bill: That it is real, it operates, and it is necessary.

Wolinsky: And by the concept called "my" **consciousness** and the concept **I AM** believing in the concept called "It is real, it operates and is it necessary"? What have been the consequences for the concept called "my" **consciousness?**

Bill: That the **I AM** concept and the body believe *it is.*

Wolinsky: And if the concept called "my" **consciousness** believed the concept called "it is real," "it operates," "it is necessary," and **I AM** (including the "one" aware of this) and they were all made of the same **underlying SUBSTANCE** which had nothing to do with anything, then . . . ?

Bill: _____(Silence).

Wolinsky: Regarding this concept called "my" **consciousness,** which believes in a concept of a body, and **I AM,** what has a fantasized separate "my" **consciousness** imagined it has done to another fantasized separate "my" **consciousness?**

Bill: Made it believe it was, and that it was separate and existed in a different location with a past, present, and future.

Wolinsky: Regarding the body concept, what has another fantasized separate "my" **consciousness** imagined it has done to this fantasized separate "my" **consciousness?**

Bill: Made it believe it was, is, has a past, present, and future.

Wolinsky: And what did this **consciousness** imagine was true?

Bill: It was, somehow it validated its is(ness), was(ness) and will be(ness).

Wolinsky: What if all of these were concepts and were made of **consciousness** and had nothing to do with. anything, then . . . ?

Bill: _____(Silence).

Wolinsky: How has the **consciousness prior to** the I AM body concept deceived itself?

Bill: Believing it was.

Wolinsky: And what if these were concepts of the **consciousness prior to I AM** which have nothing to do with anything, then . . . ?

Bill: _____(Silence).

Wolinsky: This "my" **consciousness** concept, which looks through the concept of the I AM body, how has it deceived itself?

Bill: Believing it was the I AM body lens it was looking through.

Wolinsky: And if the I AM body lens had nothing to do with anything, then . . . ?

Bill: _____(Long silence)_____

Wolinsky:	What is the concept called "my" **consciousness,** which looks through the I AM lens unwilling to communicate about?
Bill:	That it is all just **consciousness.**
Wolinsky:	Why would the concept called "my" **consciousness,** which looks through the I AM body, be unwilling to communicate about that?
Bill:	Because if it knew it was just **consciousness,** there would be no **consciousness.**
Wolinsky:	Is there anything the **consciousness,** which looks through the I AM body concept, must now know?
Bill:	It isn't.
Wolinsky:	Is there anything the **consciousness,** which looks through the I AM body concept, must not experience?
Bill:	It isn't_____(Silence).

VITAL FORCE

What is the vital force? The vital force lies underneath and animates the vital breath. Meditation on the breath misses this basic understanding. Because it *is what animates the breath or the vital force that is prior to the breath and I AM.*

ENQUIRY INTO THE NATURE OF THE VITAL FORCE

Wolinsky:	Where is the concept called "my" **consciousness,** which forms the concept called I AM and the vital force?
Ted:	Around the body.

Wolinsky: How would the concept called "my" **consciousness** and I AM define the concept of vital force?

Ted: As its manifestation.

Wolinsky: And what have been the assumptions the concept called "my" **consciousness** has made about the vital force concept?

Ted: That the I AM concept can be aware of the vital force.

Wolinsky: And if that was an illusion and the concept of I AM came from the vital force rather than the other way around?

Ted: . . . All gone_____blank_____silence.

Note:

This, as will be noted, describes what G.I. Gurdjieff meant by the world being upside down. The I AM is a by-product of the vital force, not the other way around. This means that when the I AM continually stays aware of the breath, it can reinforce the illusion of beingness or isness, rather than realizing that the being or isness concepts **appear** from or are a by-product of the vital force.

THE VITAL BREATH

ENQUIRY INTO THE NATURE OF THE VITAL BREATH

Wolinsky: How would the concept called "my" **consciousness** and the concept I AM define the Vital Breath or Life Force?

Jake: The force or energy, which pumps the energy through the body, keeping it animated and alive.

Wolinsky: And what assumptions has the concept called "my" **consciousness** made about the vital breath?

Jake: That it needs it to live.

Wolinsky: If the concept called "my" **consciousness** that looks through the I AM body concept and the vital breath and life were all just concepts made of THE SAME SUBSTANCE and had nothing to do with anything.

Jake: (Silence). The life concept disappears.

Wolinsky: How has the "my" **consciousness** concept, which looks through the I AM and the body concept, deceived itself?

Jake: That it is and is separate from the **consciousness**.

Wolinsky: **And if all these were just a concept made of THE SAME SUBSTANCE,including the one who is aware of it, and it all has nothing to do with anything, then . . . ?**

Jake: There is no life or body or breath of I AM separate from the **consciousness**.

Wolinsky: If these were just illusions of the concept called "my" **consciousness**, which had nothing to do with anything, then . . . ?

Jake: _____(Silence).

Wolinsky: This concept called "my" **consciousness** that gives the illusion of I AM, vital breath body concept, etc., what must it not know?

Jake: That it is not the body.

Wolinsky: And, if all of these were just concepts, which were made of THE SAME SUBSTANCE, and which had nothing to do with anything, then . . . ?

Jake: _____(Silence)_____(blank)_____ (long silence).

NOTHING IS BREATHING

(Nisargadatta Maharaj's, "Focus on that which animates the breathing apparatus.")

EXERCISE #9

1) Feel your breath.
2) Rather than "you" breathing, "notice" that "you" are being breathed.

THE PERCEIVER OF THE BODY IS PART OF THE BODY FOR MOST, THE SEARCH FOR ENLIGHTENMENT IS ABOUT SURVIVING BETTER

This is a hard one for "spiritual seekers" (fans) to stomach. The nervous system uses its searching-seeking mechanism to find better and better ways to survive. In this case, enlightenment is a spiritualized survival mechanism to enhance survival. In short, "If I get enlightened, I'll survive better."

THE NERVOUS SYSTEM WILL NOT ALLOW YOU TO SEE ANYTHING BUT SURVIVAL

When there is a point of view from within the body-mind nervous system, the perception is a phenomenon, hence the point of perception, which is nervous system based, is survival based. In this way, the only thing that is allowed in our perceptions or understanding is that which supports our perceptual apparatus and its survival.

Moreover, the nervous system contains a searching-seeking mechanism, which is structured to enhance survival by avoiding pain and seeking pleasure.

Furthermore, the nervous system will "see" and be attracted to that which supports its survival, not its death. When seeking enlightenment in order to survive better is "seen through," or better said, its illusion is pierced, then "you" are no longer trying to get or attain anything.

IT'S DIFFICULT FOR THE NERVOUS SYSTEM TO TAKE IN AN "ENLIGHTENED" UNDERSTANDING BECAUSE IT IS PERCEIVED AS DEATH TO THE NERVOUS SYSTEM, THUS EVOKING ITS FIGHT—FLIGHT—FREEZE RESPONSE.

The nervous system, the "I," the I AM, the body, are one. Hence, Nisargadatta Maharaj called it the body-mind.

In this way, all "understanding," particularly "enlightened" understandings disrupt or confront this nervous system response and create a feeling of threat or attack. In this way, the "I" and the body feels like it should try to destroy the attacker and or its perception by either 1) killing it, 2) diagnosing it, or 3) destroying it in some way. In short, *kill the messenger.*

BECAUSE OF SURVIVAL, ENLIGHTENED PERCEPTIONS CAN MAKE THE "I" FEELS CRAZY, LIKE IT WILL DIE.

Student: Why do we feel so threatened when something is explained that goes against what we believe or have been taught?

Wolinsky: All learning is for survival. All learnings, therefore, are produced by the nervous system. When the nervous system "sees" or perceives something as a danger to itself, it fights, flights, or freezes. This occurs sometimes when "you" cannot understand something; "you" can feel like it is not worth knowing, or put it down in some way because the nervous system feels insulted or threatened (as in its intelligence), and so the nervous system might begin to denigrate it.

PROTO-SELF

Going back the way you came, on a physiological level, means moving from the inferential or cortical brain down to the (brain stem) reptilian brain. The proto-self is in the reptilian brain. The proto-self is the governing factor, the Fight-Flight-Freeze, the kill or be killed, which is **prior to** the inferential psychological level that arises through the socialization process, to justify, rationalize, psychologize, and mythologize animal behavior.

THE PROTO-SELF: PRIOR TO THE APPEARANCE OF THE "I"

Strategy I: Kill

If it is assumed or imagined that someone else is the source of pain, then the organism wants to kill the person. A human is an animal with a cortex. The nervous system resists **real or** imagined threats to survival.

Strategy II: Assimilate

Anything seen as separate or different can be seen as a

threat. Therefore, oftentimes the nervous system deludes itself making them (person or psycho-spiritual system) **appear** as similar to "you" in order to reduce the imagined threat.

Vedanta: Realize (Not This)—(Not That)

Now, as your nervous system gets more differentiated, it can begin to see everything as not "you" (NOT-this) and kill it. This occurs when the nervous system uses its natural process to find out who "you" are.

The nervous system will use anything it can to continue its survival, until it becomes differentiated and turns on itself. Remember, there is no "you" separate from the nervous system.

It is not that there is a "you," which judges, rejects or accepts. It is the nervous system that judges, rejects or accepts. The "I," which imagines that it judges, accepts or rejects **appears** after the judging acceptance or rejection has occurred. Then it comes up with reasons, stories, and justifications for acceptance or rejection judgements, which are even farther away in time—all this to ensure its own survival.

**THERE IS ONLY AN APPEARANCE OF "I,"
WHICH APPEARS AFTER THE FACT; THEREFORE,
THERE IS NO PERSONAL RESPONSIBILITY.
REASONS ONLY BEGET MORE REASONS.**

It is in this way that the ongoing abstracting process continues. The survival drive of the nervous system demands an ongoing organization of chaos, which yields further abstractions and and inferences for survival. In this way, there are no reasons for events or things, and yet the nervous system creates reasons, false causes, and false solutions (psychotherapy) as automatically and as easily as the digestion of food.

EVERY HIGHER ABSTRACTION OFFERS AN EXPLANATION, JUSTIFICATION, AND RE-ENFORCEMENT OF THE EARLIER ABSTRACTIONS, WHICH GETS FARTHER AWAY FROM "WHAT IS."

Simply put, as we move from the object level to the descriptive level to the inference levels, in order for the nervous system to organize the chaos, millions of stimuli are omitted and only a fraction of them are used. The result is that a world, which is fluid, causeless, purposeless, and missionless, will, to the "I" that appears, seem solid, with cause and purpose. Moreover, each movement to higher and higher levels of inference lead us farther and farther into an illusory world that does not exist. Moreover, inferences are infused with meanings, which justify a belief in words and their meanings, giving them an existence, which is not. *Learning is accumulating information for survival only.*

"... VIKALPA (THOUGHT-CONSTRUCT) ACTS AS A BARRIER AND DOES NOT ALLOW US TO HAVE A VIEW OF THE REALITY SHINING WITHIN OURSELVES. IT IS ONLY WHEN THERE IS DISSOLUTION OF VIKALPA (THOUGHT CONTRUCTS) THAT THE SCREEN THAT HIDES THE ESSENTIAL REALITY, THE ESSENTIAL DIVINE SELF FROM OURSELVES IS REMOVED AND WE HAVE A VIEW OF THAT REALITY WHICH HAS ALWAYS BEEN SCINTILLATING WITHIN IN ALL ITS GLORY. THAT REALITY IS NOT SOMETHING TO BE ACHIEVED, BUT UNCOVERED. BUT THE CRUX OF THE PROBLEM IS HOW TO MAKE THE VIKALPAFUL (THOUGHT) MIND RETIRE."
(*Siva Sutras*, pp. xxv-xxvi)

THOUGHTS→THEORIES AND PHILOSOPHIES

Abstractions create distance and divide where there are no divisions.

Abstractions must be negated.

THE NERVOUS SYSTEM CREATES ABSTRACTIONS, WHICH PRODUCE MEANINGS WHERE THERE ARE NONE.

"THE THREE LIMITING CONDITIONS ARE A KIND OF LIMITED, VITIATED KNOWLEDGE ROOTED IN WORDS WHICH HAVE A TREMENDOUS INFLUENCE ON OUR LIVES. THESE WORDS ARE FORMED OF LETTERS (KNOWN AS MATRKA). THE MATRKA (WORDS AND LETTERS), THEREFORE, FORMS THE BASIS OF ALL LIMITED KNOWLEDGE." (*Siva Sutras*, p. xvii)

AN ABSTRACTION IS AN ABSTRACTION OF NOTHINGNESS

ALL IS AN ABSTRACTION OF THE NOTHINGNESS. A CONDENSATION; BUT STILL NOTHINGNESS.

THE BODY AS A LENS

The body is not without a perceiver of the body. It is in this way that the perceiver of the body cannot be separated from the body itself. The nervous system is a lens that omits, selects-out and views its own reality, solidity, and organization out of the NOTHINGNESS.

ARE YOU FEELING "WHAT IS" THERE, OR YOUR IDEAS ABOUT "WHAT IS" THERE?

The Middle Path

The middle path has been misunderstood as being moderate and not extreme. Moderate sleeping, eating, sex, etc.

However, another view might be the following:

EXERCISE #10

The Middle Path

Middle path—the space between the knower and the known.

1) Notice an object, thought, emotion, etc.
2) Be the knower of the object, thought or emotion.
3) Stay in the space between the knower of the object and the known object.

It is by staying in the middle space between knower and known that the silence or gap is "realized."

EXERCISE #11

---

1) Notice a thought.
2) Be the knower of the thought.
3) Notice the space between the knower and the known.
4) Notice what occurs if the knower, known, and the space are made of **THE SAME SUBSTANCE.**
5) Notice the non-verbal I AM.

The middle path, as mentioned in *Quantum Consciousness*, is holding the Understanding that nothing is true – nothing is false, simultaneously.

CONTEMPLATE

1) Nothing is true – Nothing is false simultaneously.
2) Notice the non-verbal I AM.

IMPULSES ARE AN OUTWARD MOVEMENT OF CONSCIOUSNESS. IT IS PART OF THE PULSATION CALLED SPANDA. IMAGINING THAT AN "I" OR "YOU" CAN OR SHOULD CHANGE OR ALTER SOMETHING IS TO DENY THE IMPULSE, WHICH IS LIKE TRYING TO SWIM UPSTREAM, LIKE A WATER DROPLET IN THE OCEAN, TRYING TO MOVE IN THE OPPOSITE DIRECTION AS THE OCEAN. WHEN "YOU" TRY TO CHANGE, ALTER, OR DENY THE IMPULSE, IT YIELDS MORE THOUGHTS AND IDEAS. ONE MUST GO WITH THE IMPULSE, REALIZING THAT THE IMPULSE AND THE EXPERIENC_ER_ OF THE IMPULSE ARE MADE OF THE SAME SUBSTANCE, "THEN" YOU ARE NOT.

IT'S EASIER TO RIDE A HORSE IN THE DIRECTION IT IS GOING.

—Zen

EXERCISE #12

BEYOND LOCATION

What is "I" Rather than Who AM I?

Once the I AM appears, then the sense of I AM here—now—in a particular location, naturally arises. In fact, the whole notion of BE HERE NOW — implies time and space, which are "I" related and appear and are intrinsic to the beingness of I AM as well as the "I" thought. Many philosophers (Immanuel Kant for one) believed that space and time were *a priori*, or existed **prior to** experience. Actually, the concept of space and time **appears** with the **I AM** and the perceiver or being itself and does not exist *a priori* (**prior to** the experiencer–experience dyad). For "me" to be here now is impossible since the "I" **appears** later and only imagines itself in time. Paradoxically, Be here now is not possible, yet to be here now would mean no-space (no here), no time (no now as in past, present and future), and no Be (because *there is no separate being*). Hence, BE here now *IS NOT* (Neti-Neti). *To be here now, we need to be in NO I AM–NO SPACE—NO TIME—NO BEING. WOW!!!*

In order to consider this shift, the question, Who AM I? can be changed to *What is "I"?* Because the enquiry of Who Am I? *implies a who, or an "I" that I am.* There is no "I." What is "I," *might* "help" to address that the "I" is NOT, thus eliminating the concept of "I" and the concept of "is."

ENQUIRE:

WHAT IS "I"?

EPILOGUE

"WHERE" "DO" "WE" "GO" "FROM" "HERE"

The *Siva Sutras* of Kashmier might leave us with a few contemplations:

"The three limiting conditions are a kind of limited, vitiated knowledge rooted in words which have a tremendous influence on our lives. These words are formed of letters known as Matrka. The Matrka, or sound, therefore, forms the basis of all limited knowledge." *(Siva Sutras,* p. xvii)

This is the essence of **ADVAITA** (one-substance Vedanta). It is through the dissolving of I-dentity and ultimately the **I AM**, the primal I-dentity, which must occur for the "realization" of *spanda* to emerge.

"The knowledge and activity of the empirical individual is (artificial) because firstly they are limited, secondly they are borrowed, i.e., derived from another source, viz., the Spanda principle." (*Spanda Karikas,* p. xx)

All knowledge based on sounds, letters, words, and language is made of **consciousness**. To believe in knowledge or to be the hav*er* of knowledge is itself bondage. Why is the cause of bondage sound? Because sounds form letters, letters form words, and words form concepts, which by their nature, bind. Moreover, the "I" is formed from sound→language.

All language is metaphor. The I AM is an abstraction, a metaphoric **appearance** produced by a chemical reaction. There is neither bondage nor the hav*er* of, or an "I" which possess it.

"THUS THE PSYCHOSOMATIC SUBJECT IS NOT REALITY."

(Spanda Karikas, p. 50)

Only a water droplet in the ocean (**I AM**) imagines it is separate and has a will, volition, lessons, a mission, or a purpose. If everything is the ocean (**THE SUBSTANCE**), how could *"the all"* have a will, a mission, or a purpose?

"I HAVE TAKEN AN AXE TO THE I AM."

—*Nisargadatta Maharaj*

See "you" in the next section.

With love,
Your mirage brother,
Stephen

PART II

The Veil of Spirituality

"I" AM IN NO WAY SUGGESTING THAT "DOING" A "SPIRITUAL" PRACTICE OR FOLLOWING A "SPIRITUAL PATH" IS BAD. HOWEVER, WHAT MUST BE GRASPED ARE THE FOLLOWING:

1) WHO (WHAT "I") IS DOING THE PRACTICE?

2) WHAT DOES THE "I" THAT IS DOING THE PRACTICE WANT TO ATTAIN, GET, ACHIEVE, OR BECOME?

AND

3) WHY WOULD AN "I," *WHICH IS NOT,* WANT TO ACHIEVE, GET, BECOME, OR HAVE A "STATE OF CONSCIOUSNESS" THAT IS IMPERMANENT AND *IS NOT?*

INTRODUCTION

"Spirituality" and "Spiritual Paths," have so many definitions and goals that it would be impossible to write them all down. For example, in Buddhism the "goal" of the "path" might be *Nirvana*; however, for most people, *Nirvana* means some kind of *beyond* or *heaven*, although its actual definition is *extinction*. In Hinduism (Yoga), the goal of its spirituality might mean liberation into some other existence *beyond* this one. In Christianity, "spirituality" could mean the realization of essential qualities like compassion, love, forgiveness, etc., so that we can enter the kingdom of heaven. Obviously the list could go on and on and on.

"Spiritual Paths" are the techniques, the approaches the ways or means, if you will, by which "you" as a participant reach these high, lofty "spiritual states."

"Spiritual" paths not only include techniques or approaches, but also underlying precepts that manifest in the form of both implicit as well as explicit *rules*. For example, from celibacy, poverty, and charity to mantras, meditation, and service to God or being open, loving, and forgiving are just a few of the possibilities.

However, what is spirituality or a spiritual path other than a *veiled* remedy? Nisargadatta Maharaj put it this way:

> "I do not accept paths . . . All paths lead to unreality, paths are creations within the scope of knowledge, therefore, paths and movements cannot transport you into reality. Because their function is to enmesh you within

the dimension of knowledge, while reality prevails prior to it." (*The Nectar of Immortality*, p. 40)

This provocative statement provides us with more than we might ever need. For, if "Spiritual Paths" ultimately can only entrap, giving us a like-minded community a spiritual life(style) which enhances the illusion that eventually we will "get" something, the path serves not only as a **veil**, but also as a *trap*. So many people after so many years of following a path have felt and continue to feel trapped at worst, or basically the same at best. Moreover, the question arises, "If all is illusion, whereby the starting point is the "belief" called **I am**, (another illusion), how can one illusion, which originates in the place where the spiritual path begins (with the false concept **I am**, i.e., **I am** doing, going to attain or have something) lead you out of the illusion of **I am**?"

The answer to these rather blasphemous questions, which we dare to ask, leaves us with several important answers:

1) *All* spirituality and spiritual paths have as there beginning point **I am**.

2) *All* spirituality is part of the illusion, or mirage, and as such, each form of spirituality contains within it the implicit promise of some altered reality—where "I" can be, do, or have _____ (fill in the blank). Thus it hooks people into believing that "they" will attain or get something like a state, which is also part of the transient mirage.

and

3) Spiritual paths, too, are part of the mirage or illusion and hence keep us in their wishful, hopeful context, trapped within the mirage.

"Later I understood the meaning of spirituality and came to the conclusion that it is as discardable as dish-

water. Therefore, I am in no way concerned with spirituality." (Nisargadatta Maharaj, *The Nectar of Immortality*, p. 177)

Now, not to throw out the baby (spirituality) with the bathwater (spiritual paths), we can begin to understand that attempts at "spirituality" through a "spiritual path" to *attain* or *get* something are ego driven or better said, driven by the illusionary body's nervous system and its desire to survive. It is, therefore, suggested that to understand this could be enough. This "I" do not know, however, the survival need of the I am is so strong and deep that to "get" this understanding, a little enquiry might be helpful. Regarding meditation, Nisargadatta Maharaj said this:

"A little daily housecleaning might be helpful."

But, for all, including the enquir<u>er</u>, negat<u>or</u> and seek<u>er</u>, I-dentity, too, ultimately must be discarded. When asked what is the most difficult to discard, Yogananda Paramahansa said it is the *spiritual ego.*

Not only does "spirituality" and the "spiritual path" contain this illusion of an "I" getting something, but psychology, too, which has now been sanctified and is often followed with the fervor of a religion also imagines and believes so much in its theories, conclusions, diagnoses, treatment, and unquestioned slogans and rhetoric that analysts and therapists do not realize that these theories and abstractions are manufactured through the I am by a chemical reaction. Moreover, they are inferences; abstractions of abstractions of abstractions with so much more omitted than "seen," so that naturally, the theories would have to be limited, inaccurate, and in a word, unreal.

When asked about analyzing psychological material for meaning, Ramana Maharishi replied this way:

"When cleaning your house it is not necessary to analyze the dirt."

In this context we will attempt to discard and "see" through and beyond the **Spiritual Veil made of consciousness** by exploring what "spirituality" calls techniques, signposts, or approaches on the spiritual path, but which we refer to as **obstacles**.

Good Luck,
Your **mirage** brother,
Stephen

CHAPTER 7

The Self-Centered "I"

"The . . . self or "I" is always a representation, a story we tell ourselves about ourselves in an effort to capture the "true self" or the "real self." Just as there is no way to establish a precise correspondence between what we say about the world and what is actually going on in the world, there is no way to establish a precise correspondence between what we say about ourselves and what is actually going on in ourselves." (Joseph Natoli, *A Primer to Post Modernity*, p. 19)

Probably the two most confusing questions in the psycho-spiritual game are 1) "What is ego?" and 2) "What can "I" do about it?"

Ego at one level is the "I" that **appears** naturally from the body as a way to enhance the body's survival. In short, the "I" and all its abstractions serve only to reinforce itself or its survival. To illustrate, the thought "I am good," reinforces **I am**, and its survival. The thought "I" am bad," also reinforces the **I am**.

In other words, intrinsic to all "I" thoughts is that they reinforce the concept of existence and **I am** and hence the survival or **isness** of itself; in this case the **I am**. Simply put, the "I" thoughts support and reinforce the **I am**'s "belief" that it is.

In spiritual practice, it is often suggested that we must "get rid of the ego." But is not ego "I" _____ (fill in the blank), and how can one "I" (ego) gets rid of another "I" (ego)?

To illustrate, while "I" was in India, after 5 years a newly arrived student approached me and said, "Wow, you've been here for 5 years. You'll probably stay forever." "I" replied, "No. I'm leaving in June." The student said, "Oh, that's just your ego." "I" said, "I" used to have the ego called ""I" want to stay," now "I" have the ego called, ""I" want to leave." It's all "I," only ego."

This understanding is paramount to decipher the enormous amount of misinformation in "spirituality." We must understand that "I" hate God," is as much ego as, "I" love God," or "I" want to serve God and get enlightened," is as much ego as "I" don't want to serve God."

Many people think that the thought, "I am great," suggests a big ego, and "I am worthless," a small ego. However, "I am worthless" can suggest as big or even bigger an ego than the "I am great," depending on the degree to which someone believes that is who they are.

How then can we come to a place of trying to "get rid" of ego, when the "one" doing the "getting rid of ego" is a new ego that was placed there by the nervous system with a new "spiritual" philosophy and life(style)—in short, a new hidden agenda, which is to help the ego survive. In other words it is an "I" that believes unknowingly that if we get rid of the ego "I," then "I" will become "enlightened" and we will survive better.

Your "external world" exists only as long as "I am" is there. And since the "I am" appears after the act is done, it is, therefore, an illusion to believe that "you" do or imagine that "you" do. Because everything that this "you" perceives or imagines it chooses only appears after the perceived (imagined) choice has already taken place.

The "I" ego is not bad; saying it is bad would be like saying that digestive enzymes are bad when they occur naturally to digest the food that was eaten.

THE VEIL OF EGO YOGA

Doing to *Get* Rather Than Doing to *Do*

These questions must be asked, Who is meditating? Do we do spiritual practice?

This can be best illustrated by what "I" wrote in *Quantum Consciousness*:

"In 1988, I was meditating and began to become curious about who was meditating? When the awarer turned its attention around; there was nothing . . . nobody was there and nobody was meditating."

If you are doing spiritual practice to get something, there is a subtle belief that *you are*, and a belief in the non-existent self-body that does this practice and will *get* something.

Spiritual practice can occur without any intention of doing or getting anything, when it just happens with no more or no less significance, or importance, then brushing your teeth, making love, or going to the bathroom. Why? Because in reality, the "I" is a representation, or "picture," produced by the nervous system and *is not*. It would be like drawing a picture of a person (representation) of "you" on paper and then imagining that it can do a spiritual practice and get something. Most spiritual practice is a "spiritualized" survival mechanism; i.e., if "I" get enlightened, then the new and improved spiritual "I" will somehow survive better.

However, beware of the subtle body-mind survival traits.

EGO YOGA

If you're doing to get (like doing service or meditation to get peace or liberation) it is ego yoga.

"This cannot be done by force, for that creates resistance. This can be achieved only by alert passivity, by relaxing the citta or mind, by not thinking of anything in particular, and yet not losing awareness."
(*Pratyabhijnahrdayam*, p. 31)

Staying in awareness, noticing how the abstracting of the nervous system continues to abstract, like the digestive system continues to metabolize food, and that the "awar<u>er</u>," along with what it is aware of, are made of THE SAME CONSCIOUSNESS.

In this way, in this context, throughout this section we will examine the "I" seeking enlightenment, and doing spiritual practice. Moreover, how spiritual practice further entraps the "I," reinforcing the belief in its existence, and that the "I" is the doer, and that somehow the "I" will get something.

THE "I AM" IS THE ROOT OF ALL SPIRITUAL PRACTICES, SPIRITUAL PRACTICE IS DEPENDENT UPON THE EXISTENCE OF THE "I AM" AND AN "AWAR<u>ER</u>"— NO "I AM" OR "AWAR<u>ER</u>," NO SPIRITUAL PRACTICE

CHAPTER 8

The Veil of the Concept of the Gunas

*ALL IS A PLAY OF THE ELEMENTS
AND FORCES. THERE IS NO "I."*

Whether we take the position of the physics dimensions as "I" did in *The Way of the Human: Volume III*, or the yoga perspective that all is a play of the elements and forces (Gunas), what we notice as "we" go **prior to** the I am object level (Section I), there is the microscopic level of NO-I. If "we" also go **prior to** the microscopic level, as it says in the Bhagavad Gita, "Everything [including "I"] can be seen as a play of the elements," and hence, *there is no "I."*

WHAT ARE THE GUNAS?
IN HINDU YOGA, THIS IS THE DEFINITION:

The Gunas

"Fundamental quality"; all objects of the manifest world are structurally composed of the three *gunas: sattva, rajas,* and *tamas.* As qualities of *māyā* [the condensation], the *trigunas* are dependent on *brahman* [THE

SUBSTANCE], but they veil the reality of *brahman*. If they are fully in balance, nothing appears—neither manifestation nor creation. Once this balance is disturbed, however, the creation appears. In the physical world, *sattva* embodies what is pure and subtle [e.g., sunlight], *rajas* embodies activity [e.g., a volcano], and *tamas* embodies heaviness and immobility [e.g., a block of granite].

From the point of view of human development, *sattva* is the nature of that which must be realized; *tamas* is the obstacle that opposes this realization; and *rajas* is the force that overcomes *tamas*. In terms of human consciousness, *sattva* is expressed as peace and serenity; *rajas* as activity, passion, and restlessness, and *tamas* as laziness, lack of interest, and stupidity. A person's character and mood are determined, at any given time, by the dominant *guna*. The spiritual aspirant must overcome *tamas* with *rajas,* and *rajas* with *sattva*. For the realization of the *ätman* [THE SUBSTANCE], even *sattva* must be overcome." (*The Encyclopedia of Eastern Philosophy and Religion,* p. 121)

THE GUNA CONCEPT

This standard definition of the concept of the *Gunas* is a cornerstone of many Hindu Yoga practices for millennia.

The Miss-understanding

The misunderstanding that the attempt to change, alter, or imagine that a *Guna actually is, is where* the problem lies, when in order for the Guna concept to be, the I am must be there to say it is so. Why, because, **prior to the I am, YOU ARE NOT,** and there is no Guna concept.

Where does misunderstanding occur in relation to the concept of the Gunas? It is the attempt to change a force

(Guna), "as if" one aspect (Sattva) of the ONE SUBSTANCE is better than another aspect of the ONE SUBSTANCE (Tamas).

This "spiritual" confusion leads seekers into trying hard to change and control their actions and personalities and presentations—in short, the "I," which *they are not*. Moreover, it adds the judgment that sattvic behavior is better than rajasic behavior "as if" either one is more than a concept and has something to do with who you are. This belief that somehow magically, by an "I" becoming more of one (sattvic) and less of another (tamasic) or, if they are balanced in some way, "realization" is assured is an illusion. It is this focus on the outer manifestation or "I" representation that forces the "seeker" to lose sight of the underlying SUBSTANCE the Gunas are made of.

Simply put, it is like trying to change a reflection in a mirror rather than notice the I am that is looking into the mirror is **prior to** its reflection.

Recently, "I" was having a conversation with a yoga practitioner of some 25 years. We were talking about one Indian Guru who was accused by another Indian Guru of having *blown it* because "He had a lot of anger."

This implication that anger is rajasic and that harmony is sattvic, and somehow one is better than the other, leads one to believe that there is more than ONE SUBSTANCE—there are two, three, or more, which could be or should be *balanced*. This contains within it the *veil or trap* of trying to change what is not you. This would be like drawing a picture of a person wearing a loud red shirt with lime-green strips (rajasic), and then imagining that by changing the colors of the shirt in the picture to crystal blue, it will somehow change "you." In this way, just as you are not the person in the drawing— you are not the person nor the qualities of the person represented in the picture.

There is only THAT ONE SUBSTANCE, and believing in

the concept of Guna theory and not seeing it also, as a *veiled trap*, forces the seeker into trying to change "himself," or a "self" that is NOT. Believing in improving or changing yourself is a red flag of this "spiritual" veil that you are believing *you are* and *it is*, which leads to this seductive metaphysical trap: "If I do this or that, all will be okay, and I will become enlightened."

Moreover, the "movement" of the Gunas *is a process.* One Guna turns into another Guna, which turns into another Guna. It is not static, but a dynamic process, a movement, which **YOU ARE NOT.**

For this reason, in the enquiry "we" have done, not only does one Guna turn into another, we see that actually contained within Sattva is Raja, and contained within Raja is Sattva and Tamas. Stated another way, a seed contains within itself not only its sprouting into a tree, but its growth, its bearing fruit, its leaves turning brown, and ultimately its death. So too, each of us began as a seed and so, everything we are in terms of "good," "bad," "pretty," "ugly," etc., was in that seed.

There are some who say we can choose to be "good" or "bad," "sattvic" or "rajasic." But, you did not choose to be a man or woman, or choose your height or hair color, it was all contained within the seed and *just happened.* So, too, Sattva, Rajas, and Tamas are all contained within each other. It is only an "I" that has taken on a "spiritual" philosophy that believes one should be more sattvic than rajasic. *All is contained within the seed of consciousness.*

This can be likened to meeting someone and feeling the incredible seed of love. However, as in all relationships, the love turns into hate, which turns into withdrawal, which turns into like, which turns into affection, which turns into love. The possibilities are endless because contained within love is the seed of hate, and contained within Sattva are Tamas and Rajas.

The veil in spiritual and psychological work arises because

of the following: 1) *Compartmentalization*: Love is good, hate is bad, Sattva is good, Tamas is bad; 2) Once this *compartmentalized veil* arises, one is sought over the other and is not seen as contained within each other; and 3) You begin to believe *YOU ARE* when *YOU ARE NOT*.

This section intends to dismantle these concepts and shatter the "I" that believes in different qualities or the concept of forces called Gunas.

TAMAS

Tamas is one of the three forces. Tamas represents the concept of inertia. The enquiry below demonstrates how contained within the seed of Tamas are Sattva and Rajas.

ENQUIRY INTO THE NATURE OF THE CONCEPT OF TAMAS OR INERTIA

Wolinsky: Where is this concept called "my" **consciousness**?

Student: In the back of the head.

Wolinsky: Now, this concept called "my" **consciousness**, which also then believes in the concept called **I am**, where is the **I am**?

Student: The **I am** is in and out the physical body, in and out.

Wolinsky: And the "my" **consciousness** is behind your head, in back of your head?

Student: Yes.

Wolinsky: So, this concept called "my" **consciousness**, which believes in the concept of **I am**, how would the concept called "my" **consciousness** define the concept called inertia?

Student: It appears to be sucked back into shape of matter, I feel a kind of supreme form of laziness, with some dark aspects.

Wolinsky: So, this concept called "my" **consciousness**, which believes in the concept called **I am**, believes in the concept of inertia; and this concept of inertia defines it as sort of a process where you get sucked back into matter and become extremely lazy, and it has some kind of dark quality to it. Are there definitions of the concept called "my" **consciousness** other than this process of condensing down and being sucked back into this?

Student: The opposite of being very at peace.

Wolinsky: Now, regarding the concept called "my" **consciousness**, which believes in the concept of **I am**, made about the concept of inertia and condensing down and being sucked into matter in some kind of dark element, what assumptions has it made?

Student: One assumption is that there are two extremes, one is extreme out going and activity and a richness and colors and the other extreme, there is the opposing force, it is very powerful.

Wolinsky: This condensing?

Student: Yes.

Wolinsky: Contracting?

Student: I would say condensing, sucking back, back into darkness, back into formlessness.

Wolinsky: Now, when it condenses down, does it become more solid, and dense, or does it become more formless?

Student: Formless but very thick, like mud, very thick mud that calls you back and sucks you back, then you lose your form completely. You reach it and you don't care, full of troubles, questions.

Wolinsky: Now, the concept called "my" **consciousness**, which believes in the concept called **I am**, which believes in the concept called inertia and being sucked back into this muddy lazy sleepy, thick mud thing, by the **I am** concept, and the "my" **consciousness** concept, believing in all of these other concepts, what have been the consequences for the concept called "my" **consciousness**?

Student: Loss of alertness because if you are sucked back totally you disappear, also some moral things come up like in the Christian or New Age, it is not okay to be so lazy and so formless, you have to react, you have to stop it, you should go out, and be alive again, and go out again, it is one moral principle and one also physiological in the sense of loss of alertness, I have to stop this, I don't have to react anymore, I die.

Wolinsky: This condensing process also resists the condensing process by trying to be more active and alive comes out of this too? That goes on too?

Student: Yes, on all sides, it is like an incredible pulling.

Wolinsky: So, intentionally, very slowly, with awareness, condense down, into this muddy, formlessness, and then resist it.

Student: Resistance is there.

Wolinsky: When there is condensation and then resistance to the condensation, in the resistance, does it make this process seem more painful, more solid?

Student: Yes, it's more tense.

Wolinsky: Intentionally, have the emptiness, and have it intentionally become more like form, and muddy, and then have the resistance to it. Take this space and intentionally do this process of having it condense down and resist the condensing.

Student: Yes.

Wolinsky: Okay, now do it over there (another part of the room).

Student: Okay.

Wolinsky: Now do it on the ceiling. Now do it over here. Now without looking, just have it done behind your head. Take your attention to all of this and allow it to disappear. How does this condensing down and resistance to condensing process seem now?

Student: The inertia part is gone and there is a little tight or still a little tension.

Wolinsky: Over here condense down and create this inertia, this condensing process, and notice how out of that comes the process of activity (Rajas). That springs naturally from it. Do that several times, notice the inertia and how it springs into activity (Rajas).

Note:
Contained within Tamas (inertia) is activity (Rajas). They are contained within one another and move into one another.

Student: Feels like a very natural process.

Wolinsky: And now?

Student: I see the whole loop, there is just a moment where there is a space, like a transition point.

Note:

The subtle space or transition point could be (?) the *purity* in terms of the Guna concept the quality of space or Sattva.

Wolinsky: Let's do it very very slowly and have this condensing process condense down and just notice the *point* where it *changes from condensing to activity*; notice at what point it changes, notice that point where this is a change, just watch, it didn't make that change, but notice the *subtle transitions*.

Student: I can see two different processes, and the *transition point*. The process is natural and hard to conceal.

Wolinsky: Is it hard for you or is it hard for it?

Student: It is hard for me.

Wolinsky: So where in the body do you feel that concept called a "me" that says this little gap here, transition is hard?

Student: It somewhere here (chest).

Wolinsky: Notice the condensation, notice that little transition point and take the label off this thing here, and naturally allow it to go into activity, back into condensation, *transition* activity—transition, condensation—just have it do that several times.

Student: Something totally new. It's like facing life, terribly terrific freedom.

Wolinsky: So allow this process, a terrific freedom.

Student: There is a lot of charge attached to these movements.

Wolinsky: A lot of energy?

Student: I would say also an emotional charge.

Wolinsky: Notice the emotional charge and as you watch this process of condensation turning into activity take the label off of it and notice the energy as it goes into condensation and then back into activity. Notice how much energy is in it, the power.

Student: It has a terrific beauty, it is like being thousands of years back and seeing the earth's primal *Force*.

Wolinsky: Now if, this concept called "my" **consciousness** which believes in the concept of **I am**, also believed in this primal process of condensation and a gap and tremendous energy as going back into activity—if it believed in all that, what would be the consequences for the concept called "my" **consciousness**?

Student: If you could believe as in you believe, the consequences would be an incredible freedom and let go. I can be lazy as much as I want because I know at a certain point, something will move and change—I feel much less resistance. I can be lazy. And also stupid.

Wolinsky: Okay, now if this concept called "my" **consciousness** was to believe in the concept called **I am** which believed in the whole concept of this condensation into activity, and all of that, and this primal force were made of the SAME underlying SUBSTANCE, including the one that was aware of it, then . . . ?

Student: Somehow, it's all ONE SUBSTANCE.

Wolinsky: Now this concept called "my" **consciousness**, which believes in the concept called condensation and activity, if, the concept called "my" **consciousness**, the concept called **I am**, the concept called this condensation process coming out into activity—if all of these were just concepts made of the same substance and had nothing to do with anything, including the one that was aware of it, then . . . ?

Student: WOW, I have a new toy, it was so beautiful to think about this.

Wolinsky: If the concept called a new toy, and this concept called, condensation, activity, process, and the **consciousness** that was aware of this were all made of the same substance, which had nothing to do with anything, then . . . ?

Student: It is like there is an aliveness!!

Wolinsky: If the concept called "my" **consciousness**, which believes in the concept of **I am**, which believed in the concept called condensing process, which becomes activity, which believed in the concept called alive and not alive or sadness and not sadness—if it believed all of that, what could this concept called "my" **consciousness** do to itself?

Student: It could create a game.

Wolinsky: What kind of game would it create?

Student: A game where all things work according to a certain rule.

Wolinsky: And tell me a rule of the game.

Student: The first rule is elements of the game, and the second rule makes it as intense and ecstatic as possible.

Wolinsky: If this concept called "my" **consciousness** which believed in the concept called **I am**, which believed in the concept called rules and one of them is to make it as ecstatic as possible, and the game called condensation yielding activity and all of this stuff, okay. Now if all of this stuff was made of the same underlying **consciousness**, including the concept called "alive," including the one that was aware of it, and it had nothing to do with anything, then . . . ?

Student: _____Nothing_____Blank_____.

Wolinsky: Now if this concept called "my" **consciousness** believed in this rule, and it has to be as ecstatic as possible, and the game called condensation, which becomes activity, and life and sadness and death, how could the concept called "my" **consciousness** deceive itself?

Student: You don't want to go out and have activity and energy—but everything is made of the **SAME SUBSTANCE**.

Wolinsky: If that too, was another concept, which had nothing to do with anything, then . . .?

Student: Really!!!!!

Wolinsky: So this concept called "my" **consciousness** believed in the concept of rules of the game called ecstatic and the rule called "you can't discuss the rules," and the process or condensation becoming activity, the concept of sadness, the concept of life, the concept of **ONE SUBSTANCE**, if all of these were made of the SAME underlying SUBSTANCE, but all of it had nothing to do with anything, then . . . ?

Student: I don't know . . .
Blank_____(silence)_____laughter.

Wolinsky: If the concept called "my" consciousness believed in the concept of the game and the rules, and you should not be as ecstatic as possible, and believed in the concept called condensation, which becomes activity, which believes in the concept of life and the concept of sadness and the concept of there is only ONE SUBSTANCE —if the concept called "my" consciousness believed in all of that, what would it be unwilling to communicate about?

Student: This is the most perfect order of the possible worlds, and that it doesn't like to be discussed that this world is discussed or questioned?

Wolinsky: So the concept called "my" consciousness does not like this whole thing to be discussed?

Student: Or questioned—yeah.

Wolinsky: Tell me something that this "my" consciousness does not want discussed.

Student: The concept of "awar*er*."

Wolinsky: Tell me something else this concept called "my" consciousness does not want discussed.

Student: The concept of "my" consciousness itself, the concept of I am.

Wolinsky: Why wouldn't the concept called "my" consciousness want the concept of I am or "my" consciousness or the "awar*er*" even discussed?

Student: Because then they would be NOTHING.

Wolinsky: So, if the concept called "my" consciousness and
            the concept called I am, and the concept called
            an "awar*er*," the concept called consciousness or
            unconsciousness or no consciousness, the con-
            cept called a game, condensation and the activ-
            ity out of the game and the rules, and should not
            talk about it, and the rule that it should be ec-
            static, and all of this stuff is made of the SAME
            underlying SUBSTANCE, including the "awar*er*"
            and the "my" consciousness, and it all really had
            nothing to do with anything, then . . . ?

Student: Then every time "I" come out with something,
            then it is fake; it dissolves.

Wolinsky: Why would the concept called "my" conscious-
            ness not want to know that whatever comes out,
            is not real, and is not?

Student: It would feel incredibly frustrated.

Wolinsky: So tell me something that frustrates the concept
            called "my" consciousness.

Student: All this that you never get to an end, the more
            you steer out, the more there is; there is never an
            end.

Wolinsky: So this concept called "my" consciousness be-
            lieved in the concept called the more you start
            there is never an end, believed in the concept
            called there is a beginning, "I" just want to get an
            end, So "I" can relax, the concept of a game, it
            has to be ecstatic, and you can't talk about it, and
            it has to have rules that you can't talk about, and
            the condensation process in it, coming into ac-
            tivity, and a life concept, and it's crazy, and "I"

should not talk about **consciousness**, or "my" **consciousness**, or **I am consciousness**— if all of these were just concepts made of the SAME underlying SUBSTANCE, all of which had nothing to do with anything including the "awar*er*," then . . . ?

Student: I am afraid to say something.

Wolinsky: So tell me something you are afraid to say.

Student: All this effort, without anything to grasp, all these years of effort, this is painful. Another thing is, since the things that seem so obvious and clearcut lose their border, and another thing is if they lose their border, It just becomes inertia again, let's just disappear back into matter.

Wolinsky: Okay, two things, one is if we were to separate the concept of inertia, which is obviously something bad, condensation and inertia separated from the concept of lazy—if these were separate concepts, what occurs?

Student: Lazy seems something human, that you can allow yourself, to fuse together.

Wolinsky: And finally, this concept called "my" **consciousness** that believed in the concept called something going on, believed in the concept of ONE SUBSTANCE, the concept of **I am**, or not **I am**, the concept of "awar*er*" or not "awar*er*," the concept of **consciousness** or not **consciousness**, the concept of "my" **consciousness**, and "I" should not talk about all of these, the concept called condensation yielding activity, the game—if you believed all of these, what would it be unwilling to experience? Gain or loss, get something, concept of frustration, if it believed all this stuff, what would it be unwilling to experience?

Student: Whatever I did not want to experience. Somehow, I am looking for something. Actually, so many things.

Wolinsky: Okay, so if the concept called "my" **consciousness**, which you are not supposed to talk about, the concept called "awar*er*," which you shouldn't talk about, the concept called **consciousness**, which you shouldn't talk about, the concept called **I am**, which you shouldn't talk about, the concept called condensation process which forms the activity and you shouldn't talk about that, the concept called meaninglessness and meaningful, and the concept called useless and the concept called useful, the concept called grief, the concept called life, concept called "awar*er*"—if all of these concepts were made of the SAME SUBSTANCE, including the one that was aware of it, and it all had nothing to do with anything, then . . . ?

Student: Laughter_____NOTHINGNESS.

ENQUIRY INTO THE NATURE OF THE CONCEPT OF SATTVA: PURITY, HARMONY, COMPOSURE

The concept of a force called Sattva can be described as purity, pure reason, harmony, composure. Moreover, it is an ideal of a "high virtue," which is always true, regardless of the situation. (See Section II on the *Virtues Trap* for an enquiry on the *virtue* of *pure reason*).

Wolinsky: Where is the concept called "my" consciousness, which believes in the concept of I am, which believes in the concept of pure reason?

Student: My head.

Wolinsky: Ask the concept called "my" consciousness, which believes in the concept called I am, to define the concept of pure reason.

Student: A pure rational thought based on rational thinking and theories that yield conclusions.

Wolinsky: What assumptions about the concept of pure reason have been made by the concept called "my" consciousness, which believes in the concept called I am?

Student: That everything has reasons, causes, and an underlying rationale, which, if you understand or are in tune with it, brings about very predictable results.

Wolinsky: And, right now, "where" is this concept called "my" consciousness, which believes in the concept of I am, which believes in the concept of pure reason?

Student: Still in the head, in my intellect.

Wolinsky: And what have been the consequences for the concept called "my" consciousness, which believes in the concept of I am, which believes in the concept of pure reason?

Student: The I am seeks out and has a rationale, which explains and justifies everything.

Wolinsky: What happens to the concept called "my" consciousness, which believes in the concept of I am, which believes in the concept of pure reason when this rationale doesn't work or doesn't apply?

Student: It gets confused and can even feel a little crazy.

Wolinsky: And what is the basic underlying rationale of this concept called "my" consciousness, which believes in the concept of I am, which believes in the concept of pure reason?

Student: That everything has a reason, purpose, and explanation. ·

Wolinsky: And *if* all of this was a concept of the concept called "my" consciousness, which believes in the concept of I am, which believes in the concept of pure reason, all of it had nothing to do with anything, . . . then?

Student: _____Absolute blank.

Wolinsky: Regarding the concept of reason in all of this, what has the concept called "my" consciousness, which believes in the concept of I am, which believes in the concept of pure reason and explanation done to itself?

Student: Stayed non-verbally fixated on this space, which believes that *it is*.

Wolinsky: And where is this concept called "my" consciousness, which believes in the concept of this non-verbally fixated space, which believes in this underlying rationale?

Student: In this space, which is fixated by awareness.

Wolinsky: Notice a difference between you and the "awar_er_" of this fixated space.

Student: O.K.

Wolinsky: If the "awar*er*" and the fixated space were by-products of consciousness, which "looks" through the I am, and had nothing to do with anything, then. . . ?

Student: (Silence)_____ . . . then something keeps checking to see that "it" is still there.

Wolinsky: Is it the "awar*er*" and/or the space?

Student: Both.

Wolinsky: If the "awar*er*" and the space are NOT, then is there a YOU?

Student: No, there is no "I" if there is no underlying rationale.

Wolinsky: Now if the "I" was part of the "awar*er*," and the concept of space, and the non-verbal rationale, and all this was made of the SAME underlying SUBSTANCE, including the I am, and had nothing to do with anything, then . . . ?

Student: _____(Silence).

Wolinsky: How has this concept called "my" consciousness, which believes in the concept of I am, which believes in the concept of *is* that *it is* fixated location deceived another?

Student: Getting it to believe it is based on location.

Wolinsky: If this I am, "I," "awar*er*" location and philosophy was separate from the concept of location, then . . . ?

Student: Then there is nothing, I am NOT.

Wolinsky: How has the concept called "my" consciousness, which believes in the concept of I am, which believes in the concept of this whole thing, deceived itself?

Student: Believing there was a thing called location.

Wolinsky: And if it *was not*?

Student: It is all perceptual, facing outward, *nothing is*.

Wolinsky: If we separate "awar*er*"-location, space with fixated philosophy?

Student: Puff-gone. _____(Silence).

Wolinsky: Is there anything that the concept called "my" consciousness, which believes in the concept of I am, which believes in the concept of this whole thing, must not know?

Student: That it is perceptual and *is not*.

Wolinsky: And if the concept called "my" consciousness, which believes in the concept of I am, which believes in the concept of all of this and even the concept of IS and IS NOT were perceptual and had nothing to do with anything, then . . . ?

Student: But the "awar*er*" keeps going there.

Wolinsky: If the "awar*er*" kept doing that, but it had nothing to do with anything?

Student: _____(Silence).

ENQUIRY INTO THE NATURE
OF THE CONCEPT OF RAJAS

The concept of *Raja Guna*, or force, represents the force of activity and doing. It is said, when someone has too much Rajas, it is best to get out of their way.

Wolinsky: Where do you feel the concept called "my" con-sciousness, which believes in the concept of I am, which believes in the concept of an "I," which is doing and has activity?

Student: In my lungs and chest.

Wolinsky: Anywhere else?

Student: No, it's like the rest of the body, anus, ... etc., has to go along for the ride.

·Wolinsky: Ask the concept called "my" consciousness, which believes in the concept of I am, which believes in the concept of an "I" doing and activity to define Raja's (doing-activity).

Student: It is this on-going that I must do-do, engage in projects, but *do*.

Wolinsky: And, what assumptions has the concept called "my" consciousness, which believes in the con-cept of I am, which believes in the concept of an "I doing" made or decided about doing?

Student: That it must *do* in order to survive.

Wolinsky: And what has been the consequences for the concept called "my" consciousness and the con-cept called I am regarding these assumptions?

Student: It must always create projects to do.

Wolinsky: What has the concept called "my" consciousness, which believes in the concept of I am, which believes in the concept of an "I" doing and hav-ing to do, done to itself?

Student: Believed its reflection.

Wolinsky: Regarding this doing thing, how has the concept called "my" consciousness, which believes in the concept of **I am**, which believes in the concept of an "I" doing, deceived another concept called "my" **consciousness**, which believes in the concept of **I am**, which believes in the concept of doing?

Student: Doing is the way; that it was the doer doing, not the **I am**'s reflection.

Wolinsky: How has this concept called "my" **consciousness**, which believes in the concept of **I am**, which believes in the concept of an "I" doing, deceived itself?

Student: By teaching that it can have whatever it wants if it does.

Wolinsky: How has this concept called "my" **consciousness**, which believes in the concept of **I am**, which believes in the concept of an "I" doing, tried to control itself?

Student: If it controls itself, it will "get" from the doing, that there is an individual doing.

Wolinsky: And *if* these were just concepts, which belonged to the concept called "my" **consciousness**, which believes in the concept of **I am**, which believes in the concept of an "I" doing, and they had nothing to do with anything, . . .then?

Student: _____Blank_____(silence).

Wolinsky: What is this concept, called "my" **consciousness**, which believes in the concept of **I am**, which believes in the concept of an "I" doing, unwilling to communicate about or experience?

Student: That it is not the doer—that there is no doer.

Wolinsky: And if the concept called "my" **consciousness**, the concept called **I am**, the concept called doer or no-doer and the "awar*er*" that is aware of all this, were all made of the SAME underlying SUB-STANCE, which has nothing to do with anything, then . . . ?

Student: _____(Silence).

Wolinsky: What must this concept, called "my" **conscious-ness**, which believes in the concept of **I am**, which believes in the concept an "I" doing, not know?

Student: That there is no doer or doing.

Wolinsky: And if all this was just a concept of a concept called "my" **consciousness**, which believes in the concept of **I am**, which believes in the concept of an "I" doing and the "awar*er*," and these were all made of the SAME underlying SUBSTANCE, which has nothing to do with anything, then . . . ?

Student: _____Blank_____

CHAPER 9

The Veil of the Concept of Mantras— Yantras—Tantras

THE ILLUSION OF GETTING OR HAVING A PERMANENT EXPERIENCE

THE CONCEPT OF MANTRA

THE ILLUSION OF THE CONCEPT OF SOUND AND WORDS[1]

"The essence of all mantras consists in letters or sounds, [and] the essence of all letters or sounds is Siva [THAT ONE SUBSTANCE]."

(Singh, *Pratyabhijnahrdayam*, p. 79)

Once the abstracting continues beyond the object level, **I AM**, the verbal I am arises. From the verbal I am arises an infinite number of possible inferences. It is, therefore, clear that the concept of sound and the concepts and inferences,

---

[1]See *The Way of the Human: Volume III* (Chapter III: The Collective Unconscious and the Archetypical Dimension) for a deeper explanation of the concept of sound. Also see page 177 in this book, *You Are Not*, for an enquiry into the nature of sound.

which arise out of the concept of sound, are abstractions of the nervous system that originate from the concept of sound. The concept of sound as mantra cannot liberate "one" from the effects of the concept of sound or its inferences. Why? Because if there were no nervous system, there would be no sound. Sound is a concept, as is mantra, which is constructed by a nervous system and interpreted by an "I," which is a by-product of the nervous system. This addresses the famous question: "If a tree falls in the forest and no one is around to hear it, does it make a sound?" No, and once this is "understood," then "we" can "see" that an "I" repeats the concept or symbol of mantra in hopes of getting something—but it is still an "I" (which is consciousness) repeating a sound (which is consciousness) in hopes of getting something in the fantasized future (which is still consciousness).

"The three limiting conditions are a kind of limited, vitiated knowledge rooted in words which have a tremendous influence on our lives. These words are formed of letters known as Matrka. The Matrka, or sound, therefore, forms the basis of all limited knowledge." *(Siva Sutras*, p. xvii)

This includes mantra, which is a condensed and symbolic representation of the concept of sound, Moreover, the *Siva Sutras* state that *all bondage is caused by sound*. Why? Because sound creates letters, letters create words, words create ideas and concepts. Hence, since the repeater of the mantra and the mantra are both abstractions of the concept of sound, how can one abstraction (mantra) liberate another abstraction ("I") that repeats the mantra?

THE VEIL OF MANTRAS

Mantra: "A name for God . . . . The mantra, which is held to be one with God, contains the essence of the guru's teachings. The pupil is asked to meditate continually on this aspect of God. Regular repetition of the mantra (*japa*) clarifies thought, and with steady practice will ultimately lead to God-realization ... a power-laden syllable or series of syllables that manifests certain cosmic forces and aspects ... Buddhist schools ... mantra is defined as a means of protecting the mind. In the transformation of "body, speech, and mind" that is brought about by spiritual practice, mantra is associated with speech, and its task is the sublimation of the vibrations." (*The Encyclopedia of Eastern Philosophy and Religion*, p. 220)

Mantras, oftentimes, are used as talismans of protection and are often referred to as sacred sounds. Many people incorrectly think or imagine that the purpose of mantras, called the divine sounds, is to focus the mind and relax the body, which is *supposed to lead to "realization."*

CONTEMPLATION: HOW COULD RELAXATION OR FOCUSING THE MIND, WHICH REQUIRES AN "I" TO FOCUS OR A FOCUS_ER_, HAVE ANYTHING TO DO WITH FINDING OUT WHO YOU ARE, OR I AM THAT—YOU ARE NOT; WHEN AN "I" OR FOCUS_ER_ IS STILL IMAGINING IT IS DOING IT?

THE VEIL OF THE CONCEPT OF YANTRAS[2]

"Yantra is a "support instrument," a mystic diagram used as a symbol of the divine as well as of it powers and

_____

[2]See *The Way of the Human: Volume III* (Chapter III: The Collective Unconscious and the Archetypical Dimension) for a deeper explanation of the formation and concept of light.

aspects, employed above all in Tantra. The Karma-Kanda, the portion of the Vedas that deals with practice, discusses the performance of sacrifices, rites, and charms. To support their execution, cult images, *yantras* and *mandalas* constructed of geometric shapes, were later developed. In the meditation practices of Tantra (e.g., in Kundalini-Yoga), these play an important role as "supports"; they are models for "visualizations," whereby the mediator inwardly pictures various aspects and powers of the divine. The best known of all *yantras* is the Shri-Yantyra." (*The Encyclopedia of Eastern Philosophy and Religion*, p. 425)

The concept of a yantra as a light pattern, is similar to Om as the primal sound, it is suggested that *Shri-Yantyra* is the primal light form (first abstraction or condensation from the concept of light). You could say that the light pattern precedes the actual deity. For example, if you could focus attention on the condensed light as a pattern (Yantra) called Kali, you could see that the condensed, abstracted light pattern (Yantra) is more solid than **emptiness,** and less solid than the deity Kali.

The concept of a light pattern (Yantra) symbolically representing a diety like Kali is a more subtle or less condensed form of the physical form of Kali herself. Theoretically, the more subtle the representation, the "closer" to **THE SUBSTANCE.** It is through Focus of Attention and being it, which is worship, that this process is supposed to be done, with the understanding that this worshipper, as well as the worshipped (Yantra, deity), in this case Kali, are *one.*

However, like Mantras, Yantras should be done knowing that the Yantra deity is made of the **SAME SUBSTANCE** as the viewer of the Yantra.

Problems arise because, an "I" believes it is doing the focusing or concentrating and that the "I" is separate from its object. The "I" mediator then imbues the symbolic representation of the concept of light or Yantra or object or picture with magical powers to save, transform, give, protect, redeem, grant grace, liberate, etc.

Yantra worship is a preliminary practice, which leads (hopefully) to Samadhi (with seeds). However, *the Veil of consciousness is that the "I" imagines it is doing something, will get something, and that it is made of a different substance than the Yantra*, which will bestow some form of "enlightenment." Moreover, it must be understood that the concept of light and its condensed-abstracted symbolic representation called Yantra as solidified light is still part of the **mirage**. In other words, meditating on a Mantra, its meaning, or to develop a "spiritual" quality still presupposes and represents an "I" in the **mirage**. The Yantra is a symbol, which exists only through the nervous system, and hence, **prior to** it is NOT. **Moreover, the symbol has no connection to the symbolized!!**

"There is . . . no necessary connection between the symbol and that which is symbolized. . . . Symbols and things symbolized are independent of each other; nevertheless, we all have a way of feeling as if, and sometimes acting as if, there were necessary connections. . . . The habitual confusion of symbols with things symbolized, whether on the part of individuals or societies, is serious enough at all levels of culture to provide a perennial human problem." (Hayakawa, *Language in Thought and Action*, pp. 22-24)

An archetype is intermittently made of light, and ultimately is ONLY NOTHING. The concept of light cannot be without an **I am**, which is a by-product of a nervous system that "says" "this is light"; hence, *no I am concept, no light or Yantra concept*—and No-You.

THERE IS AN ON-GOING ILLUSION THAT SOMEHOW THIS "YOU" OR OR EVEN AN ENLIGHTENED "YOU" WILL EXIST, COULD EXIST AND WILL CONTINUE TO EXIST.

THE VEIL OF TANTRA

Tantra (Sanskrit for "weft, context, continuum")

"Next to the Veda, the Upanishads, the Puranas, and the *Bhagavad-Gita*, Tantra is one of the fundamental elements in *Sanatana-Dharma*, the "eternal religion" of Hinduism. Its central theme is the divine energy and creative power (Shakti) that is represented by the feminine aspect of any of various gods; personified as a *devi*, or goddess, she is portrayed as his wife, above all as the wife of Shiva. Corresponding to the particular form taken by Shiva, his Shakti may be a fortune-granting figure, such as Maheshvari, Lakshmi, Sarasvati, Uma, or Gauri, or may be a terrifying figure, such as Kali or Durga.

The term *Tantra* also refers to a group of texts and a practice that are fraught with danger for anyone who is not prepared to be subjected to strict spiritual discipline. Two Tantric schools have evolved: (1) the impure, perilous path of Vamachara ("left-hand path"), devoted to licentious rites and sexual debauchery; and (2) the Dakshinachara ("right-hand path"), featuring a purification ritual and a strict spiritual discipline that requires absolute surrender to the Divine Mother in her multifarious forms.

Each of the Tantric texts is supposed to contain five themes: (1) the creation of the world; (2) its destruction or dissolution; (3) the worship of God in his masculine or feminine aspect, i.e., the worship of one of the numerous male or female divinities; (4) the attainment of supernatural abilities; (5) the various methods of achieving union with the Supreme by means of the appropriate form of meditation. These means consist of the various older yoga disciplines such as Karma-Yoga, Bhakti-Yoga, Kundalini-Yoga, and other paths.

The Tantric texts usually are in the form a dialogue between Shiva, the divine lord, and his Shakti, divine energy. They attempt to raise all of humanity to the level of divine perfection by teaching human beings how to awaken the cosmic force that lies with (*kundalini-shakti*) by means of particular rites and meditation practices." (*The Encyclopedia of Eastern Philosophy and Religion*, pp. 354-355)

Tantra can be defined as the "expansion of knowledge." However, all actions or Tantras should or must be performed with this understanding. Sexual Tantra, which is where sexual energy is utilized to merge or become one with THE SUBSTANCE, is an action performed with this intent.

Tantra, loosely defined as actions and more closely defined as "expansion of knowledge," is a *theory* whereby the experiences of life are utilized to realize THAT SUBSTANCE or **consciousness**.

Northern Kashmiri Tantra, also known as Kashmir Shavism, has *The Siva Sutras* as its cornerstone. *The Siva Sutras*, as a document believed to be discovered under a rock in Kashmir, described the most basic teaching and philosophy of Siva. Its counterpart, the *Vijnanabhairava*, describes the 112 dharanas (which means the way, or "how" to focus attention or awareness as the way of realizing THAT underlying **consciousness**) and the **divine throb** or **pulsation**, known in Sanskrit as *spanda*.

In recent years, although less than 1% of the 112 yoga Tantras is sexual, sexuality has been used to characterize Tantra and the path of Ecstasy. Let us be clear now. *THIS PATH OF*

ECSTASY IS A GREAT TRAP. Why? 1) Because an "I" is seeking or doing it to *get* something, which is an "I" wanting a permanent state, yet all states are transient—non-permanent; 2) All ecstasy is sense-dependent; 3) The ecstasy "supposedly" is the vehicle to THAT; but, at best, the vehicle leads to Samadhi with seeds; 4) There is a high probability, as in all systems, of getting attached to the vehicle—in this case, it is a vehicle of pleasure; 5) One must ask oneself this question: Can Tantra "the expansion of knowledge" lead an "I" beyond the concept of knowledge itself, or does it lead an "I" into more subtle "spiritual" concepts that are **mirage**-based? and finally, 6) There is a strong chance, as most of us have seen through the years, that desire for sex gets "spiritualized" as Tantra in order to justify, reframe or give sexual desire some "spiritual" purpose.

To illustrate, why is it that all gurus "I" have known, regarding sexual Tantra, chose young, beautiful girls? If it is all **ONE SUBSTANCE**, why would it matter to the "Enlightened Guru," who is just doing it for the disciple (a young woman)? Why didn't he choose a woman 40, 50, 60, or 70 years old? Is it sex or Tantra? I'll vote that it is sex masquerading as, and spiritualized as, Tantra.

In this way, Tantra and the search for ecstasy can become an illusion within the context of the **mirage**, and hence, among yogis in India, it is often times referred to as "the left-handed path," denoting its illusory nature, "as if" to take a wrong turn.

THE TANTRIC PATH

The Tantric Path is the utilization of daily experience to realize the underlying **consciousness** or VOID. In the *Tantra Asana*, it says "One rises by that which one falls." However, along the way it is quite easy to get *ensnared* or *entrapped* into the desire for the *ecstasy* of the bodily experience of sensation or into the ecstatic experience itself, simply because they are fun and it feels good. This illusory mistake is the hallmark of a way station or a state that one must go beyond to "*apper-*

ceive" the VOID. As all of us know, the desire for *bliss* often leads to piss. However, since there is only ONE SUBSTANCE, it is crucial to focus on the *piss* as "energy," without any desire to change or alter it in any way.

To best illustrate this, the most powerful Tantric sex "I" ever had did not even include intercourse. Another time, "I" recall having Tantric sex with a woman who really was there only for the sex. For her, there was sexual ecstasy and body bliss, for me, there was only VOID, without even going to or through the *intermediate* bliss.

THE AGONY AND THE ECSTASY

All ecstasy leads to agony, all bliss leads to piss. It is two sides of the same coin of experience because all experiences are made of **consciousness** and they take place within the **mirage.** As Buddha's first noble truth was "Life is suffering," so Nisargadatta Maharaj said, "Living in **consciousness** is suffering."

On the other hand, the "VOID," beyond **consciousness,** bliss, ecstasy, piss, and agony is the VOID that **appears** when all states are "seen" as made of THAT ONE SUBSTANCE.

And so the "trick" is to not get caught in or within anything that **appears** *to be* or *that is.* Beyond the concept of IS or NOT IS lies the VOID. The blank, pre-creative, **pre-consciousness unawareness.**

And "what is" pure TANTRA "apperceiving" the VOID that looks through "your eyes" and meditates and witnesses and is part of this dream world.

AND WHAT OCCURS WHEN YOU LOOK INTO THE EYES OR PUPILS OF "ANOTHER"? YOU CAN SEE INTO THE BLANK VOID OF PRE-CONSCIOUS, THE PRE-CREATIVE VOID. THE FORMLESS THAT.

SHIRDI SAI BABA

CHAPTER 10

The Veil of a Big Outside God

THE GODS MUST BE CRAZY

This "veil" or illusion illustrates one of the most interesting concepts conceivable. It is that, from "another" place, location or existence, sits God or *masters*, the ultimate *master* being Lord Siva himself, which, anthropomorphically, is pictured as a person.

And, it is from this "other" world or meditation that this world **appears** out of **nothing**. But how could this be? For example, when we sleep, a dream world with dream characters arise, out of NOTHING.

In the same way, this world arises.

"Apperceiving" this, people and things **appear** as a piece of flat, one-dimensional "cardboard" floating in **NOTHING**.

One day, while "I" was awakening, an image of Shirdhi Sai Baba **appeared**.

Out of the "infinite" beyond, NOTHINGNESS, came Shirdi Sai Baba. He was holding a particle of sand in his hand. This particle was the physical universe.

Now, as "I" sit and write, it is like the pure "infinite" NOTHINGNESS has shrunken down, and my eyes, see through this limited lens, and then, "I" AM.

Outer Gods creating the universe is yet another veil or illusion of **consciousness**. A God that is beyond creating this universe, is an archetype, and as we will see later, *ultimately there is no beyond.*

CHAPTER 11

Beyond the Blankness

Oftentimes when people do not use their thoughts, memories, emotions, associations, perceptions, attention, or intentions, a blankness-no-state state of the non-verbal **I am** is "there." Beyond this, however, is **consciousness**.

ENQUIRY INTO THE NATURE OF THE CONCEPT OF THE NON-VERBAL I AM

Wolinsky: Where do you feel the **consciousness** that **appears** as blankness.

Student: The whole body?

Wolinsky: How would **consciousness** define this concept of blankness?

Student: As nothingness, no emotions (just nothingness).

Wolinsky: So this spot of blankness with no thoughts, no memories, is it kind of in the middle of **consciousness**, like a point in the middle of **consciousness**?

Student: It's just like a blank cloud.

Wolinsky: Now if the "awar<u>er</u>" moved its awareness a little bit further out to where it ends, is there anything else after that?

Note:

The "understanding" must be communicated with very subtle language. Here, we are not suspecting that "you" have awareness that you can move; rather, there is an "awar<u>er</u>" that has awareness, and it is the "awar<u>er</u>" that moves or "sees"; you do not. You are neither the "awar<u>er</u>" nor awar<i>eness</i>. You are beyond the "awar<u>er</u>" and *ARE NOT.*

Student: It's something like a blank box.

Wolinsky: If the "awar<u>er</u>" moves its awareness further out, is this blank thing floating in something?

Student: It goes up in the middle and then it's now bright.

Wolinsky: So there's this blank thing here, and then as "you" go a little further out there's an expansion outside of it, but the blank thing is still in the middle, correct?

Student: Yeah, the blankness is like a blank box in the middle of this bright thing.

Note:

As the "awar<u>er</u>," *which is not you,* expands its (not your) awareness, the **consciousness**, which the **nothingness** is floating in, is like a still point or a spot still within **consciousness**. As we will see, as this develops within this stillness, which is contained within **consciousness**, the universe **appears**.

Wolinsky: Now what assumptions has this **consciousness** made about this blank nothingness thing in the middle?

Student: No separation, no walls, it's something nice, it's something I like. It is not disturbing, it's quiet, still. Quiet. It doesn't bother me.

Note:
Most "people" do not like the **emptiness**, and it is within the **emptiness** that images arise. The student, however, seems to be fine with just the **emptiness**.

Wolinsky: For this **consciousness**—which surrounds this blank, nothingness, which is something that you like, something you can go into, and "doesn't bother me," just hangs in there—what consequences has it been for the **consciousness** having those assumptions around the concept of blankness?

Student: I like to be there all the time, but I've been there only when I'm here, or when I'm meditating, it's always there.

Wolinsky: If the **consciousness**, which surrounds the blankness and the blank spot in the middle, were all made of the same **consciousness** what would that be like now?

Student: I want to stay there forever and not come out.

Wolinsky: Regarding this **consciousness** with the concept of blankness, nothingness in the middle, and you'd like to stay in there forever and not come out, what has the concept of **consciousness** done to itself?

Student: It looks like **consciousness** is always creating a new craziness, a new running around, a new kind of addiction of suffering.

Wolinsky: Now as "you" look at this **consciousness** and the blankness in the middle of it, it **appears** that, whatever craziness comes up, it **appears** in the blank space. If the screen (concept of blankness) and the one that's aware of this whole thing were all made of the same **consciousness**, then . . . ?

Note:

This is mentioned quite frequently in *The Tibetan Book of the Dead*. At death, most people will not "see" blank-nothingness; rather images of pain or pleasure will **appear** on the blank screen. If, "one" can apperceive that whatever **appears** on the screen, and the "awar*er*" of it, is made of the same **consciousness**, then **Nirvana** (extinction) is assured. (See the section on Realizing Death).

Student: Nothingness_____.

Wolinsky: So it has gotten even bigger, now this **consciousness**, which is **appearing** as blankness, or can **appear** (become) as craziness, or just remains as a void, or become whatever it **appears** as. How has this **consciousness** deceived itself?

Note:

It is important to "understand" that the VOID, or whatever **appears**, or whatever the VOID becomes, is still only **consciousness**. This is critical and is clearly emphasized when the H. H. Dalai Lama said, "The mind is devoid of mind." Why? Because the mind is made of VOID, and ultimately the same **consciousness**, hence NO-MIND.

Student: By making it believe that all the craziness I have is here.

Wolinsky: Is there an idea that craziness has to be there, and only if craziness is there, then **I am**, and if craziness is not there then **I am Not**? Does that go along with it, too?

Student: Yes, because the **I am** thinks that; otherwise, there's no **I am**, I'm not there.

Note:

That's a really important thing to notice. The only way that **consciousness** even really knows that it is, is to have craziness: If there's no craziness, then *it's not!*

Wolinsky: So if the concepts of crazy or not crazy, or **I am** or **I am Not**, and the one that's aware of it were all made of the same **consciousness**, then . . . ?

Student: Once I hear the question, I'm already gone— there's no-me.

Wolinsky: Blank and expanded?

Student: Very expanded.

Wolinsky: Now regarding this **consciousness**, which **appears** now as this incredibly spread out void, which goes on and on, what must this **consciousness** not know?

Note:

Consciousness veils itself, by asking what must **consciousness** not know, it reveals itself as **consciousness**.

Student: That she is not.

Wolinsky: If the **consciousness** and the big void emptiness and this concept called "She" were all made of the same **consciousness**, including the one that's aware of all this **consciousness** is made of the same **consciousness**, then . . . ?

Note:
Unfortunately, oftentimes we are stuck with the word "experience," which is a "bad" word. We are all stuck in a language, which is idealytic.

Student: Everything disappears, goes.

Wolinsky: Is there any particular reason why the **consciousness** isn't "wanting" to experience "everything disappears?"

Student: Because of the body, the breath, cause and effect, the stories—want to stay and not disappear.

Wolinsky: If all of that, the cause and effect, and the **consciousness**, and the stories, and the void, and the **consciousness** around, and the I **am** and I **am** Not, including the one that's aware of all this, was all made of the same **consciousness**, then . . . ?

Student: Nothing_____(Long silence).

THE KNOWER

EACH KNOWER HAS ONLY SPECIFIC, LIMITED KNOWLEDGE. WHEN INQUIRIES INTO THE NATURE OF THE KNOWER (WITH ITS LIMITED KNOWLEDGE), THE KNOWN (THE OBJECT OR THE KNOWLEDGE ITSELF), THE KNOWING (PROCESS OF "HAVING THAT KNOWLEDGE") DISAPPEAR, THEN THE PURE I AM OF NO THOUGHTS, MEMORIES, EMOTIONS, ASSOCIATIONS, PERCEPTIONS, ATTENTION OF INTENTION IS REALIZED.

"At each stage of condensation a subjective-objective relationship is established between the more condensed and the less condensed aspects of consciousness, the less condensed assuming the subjective and the more condensed the objective role . . . wherever the subjective-objective and the more condensed the objective role . . . wherever the subjective-objective meeting takes place, a definite relationship is established between the two. So the manifested universe if not a duality but a triplicity and that is how every manifestation of reality at any level . . . has three aspects . . . and may be translated as knower, knowing, known, cognizer, cognition, cognized or perceiver, perceptions perceived . . . . The one has become three." (Taimini, *The Science of Yoga*, p. 96)

CHAPTER 12

Realizing Death

THE MOST DISSOCIATED EXPERIENCE OF ALL

Acknowledging, confronting, and realizing the concept of death and the resistance to the concept of death are imperative in order to "go beyond" all the after-death resistance which manifests death theories called religious metaphysics, that range from Heaven and Hell to reincarnation. For some existential philosophers, Martin Heidegger for one, emphasizes that in order to own or be-being or return to being, death must be absorbed and integrated. This means that not only the concept of death itself, the death concepts around the concept of death, along with the resistances to NOT being, and the feeling of fear and dread, must be looked at.

For example, how many people have considered that shortly after death, nobody would even remember you, and it would be like you never were? *What concepts does that bring up?*

This is what needs to be addressed and dismantled, so that death can be seen for what it is, a *concept within the **mirage**.*

MY FRIEND, CHRISTIAN

When my dear friend, Christian, died, at first "my" **mirage** body-mind felt its grief response.

Later that evening, however, within the EMPTINESS, while "I" was sitting in the living room of our apartment, there appeared the much less condensed consciousness called Christian.

That consciousness was floating in EMPTINESS, and that consciousness did not know it had died, and hence was in shock.

"I" spent some time with him (his consciousness, which was thinning out) letting him know what had occurred.

Over the next 24-36 hours, "his" consciousness was around until it thinned out within the BIG EMPTINESS and was no more.

It was not until that day that "I" understood the saying in India, "That the most important time for a Guru is at the moment of death."

Why? To best illustrate this, let me begin with the story that took place many years ago, a story of a man, a retired flight engineer, who was a trainee of mine in the mid-1980s. He told me that as a flight engineer, his plane had been shot down over North Vietnam. As he was automatically ejected from the plane, there was a short interval of, let's say, 10 seconds, before the parachute automatically opened. In that "short" interval, what he told me was that time slowed down so much, that he saw his whole life. In that mere ten seconds, he forgave his parents, said goodbye and apologized to his wife and baby, saw himself as a child grow into an adult—he saw the entire tapestry of his life. He did all of what we would call "personal" therapy within only a few seconds. Then suddenly, the parachute opened and he was back in "normal time." For this reason, we could say that for "me" in "normal time," it was only 24-36 hours for "Christian's" consciousness to thin out and dissolve, but "subjectively," for "him," "I" cannot say how long it was.

ON DEATH: WRITTEN FOR CHRISTIAN

Everything in the universe is made of the same **one substance**. Some call this substance God, some **consciousness**, some VOID or Emptiness, some just call it THAT.

And, what are we? We are made of THAT ONE SUBSTANCE, which has condensed down.

And, what is Death? Just as THAT ONE SUBSTANCE condenses down to form us, so too, it thins out into THAT ONE SUBSTANCE again.

Never losing its true nature, always being THE SAME SUBSTANCE.

Like gold being made into jewelry; a ring, a watch, and a necklace. However it never loses its underlying true nature as the substance called gold.

Such is Death. The melting back down into gold or the thinning out back into THAT ONE SUBSTANCE.

And Christian is THAT ONE SUBSTANCE. And so we lovingly called him VOIDIAN.

DEATH'S WINDOW

For most of my life, "I" had a huge drive to understand death. And so "I" pursued its understanding through meditation and death practices for almost three decades.

In October 2000, "I" had an opportunity to find out where the "rubber meets the road." Through a medical mistake, an inappropriate procedure was performed on me, and through this procedure "this body" experienced the symptoms of heart attack.

On a psychological level and an emotional level "I" felt nothing. However, a huge window opened and **appeared** before "me." As "I" looked through the window, there was only VOID. Sometimes during the eight days of this experience, the window was 10 feet away, at other times, "I" was half in and half out of the window. What "I" saw was the vast NOTH-INGNESS. What "I" came to realize was that at death whatever is "undigested" (unprocessed) could form (**appear**) out of the condensed NOTHINGNESS. In Tibetan Buddhism, they might call it wrathful deities, for "us" we could call it our "demons."

This window did not leave, but is part of "THAT" as "I." However, during these eight days there were two levels that were "realized"; one, *within the mirage existed the concept of death*, and on another, *there was no concept of death!!!!*

ENQUIRY INTO THE NATURE OF THE CONCEPT OF DEATH

Barbara, a longtime student, all year went through a horrific experience—her daughter was murdered. "I" thought it would be a good idea to do the enquiry with her.

Wolinsky: Where in or around this body is the concept called "my" **consciousness**, which believes in the concept called death?

Student: It's all around (most of her body), in here (stomach) and it includes some of my shoulders and upper chest.

Wolinsky: How would the concept called "my" **consciousness** define the concept called death?

Student: Death is a change from physicalness and it moves us, from having a body and a nervous system and existing in space, time, etc. It's a shift out of here, not being alive to being dead.

Wolinsky: How would this concept called "my" **consciousness**, define the concept called death—it's a shift?

Student: There is no longer a **consciousness** remaining in the structure of the body. The **consciousness** disappears, its **consciousness** disappears.

Wolinsky: Okay, how are you doing now?

Student: Okay, I am still here, struggling with this.

Wolinsky: This concept called "my" **consciousness**, which is struggling with this. What is the concept called "my" **consciousness** struggling with?

Student: "My" **consciousness** is struggling with the, it's very confusing. I am feeling very confused at this moment. That I have concepts about alive and dead. That I have concepts of a body that has a nervous system and is functioning and is heart is pumping and blood is flowing and there is mental activity going on and then my concept of death is that at some moment all that ends and the body is no longer being activated by the nervous system or the body, the mind that all of that stops at a certain second.

Wolinsky: If this concept called "my" **consciousness** believed in the concept of death, what else might it struggle with?

Student: Umm, it would struggle with certain questions about what happens after death? Is there a **consciousness** that lives on after death, is it important to stay alive? It's like, oh well, it's important to be alive rather than dead, there's a change, there's a difference there is a distinction that alive is good and dead is bad there is a whole series of concepts about that.

Wolinsky: Any other concept the concept called "my" consciousness is struggling with?

Student: Yes, the idea, does consciousness exist in some other form, rather than being a part of the body that is functioning in time and space, etc?

Wolinsky: By this concept called "my" consciousness wondering whether this consciousness exists in space/time, by it wondering about all this, what does the concept of my consciousness resist experiencing?

Student: Uhm, "my" consciousness is resisting experiencing not wanting to experience that there is no distinction between consciousness. It is like consciousness just is. There is a struggle with consciousness existing separate from "yours," you know that whole thing, the dualistic, before and after.

Wolinsky: This concept called "my" consciousness which believes in this dualistic thing called before and after, which believes in the concept of shifting from one consciousness to another consciousness and struggling with connecting with a shifting consciousness and is there consciousness?

Student: It is very complicated, it makes a fascinating story doesn't it? Wandering in a maze.

Wolinsky: The concept of "maze," the concept of "time" before the concept of "after," now if the concept called "my" consciousness were to believe this whole thing, what would be the consequences for the concept, *not for you*, but for the concept called "my" consciousness?

Student: Well, for the concept it would be a grasping, wanting to hang on to "my" **consciousness** and all these concepts and find other people to gather with you and have these same concepts and it would be a whole world. A fascinating world of explorations here.

Wolinsky: This concept called "my" **consciousness** that believes all of these things even the concept called fascinating and so on.

Student: It is exhausting even to think about it.

Wolinsky:. The concept called "my" **consciousness**, while "you" are doing all that, what does the concept called "my" **consciousness** resist experiencing?

Student: Ah, just letting go of it all and just be, just be.

Wolinsky: Why would the concept called "my" **consciousness** resist the concept of letting go or holding on and the concept of just being?

Student: Well, the resistance comes from wanting to think of oneself as a self and having the **consciousness** that there is something special to that, that you have to hold onto that, the ego is just so eager to feel like, I exist in time, space, and that I have a **consciousness**, and if I don't exist. It comes down to "I don't exist," "I have to exist," I have to do everything possible to exist and even cling to "my" **consciousness**.

Wolinsky: So just to recap, the concept called "my" **consciousness** basically believes in the concept of existence and non-existence, believes in the concept of shifting **consciousnesses**, it believes in the concept of maybe there was a **consciousness** before all this, that life is good, death is bad, etc. It believes all that. Tell me a lie that the concept called "my" **consciousness** could tell itself about death.

Student: Oh, a lie is that it is final and permanent or that there isn't any death. It is like death could either exist or not exist, the lie could be that if death doesn't exist, then there are other places that you can be if you aren't in this body, then you could be existing somewhere else. It has to do with existing.

Wolinsky: Why would the concept called "my" **consciousness** come up with that whole lie?

Student: So it would not feel so terrified about dying or not being. *To be* is so important that I have to create all of these other things.

Wolinsky: So the concept called "my" **consciousness** creates all these things, tell me another lie the concept of "my" **consciousness** could tell itself around the concept of death.

Student: A lie could be that someone you love who dies is not really gone. That they are still somewhere around to be experienced at a different level.

Wolinsky: Why would the concept called "my" **consciousness** tell itself that lie?

Student: To avoid feeling the pain of losing someone who you love and cherish because that pain is so deep that, in a way not to feel that you create all this other story. It's a way to not let go of someone in your life.

Wolinsky: So the concept called "my" **consciousness** believes in the concept called "my" life, and the concept of gain and loss, is that correct?

Student: Right.

Wolinsky: Now what other lies could the concept called "my" **consciousness** tell itself about the concept of death.

Student: Death is something to avoid as long as possible.

Wolinsky: Why would the concept called "my" **consciousness** come up with the concept of that we should avoid death as long as possible?

Student: As a way to avoid, well it has to do with loss, you know, it's almost like the concept of "my" **consciousness** has the goal of existing and surviving.

Wolinsky: Survival?

Student: Survival and also of the goal of that survival depends upon having others in my life survive as well that some have to be without those loved ones is too painful to experience. It is very complex. I am glad you asked me to come up here because it is something I would not have explored at this depth if you hadn't. I really stayed away from so I didn't have to feel all the feelings.

Wolinsky: Tell me another lie the concept called "my" **consciousness** has with the concept of death.

Student: It is like the concept called "my" **consciousness** has not had death. The concept of death, "my" death, has not seemed like an issue to me, even "my" death, being alive and dead, I have not worried about that. It is other people's deaths in "my" life that has been the issue, hanging on to the ones I love and not wanting to lose has been the issue. So I think that I had, I think that has been the issue.

Wolinsky: Would it be fair to say and check me if I am wrong, that the concept called "my" **consciousness** gets fixated or focuses on the concept of death with others to avoid the fact that it eventually *will not be?*

Student: That is true.

Wolinsky: Now this concept called "my" **consciousness**, which believes in the concept of death, the concept called gain and loss, existence and non-existence, the concept called resisting its own death. If all of these concepts where made of the same **consciousness**, which had nothing to do with anything in particular, including the one that is aware of this same **consciousness** then, . . . ?

Student: It just all disappears.

Wolinsky: If the concept called "my" **consciousness** were to believe this whole thing here, what could "it" do to itself?

Student: If it were to believe all these other things, what could it do to itself? Well, it could build a big wall around itself as a way to protect itself from having any of these concepts disturbed. It is like it has to stay alive.

Wolinsky: Does it also have to stay like in a form?

Student: A form, yes, so that it could maintain its separateness.

Wolinsky: So separateness equals existence and not death, is that correct?

Student: Right, to "my" **consciousness,** to that **consciousness,** existence is in time and space and separateness and mass and everything.

Wolinsky: If the concept called "my" **consciousness** is fused with the concept of existence, non-existence, which equals solidness, separation, and definition, then what occurs to the concept called "my" **consciousness?**

Student: Well, it can maintain itself.

Wolinsky: If all these concepts were separate, including permanent, non-permanent existence—if they were all separate concepts?

Student: Well, it just keeps getting more and more complex and more and more and more permanent.

Wolinsky: So complex means permanent?

Student: Yeah

Wolinsky: "I" didn't know that.

Student: It seems obvious to me.

Wolinsky: Okay, so if the concept called "my" **consciousness** fused together the concept called permanent equals complex equals existence, okay, you notice what occurs.

Student: It just is a fascinating mind trip.

Wolinsky: Right.

Student: I can just get so involved mentally up here and you don't have to feel a thing.

Wolinsky: Now if the concept called "my" consciousness separated the concept of existence from the concept of permanent from the concept of solid, separate, walls, and so on, they are all separate concepts which had nothing to do with anything, then . . . ?

Student: This is kind of disappears, everything just kind of disappears into nothingness. It is gone.

Wolinsky: **Prior to** the emergence of this concept called "my" **consciousness,** are you?

Student: No.

Wolinsky: Okay.

Student: So I can see how the whole false identity of "not exists" is so woven in with death.

Wolinsky: Now this concept called "my" **consciousness,** which believes in this whole universe, everything from complex, as it exists, not complex as death, complex on and on and on. How could the concept called "my" **consciousness** deceive itself?

Student: Well, it is all a deception. The whole thing is a deception.

Wolinsky: Tell me a deception the concept of "my" **consciousness** could pull over on itself.

Student: The deception is, it is important to exist at all costs and to formulate all these ideas in order to further the cause.

Wolinsky: The cause of existence?

Student: Of course, existence.

Wolinsky: So, this is how it deceives itself.

Student: Yes.

Wolinsky: Tell me another way the concept called "my" consciousness deceives itself.

Student: Well, it deceives itself into believing that there is a distinction between **consciousnesses**.

Wolinsky: Why would it do that?

Student: So that it could experience itself as existing.

Wolinsky: So if the concept called "existence and non-existence," even the concept called "soul" so that it could experience itself as a concept called existing, if all of those were made of the same **consciousness**, which had nothing to do with anything, including the one that was aware of all of this, then . . . ?

Student: Nothing.

Wolinsky: How are "you" doing?

Student: It was like okay. It's all just an elaborate complex survival thing.

Wolinsky: If the concept called "my" **consciousness** was just condensed **consciousness** and had nothing to do with anything, then . . . ?

Student: _____Blank_____

Wolinsky: If the concept of **consciousness** condensed down and formed a concept called "my" **consciousness** and it believed this whole thing, what could this concept called "my" **consciousness** not want to communicate about?

Student: The psychic I saw imagines this **consciousness** as separate from this **consciousness**, is separate from that **consciousness**; then the psychic had an elaborate world of ideas about *this* consciousness existing after death and communicating with *this* consciousness, and there are these different concepts of **consciousness**, then a whole elaborate story builds up, you write books about, and on and on.

Wolinsky: So, for this concept called "my" **consciousness**, if all of these concepts were just stories, were made of the SAME SUBSTANCE, or the same condensed **consciousness**, which had nothing to do with anything, including that which is aware of it, then . . . ?

Student: It is kind of a, you know. It is a letting go, just total letting go. No interest in the stories. It is just like, oh, I am okay.

Wolinsky: If a concept called "my" **consciousness** believed all of this stuff what would this concept called "my" **consciousness** be unwilling to know about, then . . . ?

Student: It would not want to know that it was condensed **consciousness**.

Wolinsky: Why would the concept called "my" **consciousness** not want to know that is was made of condensed **consciousness**?

Student: Because then, all the stories would collapse and disappear.

Wolinsky: And if this concept called "my" **consciousness** was not separate and made of the same **consciousness** as everything, including the "awar<u>er</u>" of all of this, then . . . ?

Student: It would not have any reason for being.

Wolinsky: So, the concept called "my" consciousness has this idea that it has to have a reason for being?

Student: Right, it is survival.

Wolinsky: So why would a concept called "my" consciousness believe in a concept called "it has to have a reason for being?"

Student: It just keeps twisting back on itself.

Wolinsky: So if the concept called "my" consciousness did not have a reason to justify its being, then . . . ?

Student: Right, there are not words, It is just like, it all just kind of disappears. The concept of "my" consciousness disappears, it all just disappears and there isn't any such thing as death.

Wolinsky: So, one more question, If this concept called "my" consciousness condensed down, and formed an idea called "my" consciousness who believed all this stuff, what would this concept called "my" consciousness be unwilling to experience?

Student: I just put it together with the death of my daughter. It is like somehow the unwillingness to, somehow if all of this disappears then somehow the memory of her; it's like hanging on to her memory.

Wolinsky: The concept called of "my" consciousness is hanging on to the memory of "that" consciousness.

Student: Of that consciousness, you know she was an important part of my life and I want to remember her and I want to remember. It has all to do with that. That it is important somehow to . . . (crying).

Wolinsky: The concept called "my" **consciousness** which
              wants to keep the memory of her solidified, if
              for this concept called "my" **consciousness** could
              not keep the memory of her solidified, then what
              would that mean to the concept called "my"
              consciousness?

Student: It gets back to existence and somehow the exist-
              ence, to exist. Existing includes having memo-
              ries and not forgetting the memories and expe-
              riences and the importance of existing, the im-
              portance of one's life, it all fits in there, it is so
              fascinating to sit here and just experience this.
              And think about that and to be, it gets back to a
              purpose in life, what life is about, what is impor-
              tant in life, how to prove that my life is worth
              living, it is all that stuff. It gets back to that whole
              thing that we weave, that I have woven in my life,
              that somehow I have to drag, "my" memory with
              me all the time so I can remember that I exist.

Wolinsky: So you exist. So the way that you exist is through
              the concept called memory.

Student: Right, that I have had all these experiences, and
              this and this and this; therefore, I exist.

Wolinsky: Now, for this concept called "my" **consciousness,**
              if it were to separate the concept called existence,
              and separate that concept from the concept called
              memory to justify existence, if it were to separate
              that from I am—if that were separated from, in
              order to know that "I" have some kind of value
              or worth or something, or that I am this memory;
              if all of these concepts, were separate; if existence
              is dependent upon memory, we are going to sepa-

rate memory and existence. Rather than **I am**, I must have memory, we are separating memory and **I am**'s. We are separating memory-of-daughter in order to prove that she existed just as you existed. If all of these were separate concepts, made of the same **consciousness**, then . . . ?

Student: It is such a relief, it is just like all the tension in my body just goes out. I could be like a puddle on the ground.

Wolinsky: Now, if all of these were just concepts being the same **consciousness**, including the "awar<u>er</u>" of all of this, and it had nothing to do with anything, then . . . ?

Student: Just, there is a feeling of joy that I am experiencing now, like a joy in it, letting it all just kind of go and I feel a lot of tears about it, maybe there has been a fear about letting it all go, somehow, I have to hang on to it and I don't know why I feel like crying and letting it all go. I think I have been holding myself together a lot.

Wolinsky: Would you be willing to allow the concept called "my" **consciousness** to just fall apart?

Student: Right, just to fall apart. Yes, I have to hold myself together a lot . . . (crying).

Wolinsky: So notice how the concept called "my" **consciousness** holds itself solid.

Student: To not feel, not to feel what I am feeling.

Wolinsky: See if you can allow the concept called "my" **consciousness** to just shatter. So, if this concept called "my" **consciousness** were to shatter into pieces, what would be so bad about that?

Student: It feels like a tremendous relief. It does feel like a tremendous relief. Like letting go of all the solid walls that held me together. That kept me from, I guess the fear was, you know, I don't know what. Shattering. I don't want to reveal that at this moment . . . (crying).

Wolinsky: Now if the concept called "my" **consciousness** and shattering or not shattering or grief or relief, and all of these other concepts were all made of the same **consciousness**, including the "awar<u>er</u>" of all of that, then . . . ?

Student: I could just be with whatever.

Wolinsky: And **prior to** the emergence of the thing called "my" **consciousness**, were you?

Student: I feel like I am swimming. Swimming in a sea, with this. Thank you. I certainly did not expect this today._____Long silence.

QUESTIONS AND ANSWERS

Question: My thoughts seem random?

Wolinsky: They are.

Question: What can I do to stop them?

Wolinsky: **Put your attention on the back of your tongue and it will stop them, or put your tongue on the roof of your mouth.**

Question: It sounds like a mudra.

Wolinsky: It is.

Question: Why do it?

Wolinsky: Just do it as an experiment. You will notice that the brain is very connected to the auditory and visual centers. If your tongue does not move, it is more difficult for thoughts to arise.

Question: But I thought that thoughts are universal.

Wolinsky: That is at a different level. Thoughts are *collective*, yet the "I" thinks it has them.

Question: What is sleep?

Wolinsky: When the body goes into deep sleep, the **I am**, which is made of **consciousness**, thins out; hence, you lose body **consciousness**. This is sleep. When body **consciousness** begins to solidify more, you get into the Dream State, and when it solidifies more, you get the waking state. When **consciousness** thins out even more, there is unawareness. This, too, is Samadhi or as Baha Prakashananda called it, sleep Samadhi. When the **consciousness** thins out, yet a knowing **consciousness** is still there, you have Samadhi. With witnessing, which is where you witness the no-state and/or are **conscious** of everything as the same substance. When the **consciousness** totally dissolves, you get Nisargadatta Maharaj's question: "Eight days prior to conception, who were you?"—this unawareness **prior to** the **appearance** of the I AM or the "awar<u>er</u>." When it totally dissolves along with the **consciousness** of the emptiness and the ONE SUBSTANCE that is total Samadhi without seeds.

CHAPTER 13

The Concept
of the Skandhas

*"Sadhana (spiritual practice) is the search for
what you have not given up and then giving it up."*

—Nisargadatta Maharaj

The Skandhas in Buddhism are the five parts that comprise the personality. In the following pages, we will explore a few enquiries into different aspects of the Skandhas. Unfortunately, space allows only a few such enquiries, which, hopefully, will provide an overall context.

THE GROUP OF CORPOREALITY
(FORM OR MATTER)

Four elements (firm, fluid, heating, movement)

ENQUIRY INTO THE NATURE
OF THE CONCEPT OF MOVEMENT

Wolinsky: How would the concept called an "awar*er*" define the concept called movement?

Student: The ability to change position, the ability to go from one place to another. Change position mostly, that takes care of it, I think.

Wolinsky: Anything more?

Student: One location to another or there can be movement in a sense of ideas, cause, emotion, movement in the sense of searching for things necessary for survival.

Wolinsky: Could there also be movement for example, what is commonly called in our *lingo*, "evolution," I don't mean evolution like monkeys into humans.

Student: I think that is the movement that I say is the movement of ideas, evolution, moving forward, thinking of, almost like *change*.

Wolinsky: So change also implies some kind of a movement from one thing to another?

Student: Yes.

Wolinsky: What assumptions has the concept called an "awar*er*" made about the concept called movement, the concept called moving from one location to another location, the concept called change, the concept called movement of thoughts, the concept called evolution and things changing, moving forward as you said, which also means it had to go from a backward to forward, from a position here to over there, what assumptions has the awar*er* made about all of these concepts?

Student: Well, there is a starting point. That is the first assumption.

Wolinsky: So a place where it began or originated.

Student: The second assumption would be that it could move at all.

Wolinsky: Is there also an assumption that it had independent movement?

Student: Sure, that ties up with volition, kind of.

Wolinsky: So this is separate from you, which moves independently from me.

Student: Absolutely. In fact movement, the assumption was made that the movement was independent—that is the only kind there was.

Wolinsky: Now if the concept of an "awar*er*," has the concept of independent movement, the concept of moving from one location to another location, the concept of illusion or change, the concept of ideas moving, the concept of a starting point, which started here and ended here or something—if all of these concepts were made of the same substance, same **consciousness**, including the concept of an "awar*er*," and it all had nothing to do with anything, then . . . ?

Student: It feels frozen.

Wolinsky: What is the *it*?

Student: I don't know—just frozen, like maybe the space or the blank all of a sudden changes from the space to frozen.

Wolinsky: Okay and if the concept of an "awar*er*," which is aware also of the concept of frozen, or fluid, and the movement from either frozen to fluid or fluid to frozen, if those too, were concepts all made of the same substance as the "awar*er*," which had nothing to do with anything, then . . . ?

Student: There is the breath.

Wolinsky: So, the "awar*er*" has the concept of breath, which is constant movement.

Student: I try to get away from all and I got right into the breath.

Wolinsky: If the concept of movement was fused with the concept of breath and the concept called **I am** moving my breath, if these were all fused together then, . . . ?

Student: Well, fusion is obviously as long as there is breath, there is life and the whole thing is held together and that keeps you forward.

Wolinsky: And if we separated the concept of movement, concept of breath, concept of life, concept of moving forward—if they were all separate concepts, and if all of those concepts along with one location moving to another and e volution changing, starting point, forward, backward—if all of these now were concepts made of the **SAME SUBSTANCE** as the "awar*er*," which had nothing to do with anything, then . . . ?

Student: Holding very tightly onto that concept

Wolinsky: What is?

Student: I imagine it is some part of the **I am.** Holding on very tightly to the breath and the movement and it can't be a concept or else you die, that's it. I almost feel like white fingernails falling off the **I am.**

Wolinsky: Holding on for dear life. If you separate the concept of life, the concept of death, and the concept of movement, if they are all separate concepts, then . . . ?

Student: I don't get any words.

Wolinsky: If the concept called an "awar_er_," believed in the concept of life, the concept of death, the concept of movement, the concept of a starting point, a forward and a backward, a concept of an evolution or change from one thought to another, one level to another—if it believed in all those concepts, what would be the consequences for the concept called the "awar_er_" if it were to believe all of that?

Student: You would have to stay on the move, you would have to be in perpetual motion, you would have to be moving, need to move to breathe, you need to move to learn, you need to move to survive. It is all there together, it is constant.

Wolinsky: Now, if the "awar_er_," believed in the concept of "I" have to move in order to survive, moving from one space to another space, evolution from here to there, process in motion, forward and backward, a starting point, an ending point, and that the breathing and life and death concepts were all separated; if breath and movement were separate concepts—if all of these were separate concepts made of the same **consciousness**, all of which had nothing to do with anything, then . . . ?

Student: I am not getting any words but what I am getting is like a big blinding light, but you can't look at it, because it is blinding; you have to look to the side, like the sun can be blinding. You have to look aside. There are no words for it.

Wolinsky: Okay, so the "awar_er_," which now has two parts one is aware of it looking away, and the other part of the "awar_er_" wants to look at this incredibly bright light, if the "awar*er*" and the light, looking away part or looking at part all was made of the same **consciousness**, which had nothing to do with anything, then . . . ?

Student: It was like the "awar*er*" had an impression that you know you shine a light in a deer's eye or something, which would immobilize them. And when I could see that happening, you wouldn't look at the light for fear of immobilization; but then when you get that it is the same substance, it just kind of trailed away.

Wolinsky: And **prior to** the emergence of the **I am**, which believes in the concept of movement, the concept of life and death and the concept of you have to move, and the concept of survival, and the concept of an evolution, and the concept of change, the concept of location, the concept of from one space to another location—if all of those were made of the same **consciousness** as the "awar*er*," which had nothing to do with anything, **prior to** the emergence of the "awar*er*," that was aware of all of this, are you?

Student: NOTHINGNESS_____(Silence).

Wolinsky: Now if the concept called an "awar*er*" believed in the concept of movement from this location to another location, concept of evolution changed, changing into something else, a starting point, the concept of birth, life, death, concept of breathing and moving to survive the concept of breathing, being separated from lung and breath and so on and the concept of a light, a concept of freezing in the light, if some "awar*er*" out there were to believe all of this stuff, what could this aware concept do to another "awar<u>er</u>" concept?

Student: Try to get them to move.

Wolinsky: Why would an "awar<u>er</u>" concept try to get another "awar<u>er</u>" concept to move?

Student: Because they should be moving.

Wolinsky: That is obvious (said jokingly). Now, is this movement concept attached to the eyes?

Student: Of course because sometimes when you are very still, the eyes are still moving.

Wolinsky: Is it possible that the eyes see movement, but not necessarily "you"?

Student: That is what the eyes are doing, if the person is still, they are watching all the movement.

Wolinsky: If "you" were separate from the concept called eyes, which is separate from the concept called movement, then . . . .?

Student: It is really bad . . . it is like you are blind, you can't see, that feels bad.

Wolinsky: Let me ask you this, can the eyes see and can you allow the eyes to see what they see even though it has nothing to do with you?

Student: Hmm—Wow!!!!

Wolinsky: So the eyes can see even though, it has nothing in particular to do with anything.

Student: It feels very free. Like you can set the eyes over here

Wolinsky: If the concept called an "awar_er_" were to believe in the concept called starting point, ending point, backwards, and forwards, the concept of movement, the concept of death and survival, the concept of movement, the concept of evolution, one thing changing into another thing, if an **I am** believes all of that, what could the concept called **I am** do to itself?

Student: Well, perpetual motion machine—rolling, just keep moving, just keep moving.

Wolinsky: And **prior to** the "awar_er_"/**I am** concept which believed in the concept of this, are you?

Student: No.

Wolinsky: And if all of these concepts were made of the same **consciousness**, including the "awar_er_," which had nothing to do with anything, then . . . ?

Student: _____(Silence)_____

Wolinsky: So, if an "awar_er_" concept had the belief in moving from one point to another, the concept of evolution, the concept of a life and birth, and movement, and survival, and evolution of some kind of **consciousness**, changing from one thing to another, a starting point, a concept of **I am** seeing, rather than it sees—all these concepts— if it had all of that, how could the concept of an "awar_er_" be deceived by another concept of an "awar_er_"?

Student: No matter where you moved they would find you.

Wolinsky: What "awar_er_" said "I can see you every where and find you," and so on. Was it somebody specific?

172 / You Are Not

Student: A dark indoctrination of the cult said we were always under their control.

Wolinsky: The "indoctrination," we can see you, find you, know your thoughts. Let me be a little more specific then, if we have the cult figures fused with some God-like power, if those are fused together, then what occurs?

Student: Fear.

Wolinsky: If you separate this God-like powers from these cult figures, if they are separate, then . . . ?

Student: Then, yeah, that trickles back into movement because now it is safe to breathe. It is still some form of motion.

Wolinsky: "I" want to check a couple of things out. The first thing is those cult figures; where in relationship to their bodies are their eyes that witness this movement over here?

Student: It is almost like their bodies are covered with eyes.

Wolinsky: And where are those bodies that are covered with eyes in relationship to this physical body.

Student: They are over there, they are outside.

Wolinsky: Now, if the concept of an "awar*er*," which believed in the concept of "these people with eyes all over them that can see everything;" the concept of an omniscient God that is not separate; the concept of beginning point, starting point; the concept of evolution of some kind of **consciousness** from Point A to Point B; the concept of moving from some point to another point; the concept of death and how it is going to survive; the concept of breathing—if all of these, etc., etc., were all made of the same underlying **consciousness**, including the "awar<u>er</u>" of all of them, even the concept called "what I see, **I am** the one who is seeing," if all of those were made of the same **consciousness**, which had nothing to do with anything, then . . . ?

Student: The only thing I am noticing is a body reaction where there is more energy flowing and I am getting really hot. Other than that, it is okay.

Wolinsky: Can we say that the eyes are seeing, they see movement, the sensor of the sensations feel the heat and the movement of sensation in the body, that concept, so that occurs, but does that have anything to do with **prior to** the "awar<u>er</u>" . . . ? Also . . . **prior to** the "awar<u>er</u>" that is aware of sensations, moving, that is aware of the body all of a sudden, movement of heat or energy, eyes are still moving and doing what it is doing, **prior to** the "awar<u>er</u>" that is aware of all of those concepts, are you?

Student: (Silence)_____(long silence).

Wolinsky: Anything you want to say so far?

Student: (Silence)_____(long silence).

Wolinsky: Now the "awar<u>er</u>" concept, which believes in the concept of breathing and the concept of moving, the concept of survival, the concept of beginning point, the concept of a movement or a change process, one point changing from one point to another, believes in the illusion of an omniscient God, the concept that if there were sensations being felt or movement or heat or energy being moved that it had something to do with you, the concept that the eyes saw—if all of these were just concepts, but they were believed by an "awar<u>er</u>," what would that "awar<u>er</u>" be unwilling to communicate about?

Student: That it was all believed. The only thing I am coming up with is there is no place to hide.

Wolinsky: So the "awar<u>er</u>" believes in the concept of a place to hide and no place to hide, concept of space tied in or no space to not tie in, the concept of beginning, the concept of change, the concept of etc.—if it believed in all of these concepts, all of these concepts made of the same substance, which had nothing to do with anything, including the one that is aware of it . . . **prior to** the emergence of the "awar<u>er</u>" that awares all of this, are you?

Student: _____(Silence)_____

Wolinsky: Anything you want to say so far?

Student: No, I feel very okay and just kind of like hanging out . . .

Wolinsky: Now, if there is a concept of an "awar<u>er</u>" that believed what it saw it was seeing, what it felt it was sensing and feeling, if it believed in the concept of survival and death and breathing and the concept of starting point, and a concept of movement and evolution and change from one place to another—if it were to believe all of that, what can that "awar<u>er</u>" not know?

Student: It can't know that it is all false.

Wolinsky: How come the "awar<u>er</u>" can't know it is all false?

Student: If it knew it was all false, it would not have to do any of that stuff.

Wolinsky: And if it didn't move? If the "awar*er*" were separate from a concept called movement, then would the "awar*er*" be there?

Student: _____(Silence)_____(silence)_____

Wolinsky: If there was some "awar*er*" out there that believed in the concept called movement, and believed in the concept called birth and life and death and movement and starting points and changing and evolution, locations from one thing to another, from what it sees and all that other stuff, if an "awar*er*" were to believe all of that stuff, what can the "awar*er*" not experience?

Student: It can't experience big people, big people can stop the movement. As long as you are bigger than they are, or stronger, as long as the **I am** is bigger or stronger, it can't experience large people.

Wolinsky: First off, the "awar*er*" has a discriminative ability to discriminate small from big. So you have the concept of small, the concept of big, the concept of an "awar*er*," and you also have the concept called stopping movement. Let's make a separation here, if we have movement stopped and if we have stopping and the "awar*er*," if they are fused together, then that equals death, I am assuming, or something bad. So if we separate the concept of an "awar*er*" from the concept of movement, from the concept of something bad, they are all separate. And if we separate the concept of an "awar*er*," a concept of movement, a concept of something good or survival, all separate concepts, So if the concept called an "awar<u>er</u>" had all of these concepts going on, all made of the same **consciousness**, which including the "awar<u>er</u>" of course, which had nothing to do with anything, and if you separate the concept of an "awar<u>er</u>" from the concept of movement, could the "awar<u>er</u>" be? So **prior to** the emergence of the "awar<u>er</u>," were you? If the "awar<u>er</u>" and the concept of movement were separated, but singly were made of the SAME SUBSTANCE, are you?

Student: _____(Silence)_____(long silence).

Note to Group:

So, the eyes can move and the ears can hear, but it is a function. **Prior to** the "awar<u>er</u>" are you? Since awareness, is a biological function, ultimately, no body, no "awar<u>er</u>," therefore, *you cannot have an experience unless there is movement.* Even if it is an experience of me touching the table, at least the neurons are moving. *If there is no movement, there is no "awar<u>er</u>"—no awareness.* It is a biological function. That means that when we ultimately separate it out, *there can be no "awar<u>er</u>" if there was no movement.*

There can be no experience without movement, there can be no "awar<u>er</u>" without the movement. This idea that people have in "spiritual" circles that somehow awareness goes on, awareness implies an "awar<u>er</u>" in some place in a space-time location. If you were to say everything is just awareness, there would not be awareness. If everything is made of **consciousness**, including the one that is aware of it, then obviously there is no such thing as **consciousness** or awareness; **consciousness** is another concept conceived of by an "awar<u>er</u>." Because there has to be something separate to say that **consciousness** is—

just by definition. *When the awar<u>er</u> and* **consciousness** *are the same substance, neither* **consciousness** *nor the* awar<u>er</u> *nor awareness are.*

THE SENSATION GROUP

Sound, smell, taste, bodily impressions, and mental objects.

ENQUIRY INTO THE NATURE
OF THE CONCEPT OF SOUND

Wolinsky: How does the concept called "my" **consciousness**, which believes in the concept of **I am** define the concept of sound?

Student: As a vibration that my ear turns into a sound or words.

Wolinsky: What assumptions has concept called "my" **consciousness**, which believes in the concept of **I am** made about the concept of sound?

Student: That it is outside of myself, the vehicle for the delivery of verbal information.

Wolinsky: And what have been the consequences for the concept called "my" **consciousness**, which believes in the concept of **I am**, which believes in the concept of sound as a vehicle for the delivery of verbal information?

Student: That there exists something outside of this one that is at a distance and in another location of space-time separate from this one.

Wolinsky: If all of this was just a concept of the concept called "my" consciousness, which believes in the concept of I am and were made of the SAME underlying SUBSTANCE, including the "awar_er_" that is aware of it, and it has nothing to do with anything, then . . . ?

Student: It's still there, but its more diffused.

Wolinsky: What has the concept called "my" consciousness, which believes in the concept of I am, which believes in the concept sound, distance, separate, information, etc., done to itself regarding sound, distance, separate, information, etc?

Student: Believed and experienced all of this as true.

Wolinsky: If these were just concepts of the concept called "my" consciousness, which believes in the concept of I am and were made of the SAME underlying SUBSTANCE including the "awar_er_," which is aware of it, and it all has nothing to do with anything, then . . . ?

Student: Still, . . . a little more diffused.

Wolinsky: Regarding all these concepts around sound, how has the concept called "my" consciousness, which believes in the concept of I am, deceived itself?

Student: Believing it all is.

Wolinsky: If these were just concepts of the concept called "my" consciousness, which believes in the concept of "I" and were made of the SAME underlying SUBSTANCE including the "awar_er_," which is aware of it and it all has nothing to do with anything, then . . . ?

Student: It's getting a little harder to grasp.

Wolinsky: Regarding this sound concept, what must the concept called "my" consciousness, which believes in the concept of I am, not know?

Student: That it all isn't.

Wolinsky: If these were just concepts of the concept called "my" consciousness, which believes in the concept of "I" and were made of the SAME underlying SUBSTANCE including the "awarer," which is aware of it, and it all has nothing to do with anything, then . . . ?

Student: It's like little specks of consciousness dissolving in a cloud.

Wolinsky: If these were just concepts of the concept of the concept called "my" consciousness, which believes in the concept of I am and were made of the SAME underlying SUBSTANCE including the "awarer," which is aware of it and it all has nothing to do with anything, then . . . ?

Student: _____(Long silence).

Wolinsky: Regarding all those sound concepts, what must the concept called "my" consciousness, which believes in the concept of I am not experience?

Student: That there is no experience or knowledge or information, that an experience took place if there was no sound.

Wolinsky: If these were just concepts of the concept of the concept called "my" consciousness, which believes in the concept of I am and were made of the SAME underlying SUBSTANCE including the "awarer," which is aware of it and it all has nothing to do with anything, then . . . ?

Student: NOTHING_____(Long silence).

ENQUIRY INTO THE NATURE
OF THE CONCEPT OF BODILY IMPRESSIONS

Wolinsky: How does concept called "my" consciousness, which believes in the concept of **I am** define the body impressions?

Student: As an image, something I call a body and me.

Wolinsky: What assumptions has concept called "my" consciousness, which believes in the concept of **I am** made about this body/me/image thing?

Student: That it's me.

Wolinsky: If these were just concepts of the concept called "my" consciousness, which believes in the concept of "I" and were made of the SAME underlying SUBSTANCE including the "awarer," which is aware of it, and it has nothing to do with anything, then . . . ?

Student: I'm falling into meditation.

Wolinsky: Regarding this body image concept that calls itself me, what has concept called "my" consciousness, which believes in the concept of **I am**, done to itself?

Student: Believed it was itself?

Wolinsky: If these were just concepts of the concept called "my" consciousness, which believes in the concept of "I" and were made of the SAME underlying SUBSTANCE including the "awarer," which is aware of it and it has nothing to do with anything, then . . . ?

Student: _____(Long silence).

Wolinsky: Regarding this concept called "my" **consciousness**, which believes in the concept of **I am**, which believes in the concept of body image that calls itself *me*, how has it deceived itself?

Student: By imagining it was itself and solid, and simultaneously not **consciousness**.

Wolinsky: If these were just concepts of the concept called "my" **consciousness**, which believes in the concept of **I am**, and were made of the SAME underlying SUBSTANCE including the "awar<u>er</u>," which is aware of it, and it has nothing to do with anything, then . . . ?

Student: _____(Long silence).

Wolinsky: Regarding this body image that calls itself "me," what must the concept called "my" **consciousness**, which believes in the concept of **I am**, not know?

Student: That it is just an image made of **consciousness**, but is not it?

Wolinsky: Why must **consciousness** not know that?

Student: Because then there would be only **consciousness**, which means there is no **consciousness**, just NOTHINGNESS.

Wolinsky: If these were just concepts of the concept called "my" **consciousness**, which believes in the concept of **I am** and were made of the SAME underlying SUBSTANCE including the "awar<u>er</u>," which is aware of it, and it all has nothing to do with anything, then . . . ?

Student: _____(Long silence).

Wolinsky: Regarding this body image that calls itself "me," what must the concept called "my" **consciousness** not experience?

Student: That it isn't.

Wolinsky: If all of these were just concepts of the concept called "my" **consciousness**, which believes in the concept of **I am** and were made of the SAME underlying SUBSTANCE including the "awar<u>er</u>," which is aware of it and it all has nothing to do with anything, then . . . ?

Student: _____(Long silence).

ENQUIRY INTO THE NATURE
OF THE CONCEPT OF MENTAL OBJECTS

Wolinsky: How does concept called "my" **consciousness**, which believes in the concept of **I am**, define mental objects?

Student: Images, thoughts, fantasies, ideas, even emotions, perceivables. All I's.

Wolinsky: What assumptions has the concept called "my" **consciousness**, which believes in the concept of **I am** made about the concepts called images, thoughts, fantasies, ideas, even emotions, perceivables—all "I's"?

Student: That they are real and ARE.

Wolinsky: And what have been the consequences for concept called "my" **consciousness**, which believes in the concept of **I am**, by believing in the concepts of images, thoughts, fantasies, ideas, even emotions, perceivables—all "I's"?

Student: That they are and **consciousness** as the perceiver of them IS.

Wolinsky: If these were just concepts of the concept called "my" **consciousness**, which believes in the concept of "I" and were made of the SAME underlying SUBSTANCE including the "aware_er_," which is aware of it and it all has nothing to do with anything, then . . . ?

Student: Everything stops.

Wolinsky: Regarding the concepts of images, thoughts, fantasies, ideas, even emotions, perceivables—all "I's"—how has the concept called "my" **consciousness**, which believes in the concept of I am, deceived itself?

Student: Imagining it is and all else is.

Wolinsky: If all of these were just concepts of the concept called "my" **consciousness**, which believes in the concept of I am, and were made of the SAME underlying SUBSTANCE including the "aware_er_," which is aware of it, and it all has nothing to do with anything, then . . . ?

Student: Wow, you can really see the circular illusion of it.

Wolinsky: Regarding all these concepts of images, thoughts, fantasies, ideas, even emotions, perceivables—all "I's"—how has the concept called "my" **consciousness**, which believes in the concept of I am, deceived itself?

Student: Imagining it is and all else is.

Wolinsky: If these were just concepts of the concept called "my" **consciousness**, which believes in the concept of I am and were made of the SAME underlying SUBSTANCE including the "awar*er*," which is aware of it and it all has nothing to do with anything, then . . . ?

Student: . . . no words . . . (silence).

Wolinsky: Regarding all the concepts called images, thoughts, fantasies, ideas, even emotions, perceivables—all "I's"—what must the concept called "my" **consciousness,** which believes in the concept of **I am,** not know?

Student: That it is NOT.

Wolinsky: Why must the concept called "my" **consciousness,** which believes in the concept of **I am,** not know that?

Student: Because if it is not, then it is not.

Wolinsky: If these were just concepts of the concept called "my" **consciousness,** which believes in the concept of **I am** and were made of the SAME underlying SUBSTANCE including the "awar*er*," which is aware of it and it all has nothing to do with anything, then . . . ?

Student: _____(Silence).

Wolinsky: Regarding images, thoughts, fantasies, ideas, even emotions, perceivables—all "I's"—what must the concept called "my" **consciousness,** which believes in the concept of **I am,** not experience?

Student: That it is not.

Wolinsky: Why not?

Student: Because if it is not, it is not.

Wolinsky: If the concept of *is* and *not* were just concepts of the concept called "my" **consciousness,** which believes in the concept of **I am** and were made of the SAME underlying SUBSTANCE including the "awar<u>er</u>," which is aware of it and it all has nothing to do with anything, then . . . ?

Student: _____(Long silence).

Wolinsky: Regarding images, thoughts, fantasies, ideas, even emotions, perceivables—all "I's"—what must the concept called "my" **consciousness**, which believes in the concept of **I am**, not experience?

Student: That it is not.

Wolinsky: Why not?

Student: Because if it is not, it is not.

Wolinsky: If *is* and *not* were just concepts of the concept called "my" **consciousness**, which believes in the concept of **I am** and were made of the SAME underlying SUBSTANCE including the "awar<u>er</u>," which is aware of it and it all has nothing to do with anything, then . . . ?

Student: _____(Long silence).

THE MENTAL FORMATION MENTAL IMPULSES GROUP

Volition, attention, discrimination, joy, happiness, equanimity, resolve, exertion, compulsion, concentration.

ENQUIRY INTO THE NATURE OF THE CONCEPT OF COMPULSION

Wolinsky: How does the concept called "my" **consciousness**, which believes in the concept of **I am**, define compulsion?

Student: An act that has to be done without choice or free will.

Wolinsky: What assumptions has the concept called "my" consciousness made about the concept called an act that has to be done without choice or free will?

Student: That it has an energy of its own, it cannot stop, it has to be done.

Wolinsky: What have been the consequences for the concept called "my" consciousness, which believes in the concept of consciousness "without choice or free will and that it has an energy of its own, it cannot stop, it has to be done"?

Student: It cannot stop any thought, action, reaction, etc.

Wolinsky: If these were just concepts of the concept called "my" consciousness, which believes in the concept of I am and were made of the SAME underlying SUBSTANCE including the "awarer," which is aware of it and it all has nothing to do with anything, then . . . ?

Student: It disappears, but then I notice a resistance like I want to stop the compulsion.

Wolinsky: If resistance was just a concept of the concept called "my" consciousness, which believes in the concept of I am and were made of the SAME underlying SUBSTANCE including the "awarer," which is aware of it and it has nothing to do with anything, then . . . ?

Student: There's a pulsation, which I can witness.

Wolinsky: Regarding the concept of an act that has to be done without choice or free will and that it has an energy of its own, it cannot stop, it has to be done, what has the concept called "my" consciousness, which believes in the concept of I am, done to itself?

Student: Assumed it *was*, that it had to be done, it told itself that it couldn't stop, justified it and reacted.

Wolinsky: Why would the concept called "my" consciousness, which believes in the concept of I am, do all of that?

Student: I don't know, it just did.

Wolinsky: If these were just concepts of the concept called "my" consciousness, which believes in the concept of I and were made of the SAME underlying SUBSTANCE including the "awar*er*," which is aware of it and it all had nothing to do with anything, then . . . ?

Student: Pulsating and witnessing the pulsation.

Wolinsky: If even the pulsation was a concept of the concept called "my" consciousness, which believes in the concept of I am and were made of the SAME underlying SUBSTANCE including the "awar*er*," which is aware of it and it has and had nothing to do with anything, then . . . ?

Student: Stillness.

Wolinsky: Regarding the concepts of an act that has to be done without choice or free will and that it has an energy of its own, it cannot stop, how has the concept called "my" consciousness, which believes in the concept of I am, deceived itself?

Student: Believing it was.

Wolinsky: If the concept called *was* was a concept of the concept called "my" **consciousness**, which believes in the concept of I **am** and were made of the SAME underlying SUBSTANCE including the "awar<u>er</u>," which is aware of it, and it has and had nothing to do with anything, then . . . ?

Student: Nothingness.

Wolinsky: Regarding the concept of an act that has to be done without choice or free will and that it has an energy of its own, it cannot stop, what must the concept called "my" **consciousness**, which believes in the concept of I **am**, not say?

Student: That all this is going on.

Wolinsky: Why?

Student: **Consciousness** feels it must hide it from itself and others in order to BE or exist.

Wolinsky: If these were just concepts of the concept called "my" **consciousness**, which believes in the concept of I **am** and were made of the SAME underlying SUBSTANCE including the "awar<u>er</u>," which is aware of it and it has and had nothing to do with anything, then . . . . ?

Student: _____(Long silence).

Wolinsky: Regarding the concept of an act that has to be done without choice or free will and that it has an energy of its own, it cannot stop, what must the concept called "my" **consciousness** not experience?

Student: _____(Long silence).

ENQUIRY INTO THE NATURE
OF THE CONCEPT OF VOLITION

Wolinsky: How does the concept called "my" **consciousness**, which believes in the concept of **I am**, define volition?

Student: Will, self-determined movement.

Wolinsky: What assumptions has the concept called "my" **consciousness**, which believes in the concept of **I am** made about will and self-determined movement?

Student: That that's "what is," or what it was told it was.

Wolinsky: If these were just concepts of the concept of the concept called "my" **consciousness**, which believes in the concept of "I" and were made of the SAME underlying SUBSTANCE including the "awar*er*," which is aware of it and it has nothing to do with anything, then . . . ?

Student: _____(Long silence).

Wolinsky: How has the concept called "my" **consciousness**, which believes in the concept of **I am**, which believes in the concepts of will and self-determined movement, deceived itself?

Student: Believing what it was told and felt.

Wolinsky: If these were just concepts of the concept of the concept called "my" **consciousness**, which believes in the concept of **I am** and were all made of the SAME underlying SUBSTANCE including the "awar*er*," which is aware of it and it has and had nothing to do with anything, then . . . ?

Student: Stillness_____(Long silence).

Wolinsky: Regarding the concepts of volition, will, and self-determined movement, what has the concept called "my" **consciousness**, which believes in the concept of **I am**, done to itself?

Student: Believed in will and self-determined movement, and continually tried to move and do as if it came from me and not **consciousness**.

Wolinsky: If these were just concepts of the concept of the concept called "my" **consciousness**, which believes in the concept of **I am** and were made of the SAME underlying SUBSTANCE including the "awar*er*," which is aware of it and it has nothing to do with anything, then . . . ?

Student: It takes all the push out.

Wolinsky: Regarding the concepts of will and self-determined movement, what must the concept called "my" **consciousness**, which believes in the concept of **I am**, not say?

Student: That there are no choices.

Wolinsky: Why?

Student: Not supposed to.

Wolinsky: If *supposed to* or *not supposed to* were just concepts of the concept called "my" **consciousness**, which believes in the concept of **I am** and were made of the SAME underlying SUBSTANCE including the "awar*er*," which is aware of it and it has and had nothing to do with anything, then . . . ?

Student: Free, lighter.

Wolinsky: Regarding the concepts of will and self-determined movement, what must the concept called "my" **consciousness**, which believes in the concept of **I am**, not know?

Student: There are no choices, and the NOTHING.

Wolinsky: Why not?

Student: Because then **consciousness** would not be.

Wolinsky: If these the concepts, Be – Not Be, will, and choices were just concepts of the concept called "my" **consciousness**, which believes in the concept of **I am** and were made of the SAME underlying SUBSTANCE including the "awar*er*," which is aware of it and it has and had nothing to do with anything, then . . . ?

Student: _____(Silence).

Wolinsky: Regarding the concepts of Be – Not Be, will, and self-determined movement, what must the concept called "my" **consciousness**, which believes in the concept of **I am**, not experience?

Student: The NOTHINGNESS.

Wolinsky: Why not?

Student: Because it's beyond **consciousness**, and **consciousness** will disappear.

Wolinsky: If all of this were just concepts of the concept called "my" **consciousness**, which believes in the concept of **I am**, and were made of the SAME underlying SUBSTANCE including the "awar*er*," which is aware of it and it had nothing to do with anything, then . . . ?

Student: The NOTHINGNESS.

Wolinsky: Why?

Student: Because it's beyond **consciousness**, and **consciousness** will disappear.

Wolinsky: If **appear** and disappear were just concepts of the concept called "my" **consciousness**, which believes in the concept of **I am** and were made of the SAME underlying SUBSTANCE including the "awar*er*," which is aware of it and it has nothing to do with anything, then . . . ?

Student: NOTHINGNESS.

ENQUIRY INTO THE NATURE
OF THE CONCEPT OF ATTENTION

Wolinsky: How does the concept called "my" **consciousness**, which believes in the concept of **I am**, define attention?

Student: Attention is how **consciousness** focuses itself through a concentration of itself forming a lens to view through.

Wolinsky: What assumptions has the concept called "my" **consciousness**, which believes in the concept of **I am**, made about attention, which is how **consciousness** focuses itself through a concentration of itself forming a lens to view through? ⋅

Student: That the lens it looks through and all it looks at are not **consciousness**.

Wolinsky: And what have been the consequences of that for the concept called "my" **consciousness**?

Student: A world or differences.

Wolinsky: If these were just concepts of the concept called "my" consciousness, which believes in the concept of I am and were made of the SAME underlying SUBSTANCE including the "awar*er*," which is aware of it and it has nothing to do with anything, then . . . ?

Student: There is only consciousness with a tube-like lens floating in it.

Wolinsky: Regarding the concept called attention, which is how the concept called "my" consciousness, which believes in the concept of I am, which focuses itself through a concentration of itself forming a lens to view through, how has concept called "my" consciousness deceived itself?

Student: Imagining this lens, tube, was not it.

Wolinsky: If these were just concepts of the concept called "my" consciousness, which believes in the concept of I am and were made of the SAME underlying SUBSTANCE including the "awar*er*," which is aware of it and it has nothing to do with anything, then . . . ?

Student: Only consciousness with a slight lens tube.

Wolinsky: Regarding attention, what has the concept called "my" consciousness, which believes in the concept of I am, which believes in the concept of I am, which focuses itself through a concentration of itself forming a lens to view through, done to itself?

Student: Believed the lens tube and the looking through it was not . . .

Wolinsky: Do that now.

Student: Wow, there's the world.

Wolinsky: Do that a few times.

Student: The world disappears.

Wolinsky: And the lens tube.

Student: It is . . . as **consciousness**.

Wolinsky: Regarding the concept of attention, "what is" the concept called "my" **consciousness**, which believes in the concept of **I am**, which believes in the concept of focuses itself through a concentration of itself forming a lens to view through, unwilling to say?

Student: It is not.

Wolinsky: Why?

Student: Because it won't be?

Wolinsky: What's be?

Student: _____(Long silence).

Wolinsky: Regarding attention, what must the concept called "my" **consciousness**, which believes in the concept of **I am**, which believes in the concept of focuses itself through a concentration of itself forming a lens to view through, not know?

Student: The NOTHINGNESS.

Wolinsky: Why?

Student: Because if it does, there is no **consciousness**, just NOTHINGNESS, not even that.

Wolinsky: If these were just concepts of the concept called "my" **consciousness**, which believes in the concept of **I am** and were made of the SAME underlying SUBSTANCE including the "awar*er*," which is aware of it and it had nothing to do with anything, then . . . ?

Student: _____(Silence).

Wolinsky: Regarding the concept of attention, what must the concept called "my" **consciousness**, which believes in the concept of **I am**, which believes in the concept of focuses itself through a concentration of itself forming a lens to view through, not experience?

Student: That it's not.

Wolinsky: Why?

Student: Just NOTHINGNESS.

Wolinsky: If these were just concepts of the concept called "my" **consciousness**, which believes in the concept of **I am** and were made of the SAME underlying SUBSTANCE including the "awar*er*," which is aware of it and it had nothing to do with anything, then . . .?

Student: _____(Long silence).

ENQUIRY INTO THE NATURE
OF THE CONCEPT OF MENTAL IMPULSES

Wolinsky: How does concept called "my" **consciousness**, which believes in the concept of **I am**, define mental impulses?

Student: As this bio-electric pulse that pulses out these impulses that can take the form and represent energy, images, fantasies, emotions, etc.

Wolinsky: What assumptions has the concept called "my" consciousness, which believes in the concept of **I am** made about this bio-electric pulse that pulses out these impulses that can take the form of energy, images, fantasies, emotions, etc.?

Student: That it is, it is, and because it is, it is.

Wolinsky: If these were just concepts of the concept called "my" **consciousness**, which believes in the concept of **I am** and were made of the SAME underlying SUBSTANCE including the "awar*er*," which is aware of it and it had nothing to do with anything, then . . . ?

Student: _____(Silence).

Wolinsky: Regarding this bio-electric pulse that pulses out these impulses that can take the form of energy, images, fantasies, emotions, etc., what has the concept called "my" **consciousness** done to itself?

Student: Believed there was a self rather than a pulsating bio-electric impulse that registers as a self.

Wolinsky: If the concept of a bio-electric pulse and the concept of a self were just concepts of the concept called "my" **consciousness**, which believes in the concept of **I am** and were made of the SAME underlying SUBSTANCE including the "awar*er*," which is aware of it and it had nothing to do with anything, then . . . ?

Student: _____(Long silence).

Wolinsky: Regarding this bio-electric pulse that pulses out these impulses that can take the form of energy, images, fantasies, emotions, etc., what is the concept called "my" **consciousness** unwilling to say?

Student: That it is behind the illusion of bio-electric impulse.

Wolinsky: Why?

Student: Because if it did, it would all collapse.

Wolinsky: If these were just concepts of the concept called "my" consciousness, which believes in the concept of I am and were made of the SAME underlying SUBSTANCE including the "awar*er*," which is aware of it and it had nothing to do with anything, then . . .?

Student: It's hard to believe————(Long silence).

Wolinsky: Regarding this bio-electric pulse that pulses out these impulses that can take the force of energy, images, fantasies, emotions, etc., what is the concept called "my" consciousness, which believes in the concept of I am unwilling to know about?

Student: That bio-electric is an illusion.

Wolinsky: Why?

Student: Because if it did, there would be no self, only consciousness, and then no CONSCIOUSNESS, only NOTHINGNESS.

Wolinsky: If these were just concepts of the concept called "my" consciousness, which believes in the concept of I am and were made of the SAME underlying SUBSTANCE including the "awar*er*," which is aware of it and it had nothing to do with anything, then . . . ?

Student: But it seems to be heart or pulse connected.

Wolinsky: Regarding this bio-electric pulse that pulses out these impulses that can take the form of energy, images, fantasies, emotions, etc., what must the concept called "my" **consciousness**, which believes in the concept of **I am**, not know?

Student: That **consciousness** is what it is all made of.

Wolinsky: Why?

Student: Because then there is no bio-electric, no **consciousness**, only NOTHINGNESS, and not even that.

Wolinsky: If these were just concepts of the concept called "my" **consciousness**, which believes in the concept of **I am** and were made of the SAME underlying SUBSTANCE including the "awar<u>er</u>," which is aware of it and it had nothing to do with anything, then . . . ?

Student: _____(Long silence).

Wolinsky: *If* there is a YOU concept called "my" **consciousness**, which believes in the concept of **I am**, which believes in the concept of mental functioning, is there anything this concept called "my" **consciousness**, which believes in the concept of **I am** and were made of the SAME underlying SUBSTANCE including the "awar<u>er</u>," which is aware of it and it had nothing to do with anything, then . . . ?

Student: _____(Long silence).

THE CONSCIOUSNESS GROUP

ENQUIRY INTO THE NATURE
OF THE CONCEPT OF MENTAL CONSCIOUSNESS

Consciousness of seeing, hearing, smelling, tasting, body sensations, mental consciousness.

Wolinsky: How does concept called "my" **consciousness**, which believes in the concept of I am, define mental **consciousness**?

Student: Being conscious of mental functioning.

Wolinsky: What assumptions has concept called "my" **consciousness**, which believes in the concept of I am, made about the concept of mental **consciousness**?

Student: That there is a YOU that is CONSCIOUS of mental functioning.

Wolinsky: And what have been the consequences of that for the concept called "my" **consciousness**, which believes in the concept of I am, by believing in the concept of mental **consciousness**?

Student: There is a constant attempt to reinforce this YOU, which is **consciousness** of mental functioning.

Wolinsky: If these were just concepts of the concept called "my" **consciousness**, which believes in the concept of I am and were made of the SAME underlying SUBSTANCE including the "awar_er_," which is aware of it and it has nothing to do with anything, then . . . ?

Student: _____(Long silence).

Wolinsky: How has this concept called "my" **consciousness,** which believes in the concept of I **am,** which believes in the concept of mental **consciousness,** deceived itself?

Student: It imagined that it was separate from **consciousness** and the object, thoughts, etc., were separate from **consciousness.**

Wolinsky: If these were just concepts of the concept called "my" **consciousness,** which believes in the concept of I am and were made of the SAME underlying SUBSTANCE including the "awar<u>er</u>," which is aware of it and it has and had nothing to do with anything, then . . . ?

Student: _____(Long silence).

Wolinsky: If there was a YOU concept called "my" **consciousness,** which believes in the concept of I am, which believes in the concept of mental functioning, what has "my" **consciousness** done to itself?

Student: Believed that there was a YOU separate from "it."

Wolinsky: If these were just concepts of the concept called "my" **consciousness,** which believes in the concept of I am and were made of the SAME underlying SUBSTANCE including the "awar<u>er</u>," which is aware of it and it had nothing to do with anything, then . . . ?

Student: _____(Long silence).

Wolinsky: Considering that there is a YOU concept called "my" **consciousness,** which believes in the concept of I am, which believes in the concept of mental functioning, what is **consciousness** unwilling to say?

Student: It is not.

Wolinsky: If *not* and *is* were just concepts of the concept called "my" **consciousness**, which believes in the concept of I am and were made of the SAME underlying SUBSTANCE including the "awar*er*," which is aware of it and it has and had nothing to do with anything, then . . . ?

Student: _____(Long silence).

Wolinsky: If there is a YOU concept called "my" **consciousness**, which believes in the concept of I am, which believes in the concept of mental functioning, what is the concept called "my" **consciousness** unwilling to know?

Student: That it is all one substance and is not.

Wolinsky: If these were just concepts of the concept called "my" **consciousness**, which believes in the concept of I am and were made of the SAME underlying SUBSTANCE including the "awar*er*," which is aware of it and it has nothing to do with anything, then . . . ?

Student: _____(Long silence).

Wolinsky: If there is a YOU concept called "my" **consciousness**, which believes in the concept of I am, which believes in the concept of mental functioning, is there anything this concept called "my" **consciousness** is unwilling to experience?

Student: That it is not and is pure NOTHINGNESS.

Wolinsky: If *not* and *nothingness* were just concepts of the concept called "my" **consciousness**, which believes in the concept of I am and were made of the SAME underlying SUBSTANCE including the "awar*er*," which is aware of it and it had nothing to do with anything, then . . . ?

Student: _____(Long silence).

**PRIOR TO CONSCIOUSNESS
THERE IS NO "AWAR*ER*" OR AWARENESS.
PRIOR TO CONSCIOUSNESS IS UNAWARENESS.
PRIOR TO CONSCIOUSNESS IS
THAT ONE SUBSTANCE,
WHICH HAS NO "AWAR*ER*."
ASK: PRIOR TO THE EMERGENCE
OF THE "AWAR*ER*" . . . ARE YOU?**

**QUANTUM PSYCHOLOGY ENDS AT AWARENESS
OF THE BIG EMPTINESS, WHICH WE CALLED
AND WAS REPRESENTED BY THE CONCEPT
OF THE NOT-I-I. PRIOR TO THE "AWAR*ER*,"
WHICH IS MADE OF CONSCIOUSNESS, ARE YOU?**

**THE "AWAR*ER*" AND AWARENESS ARE MADE
OF CONSCIOUSNESS. EVERYTHING IS MADE
OF THAT ONE SUBSTANCE.
PRIOR TO THIS ONE SUBSTANCE CONCEPT, WHICH
DOES NOT CONTAIN CONSCIOUSNESS
OR AWARENESS, IS UNAWARENESS.**

CHAPER 14

The Veil of the Concept of the Eight-Fold Path

CONCENTRATION–MEDITATION–SAMADHI

n the eight-fold (step) paths of both the Hindu and Buddhist tradition; the 6th, 7th and 8th steps are concentration (in Sanskrit, Dharana), meditation, (in Sanskrit, Dhyana), and Samadhi, respectively, all of which require an "I" to do the process. Before we go into how this could be a veil of consciousness, let us first begin by defining the terminology.

Dharana (Concentration)

"Concentration is confining the mind within a limited mental area (object of concentration)." (Taimini, *The Science of Yoga*, p. 275)

Dhyana Meditation

"Uninterrupted flow (of the mind) toward the object (chosen for meditation) is contemplation." (Taimini, *The Science of Yoga*, p. 275)

Samadhi

"When there is consciousness only of the object of meditation and not of itself (the mind) is Samadhi." (Taimini, *The Science of Yoga*, p. 281)

Let us begin by seeding what will become Section III by beginning with a question: "What is *a priori*, or better said, what must be there first in order to concentrate, meditate, or "go into Samadhi"?"

The answer is an "awar*er*." In other words, the I am is, *a priori* in order to do any form of concentration or "spiritual practice," and it is the I am, which contains the structure (condensation of THE SUBSTANCE) called an "awar*er*." An "awar*er*" naturally carries out the process of awar*ing* and produces what we call awareness. In other words, the "awar*er*," is a structure made of **consciousness**, which awar*es* things, and has a location in space-time.

Ask this question: "*Prior to the emergence of an awarer, . . . are you?*" With this "understanding," concentration and meditation are a function of an "awar*er*," which is made of **consciousness**. To illustrate, **prior to** building muscles, you must have a body that exercises. **Prior to** meditation is a body and (**I am**) and the exercise of concentration. Hence, concentration and meditation followed by religious dogma can serve to strengthen the resolve of its substructure or understructure called the "awar*er*," making it (the "awar*er*") believe *it is*. This exercising of a substructure (the "awar*er*") can, *without understanding*, serve to strengthen the substructure called the "awar*er's*" ability to concentrate—BUT also runs the risk of deluding the **I am** into believing *it is* and that *it is* "getting better." At this point it is imperative to insist on a key issue to avoid miss-understandings. THERE IS NO SUGGESTION OR IMPLICATION THAT CONCENTRATION → MEDITATION IS BAD.

However, the questions and understanding that must go with this are the following: 1) Who is meditating? (What "I" is imagining it is performing the action?); and 2) For what reason is the *meditator-"I"* performing the action; i.e., what does the *meditator-"I"* imagine it will get, become, have, or be able to do better?

In both instances, there is some form of "I" that is meditating, and it is doing this to get something, both of which are counter to *Nirvana* or "No-I."

In this way, concentration → meditation can be "understood" as a possible "beginning step"; however, ultimately, along with the I am-"awar*er*" substructure, they must be understood for what they are—a *meditator-"I"*; hence, it, too, must be dissolved (this will be more central in Section III).

Samadhi is the "last" step in any eight-limb or eight-fold (step) path or yoga. Samadhi, as it is commonly used, has several earlier levels to it. For our purposes, in this section we will talk of only the first three previously mentioned Step 6 (concentration), Step 7 (meditation), Step 8 (Samadhi with seeds)—Step 6 and Step 7 contain seeds of the **consciousness** of I **am**. The last Step 8 contains the subtle seeds within the void or gap (a *meditator-"I"*), which acts and remains subtly, even during the in-between state or *void*.

"A cloud or void is also a cover on pure consciousness. It is only the blurred impression produced in consciousness when i t passes through successive "planes." This phase is like the critical state between two states of matter, liquid and gaseous, when it can neither be called liquid or gaseous." (*Yoga Sutras*, p. 40)

The "bliss of Samadhi," really cannot be described. However, that *void* still carries with it the impressions (seeds), which, in a subtle form, sprout upon arising out of Samadhi and hence brings us back to "our" psychological "experience" as "I."

It is for this reason that Samadhi, too, must be "gone beyond." In this way, although Samadhi is referred to as the eighth and final step, it is so because beyond the *state* of Samadhi *with seeds*, there is no state. In this way, the *void* contained within Samadhi contains seeds, because it contains impressions and representations of manifestation that, as potential, will manifest. From a physics perspective, metaphorically, this could be likened to this *void* being called *potential energy*, and "energy" in motion or manifestation as *kinetic energy*. The *void* of Samadhi with seeds is "energy" or impressions as *potential* manifestation and is still manifestation in seed form. The *void*, as manifestation or manifested, is impressions with motion or *kinetic*. Metaphorically, we can say that a house made of bricks and mortar is the manifestation; the mortar, bricks, and space the house will occupy is the void or potential house, which we must have in order to build a house.

In this way, Nisargadatta Maharaj, when asked, "Are you in Samadhi?" replied, **"No, Samadhi is a state; I am not in a state."**

The Yoga Sutras say it this way:

"Why is the Yogi's consciousness thrown back into the vehicles which he has transcended and why do these appear, again and again, in this stage of his progress towards Self-realization? Because the Samskaras (impressions) which he has brought over from his past are still present in his vehicle (body) in a dormant condition and emerge into his consciousness as soon as there is relaxation of effort or a temporary interruption. As long as these 'seeds' are present merely in a dormant condition and have not been 'burnt' or rendered quiet. . . . they sprout into his consciousness as soon as a suitable opportunity presents itself." (Taimini, *The Science of Yoga*, p. 430)

In Section III we will discuss Samadhi without seeds, which is "beyond" and not a state or thing. For now, suffice to say that Samadhi with seeds is "arrived" at through some form of "spiritual practice," which a *meditator-"I"* imagines "it" does.

Samadhi without seeds just **appears**, or better said, disappears (hard to express in language); but there is no "I" that can do it. In other words, all states of Samadhi are states, and are I **am** and awar*er* dependent—hence, THEY ARE NOT IT!!!! They are subtle substructures intermittently of the I **am**, and ultimately are not even **nothingness**, and ARE NOT.

THE LAST STEP IN RAJA YOGA IS SAMADHI— (DERIVED FROM AND WHICH INCLUDES SEEDS). WITHOUT THINKER SENSOR KNOWER OR "AWAR*ER*," THIS IS SAMADHI WITHOUT SEEDS. HOWEVER, IF THERE IS NO "AWAR*ER*, THEN THERE IS NO AWARENESS, AND NO YOGA.

SOME PEOPLE SAY, "IT'S ALL AWARENESS." HOWEVER, IF EVERYTHING WAS AWARENESS, THERE WOULD BE NO AWARENESS. WHY? BECAUSE THERE WOULD BE NOBODY THERE TO SAY THAT SUCH A THING AS THIS CONCEPT CALLED AWARENESS EXISTED.

THEREFORE, ALL AWARENESS IMPLIES AN "AWAR*ER*" CONCEPT, LOCATION, AND POINT OF ORIGIN. HENCE, IF THERE IS NO "AWAR*ER*," THERE IS NO AWARENESS, NO LOCATION, AND NO POINT OF ORIGIN.

CHAPTER 15

The Five-Fold Act of Consciousness

YET ANOTHER "AWAR_ER_"

"The act of *emanation*. With reference to the appearance of the objects in another space, time, etc., it is The act of *withdrawal* or absorption. With reference to the actual (continuity of the) appearance of blue etc., it is The act of *maintenance*. With reference to its appearance as different, it is The act of *concealment*. With reference to the appearance of everything as identical with the light (of consciousness), it is The act of *grace*." (Singh, *Pratyabhijnahrdayam*, p. 75)

Consciousness, no doubt, has many different steps in its traversing from THAT SUBSTANCE to the manifested universe and what we call "I." However, each witnessing of the steps or acts that **consciousness** makes requires an "awar_er_." Thus, the trap is not in mentioning or even knowing the 5-fold, 10-fold, 100-fold, or no-act act. The trap lies in two areas: First, in the misunderstanding that witnessing, noticing or being "awar_er_" of these steps or acts will liberate an "I"; second, that the "awar_er_" that is awaring these "movements," " "acts," "plays," or "phases" of **consciousness** is still and always contingent upon the presence of an "awar*er;* and third that the "awar*er* is made of a different substance than the awar*ed object.*"

First of all, the "I" can never get liberated because there is NO "I." Secondly, the "awar*er*" is made of the same subtler and less condensed substance; call it **consciousness**, as the awar*ed,* (the five-fold act), and as such it continues as long as the "awar*er*" is fixated on the awar*ed* "as if" it is made of a different substance than itself.

According to Saiva philosophy, the world is not a creation, but

1) an emanation
2) a maintenance (of the world-process)
3) a withdrawal or re-absorption. It does not mean destruction. There is no destruction of the world. It is only re-absorbed for a time. Destruction is only metaphorical.
4) concealment of the real nature of the Self.
5) "grace."
   (Singh, *Pratyabhijnahrdayam*, p. 119)

"However, if at the time of the re-absorption or withdrawal (of the experience of manifoldness or differentiation), it (i.e., the object of experience) generates various impressions of doubt etc. inwardly, then it acquires the state in germ (or seed form) which is bound to spring forth into existence again, and thus it superimposes (on the experient) the state of concealment of the real nature of the Self [THE SUBSTANCE] .... On the other hand while it (i.e., the world), which has been reduced to a (seed of) germinal form is being held inwardly and anything else that is experienced at that time, if it is burned to sameness with the fire of consciousness. He (the yogin seeker) enters the state of grace." (Singh, *Pratyabhijnahrdayam*, pp. 77-78)

This, as mentioned earlier, reiterates that the void can also be the withdrawal of consciousness and thus holds in a (potential) seed form the impressions that will later manifest. Moreover, then the "awar*er*" and "awar*ed*" are seen as THE SAME SUBSTANCE; then they disappear, and that is *grace*.

In quantum physics, David Bohm discussed the *implicit* or underlying order and the *explicate* order of names and forms. *Pratyabhijnahrdayam* divides itself into several more divisions.

However, these divisions that describe such a process are all contingent upon an "awar*er*" being aware *of* an "awar*ed*." If there is no "awar*er*," then there is no five-fold act.

In this way, like the Zen Koan; "If a tree falls in the forest and there is nobody there to hear it, does it make a sound?"

ENQUIRE

If there is no "awar*er*," is there a five-fold act?
Prior to the emergence of the "awar*er*," . . . are you?

"Pratyabhijnahrdayam lays the greatest stress on the meditation of the five-fold act which is going on constantly even in the individual." (Singh, *Pratyabhijnahrdayam*, p. 30)

In the *Pratyabhijnahrdayam*, the *spanda* is defined not in terms of two parts (appearance—disappearance), but the term is subdivided into five parts. It is the realization of these five-fold parts or "acts" or **consciousness**, which when "viewed" according to the *Pratyabhijnahrdayam* liberates "one" of their effects. **However**, please recall that the "understanding" that the "awar*er*," too, is part of this five-fold act and is essential for the "awar*er*" "*apperceiving*" **Nirvana** (extinction).

It is critical to note that the natural withdrawal process holds impressions, and when it arises again, it conceals THAT SUBSTANCE. However, if the potential, which is a seed that is held is "seen" as the same **consciousness** as the experient, both disappear; this is *grace*.

This was often the case when "I" would meet someone who knew who they were. "I" would approach them with a problem. In "their" presence, the problem dissolved (*grace*). However, *because "I" was unaware that the "awarer" of the problem and the problem were the SAME SUBSTANCE, the problem would arise again.*

In other words, the gap, space, or *void* is the subtlest form (seed) of the **I am** and thought. And, in the *void* the thought is concealed but not destroyed—merely withdrawn. This is not grace (disappearance), but rather concealment. It is for this reason, that "'people' in meditation go into the void or gap," but come out with the same problem.

GRACE IS DISAPPEARANCE; VOID-GAP IS WITHDRAWAL.

"Where, however, (when) contraction or limitation is predominant, there occurs the knowership of the Void, etc." (Singh, *Pratyabhijnahrdayam*, p. 60)

The *void*, of course, has a know*er* of the *void*. It is the know*er* of the *void* that arises along with the knowledge of the *void*. It is, therefore, a contraction that brings forth the arising of the know*er* of the *void*. Once the know*er* of the *void* and the *void* are seen as **THE SAME SUBSTANCE**, then there is neither a know*er* of the *void* or the *void* itself. In this way, the *void* and its know*er* **appear** and disappear together.

CHAPTER 16

The Heart is Emptiness

"Hrdaya here does not mean the physical heart, but the deepest **consciousness.** *It has been called hrdaya or heart because it is the center of reality. It is the light of* **consciousness** *in which the entire universe is rooted. In the individual, it is the spiritual center."*

(Singh, *Pratyabhijnahrdayam*, p. 95)

This particular statement is of the utmost significance. The *BIG EMPTINESS IS THE HEART.* It is beyond qualities and attributes. The **heart**, because of most western associations is associated with either personal love or unconditional love. Recall that the cornerstone of Buddhism, *"Form is none other than Emptiness, Emptiness is none other than Form,"* is called the *Heart Sutra,* because the BIG EMPTINESS -as THAT, *undifferentiated consciousness* is the Heart. The gnawing inner emptiness, which, because of resistance to it, causes so many problems and I-dentities, is considered a pivotal cornerstone for understanding existential philosophy. However, throughout Quantum Psychology, this inner emptiness is seen rather as a gateway to the BIG EMPTINESS. Moreover, this provides the solution to the existential problem of dread, angst, and falling from being that pervades 20th century western psychology and philosophy. Simply put, the "inner" emptiness is the "spiritual center," or *void center* "contained within each individual."

"The yogi should concentrate intensely on the idea that this universe is totally void. In that void, his mind should become absorbed. Then he becomes highly qualified for absorption, i.e., his mind is absorbed in sunyatisunya, the absolute VOID . . ." (Singh, *Vijnanabhairava,* p. 55)

Prior to all is the nothingness, the VOID OF UNDIFFERENTIATED CONSCIOUSNESS; THAT SUBSTANCE. Although present, it too can become a veil of consciousness. Why? Because it requires an "awar*er*" of consciousness, which is consciousness itself. Once consciousness itself realizes that there is only consciousness, then consciousness is no more and we are beyond consciousness, (to be discussed in greater detail in Section III).

In this way the emptiness "becomes" form (a thought) and dissolves to become emptiness, the emptiness may arise as the form of a thought again. But to whom? Since all are still made of the same emptiness, then *neither are, both are not.*

In short, all experiences of anything require an experienc*er* or "awar*er*"—no "awar*er*"—no awareness, no Form, to emptiness.

CHAPTER 17

The Bhakti Illusion

FORMS ARE SEEDS

Plato *hypothesized* (conjectured) about the existence of **forms**, or perfect prototypes, which we cannot see with our eyes. These **forms**, are the "originals," but what we see, be it a tree, a person, or a table, is merely a "copy" of this perfect original prototype. However, even if we take Plato's *hypothesis* as true, still, all **forms** are seeds of their copies, and hence lead only to the ripening of more fruit (copies).

One of the greatest spiritual illusions is to worship an "outer object" or deity, "as if" it, the outer statue, picture, deity, or "energy" can then give you something.

This is like the old story of the statue maker who makes an image of God and then worships the image—forgetting who made the image.

I was once with Nisargadatta Maharaj when an Indian man came in and began talking about how he was a devotee of the mother, and how he worships the mother and "gets" things like peace, etc. Maharaj asked him, "Who came first, you or the mother?" The man replied, "The mother came first, she created me and I worship her; and she will give me grace, bliss, and liberation." Maharaj shouted, "*NO*, first *you* had to be there; then came the mother. No you, no mother; so why don't you worship yourself which is **prior to** the mother?"

This illusion of an "I" worshipping a mother with all of these wonderful qualities not only runs the risk of psychological trance-ference of the "wish" for the perfect magical mommy and its repressed pain of separation lying in an age-regressed adult, this illusion also carries with it and presupposes three things: 1) That there is a separate substance called you and mother, 2) That there is an "I" that will get or experience something if it does the practices, and 3) Probably the most seductive of all is the premise of the feminine as opposed to the masculine. This is deeply rooted in projecting ones' feminine qualities onto an outer object or deity and then worshiping the outer deity. This is not only anthropomorphic, but it also implies more than one substance (masculine and feminine and attributing different qualities or attributes to the **ONE SUBSTANCE**), and also implies a separate "I" doing something to get something. This can be best conveyed by the words of Nisargadatta Maharaj, who said to me, "**You think you are a person, so you think Maharaj is a person; you think you are an entity or a deity, so you think Maharaj is an entity or deity.**" (*This must be gone beyond.*)

"When the realization of the inadequacy of Atma-Bhava dawns upon the Yogi, he determines to break the last fetter by renouncing the bliss and knowledge of the atomic plane. Thence forward all his efforts are directed by intense penetrating... which alone can pierce through this veil or illusion." (Taimini, *The Science of Yoga*, p. 428)

Moreover, to focus on an outer object is called, in the yoga sutras, Samadhi with (based on) seeds. If you focus on seeds, the problem is that even if you go into Samadhi, you return with seeds and the fruit of those seductive seeds.

Below is an **enquiry** that began with the concept of earth and it led to the Veil of devotion to an outer object (the mother); in yoga circles, this is called Bhakti.

Wolinsky:	The I am, which believes in the concept of Earth. Where do you feel it in the condensed **consciousness** body?
Student:	Feet.
Wolinsky:	How does the I am concept, which believes in the concept of earth, define earth?
Student:	Earth is **consciousness**, is condensed, solid, life, planet we live on.
Wolinsky:	What assumptions has the I am concept made about the planet we live on, solid, life, etc?
Student:	It is a nurturing thing, food comes from earth, makes things grow. I can really connect to this element; it has a *motherly thing, women, feminine thing, not male.*
Wolinsky:	Regarding all these concept of female, feminine, motherly, not male, nurturing, if all of these were just concepts of the I am and had nothing to do with anything, then . . . ?
Student:	It disappears.
Wolinsky:	If the I am were to believe in these concepts called solid, nurturing, motherly, female, not male, what would be the consequences for the concept of I am if it believed all those other concepts?
Student:	Makes earth very important, makes earth very solid thing, being the center of things—of everything; safe, reliable, dependable.
Wolinsky:	The I am, which has these concepts called solid, important, reliable, female, not male, nurturing, center, if they were all concepts of I am and had nothing to do with anything, then . . . ?

Student: "I" become less solid, it makes me a little thing in the universe, it's a good feeling, as if all the solidness gives a certain fear of losing it all.

Wolinsky: This **I am** concept, which believes in the concept of mother, earth, feminine, not masculine, being the center of everything, nurturing, solid, important. What has that **I am** concept done to another **I am** concept, and what did that **I am** create in response to this **I am**?

Student: The **I am** is my mother (birth), mom, mother earth stories, take care of, etc.

Wolinsky: So there's a lineage here. This **I am** (pointing to her) had to take it on to keep the lineage going? If this **I am** did not believe that (her mom) **I am** concept, which believes in the concept of mother, earth, earth is mother, feminine, not masculine, being the center of everything, nurturing, solid, important, certain, must take care of, etc. If *that* **I am** concept realized it was just a concept, which had nothing to do with anything, then . . . ?

Student: "I" disappear.

Wolinsky: If *that* **I am** concept were to believe this **I am** concept, which believes in the concept of mother, earth, feminine, not masculine, being the center of everything, nurturing, solid, important, certain, take care of, etc. What has this concept of **I am** done to itself?

Student: Taking on all this stuff, being busy all the time.

Wolinsky: If these were all concepts of **I am** and had nothing to do with anything, then . . . ?

Student: "I" disappear.

Wolinsky: This **I am** concept, which believes in the concept of mother, earth, earth is mother, feminine, not masculine, being the center of everything, nurturing, solid, important, certain, take care of, etc. How has this **I am** concept deceived another **I am** concept?

Student: Took a lot of responsibility from other **I am**'s, feels like we must take care of.

Wolinsky: If the concept of *taking care of* was a concept of **I am** and had nothing to do with anything, then . . . ?

Student: _____Nothing_____(Silence).

Wolinsky: This **I am** concept, which believes in the concept of earth is mother, mother, earth, feminine, not masculine, being the center of everything, nurturing, solid, important, take care of, etc. How has this **I am** concept deceived itself?

Student: It imagined that all those mother earth stories were true and had to be acted out.

Wolinsky: And if all those stories were just concepts of **I am** and had nothing to do with anything, then . . . ?

Student: _____(Long silence).

Wolinsky: How does the concept of earth, which this **I am** concept believes, like the concept of mother, earth, feminine, not masculine, being the center of everything, nurturing, solid, important, take care of, etc. How does this **I am** concept seem now?

Student: It's gone.

Wolinsky: This **I am** concept, which believes in the concept of earth is mother, mother, earth, feminine, not masculine, being the center of everything, nurturing, solid, important, take care of, etc.—what is this **I am** concept unwilling to communicate about?

Student: The unsafe, not solid side of earth, destructive side, volcanoes, bad mother.

Wolinsky: So why would the **I am** concept be willing to focus only on the nurturing good mother, not the destructive side?

Student: Lots of fear of death, fear of destruction.

Wolinsky: So this **I am** concept, which believes in the concept of earth is mother, mother, earth, feminine, not masculine, being the center of everything, nurturing, solid, important, taking care of, etc. Where in your body do you feel the natural destructive earth process and the resistance to things falling apart?

Student: In my chest.

Wolinsky: Take the label off, give it back to **I am**. How does it feel to you now?

Student: It went away.

Wolinsky: So this **I am** concept, which believes in the concept of earth is mother, mother, earth, feminine, not masculine, being the center of everything, nurturing, solid, important, take care of, etc., if it had nothing to do with anything, then . . . ?

Student: _____(Long silence)_____I feel it in my feet.

Wolinsky: This **I am** concept, which believes in the concept of solidness, if that was just a concept of **I am** and had nothing to do with anything, then . . . ?

Student: _____(Silence).

Wolinsky: Notice the **emptiness** within the solidness within the feet and everything else. How are you doing?

Student: _____(Long silence)_____It's gone.

Wolinsky: This **I am** concept, which believes in the concept of earth is mother, mother, earth, feminine, not masculine, being the center of everything, nurturing, solid, important, take care of, etc.—if they had nothing to do with anything, then . . . ?

Student: _____(Long silence).

THE KNOWER AND THE "AWAR*ER*"

In order for an identity of "I" to be there, there must be a knower of the I-dentity. The knower of the I-dentity is part of the I-dentity.

The knower of any I-dentity contains only that knowledge which is contained within the I-dentity.

To go beyond the knower, try to find the knower, or look for the knower, and you *apperceive* that there is none.

Or try to "see" the knower and the I-dentity as being made of **THE SAME SUBSTANCE**. Then there is **blank** and then "soon," only the pure **NOTHINGNESS** or the **vastness** remains.

THE "AWAR*ER*"

The same is true of an "awar*er*." An "awar*er*" subtly implies a "place" or origin of awareness; a location in space-time. The "awar*er*" structure, through awaring, produces awareness. As long as there is an "awar*er*," the illusion of location, origin, source, or cause of (fill in the blank) remains. The "awar*er*" structure must be dismantled.

CONTEMPLATION

As mentioned throughout, there are innumerable numbers of "spiritual practices" (in Sanskrit, Sadhana) that can be given. However, even in the ones below three dangers must always be "understood":

1) There is a separate "I" that imagines it is doing the process.
2) This "I" imagines it will get something.
3) The gap or void is IT. The void-gap holds the seeds of the "I" in subtle form.

Questions to Consider:

1) What "I" is doing the process?
2) What does the "I" want from doing the process?
3) **Prior to** the emergence of the "I"—are you?
4) **Prior to** the emergence of even the "awar*er*" of the *void*—are you?

"When the mind of the aspirant that is to quit one object is firmly restrained (niruddha) and does not move towards any other object, it comes to rest in a middle position between the two and through it (i.e., the middle position) is unfolded the realization of pure consciousness which transcends all contemplation. . . . (In whom does it arise?) it arises in the yogi who is deeply engrossed, i.e., deeply concentrated in one thought." (*Spanda Karikas*, p. 143)

Contemplations:

1) Find the space between waking and sleep.
2) "See" all desires, information, or knowledge as made of **consciousness**, including the "awar*er*" of the desires, information, or knowledge.

222 / You Are Not

3) "See" all states of mind as different states of mind, as different states of THE ONE SUBSTANCE, including the "awar*er*" of the states of mind.
4) Find the space between subject and object.
5) See or feel every sensation as an expression of universal **consciousness**.
6) Contemplate the knower and the known as the same.

THE "I AM"

**THE "I AM" IS CONDENSED CONSCIOUSNESS
AND SO ARE ITS PERCEIVED OBJECTS.
CONSCIOUSNESS "VIEWS THROUGH"
THE CONDENSED CONSCIOUSNESS OF "I AM,"
THUS PRODUCING THE ILLUSION OF AN OBJECT
WHICH IS SEPARATE FROM ITSELF.
HOWEVER, IF THERE IS ONLY CONSCIOUSNESS,
THEN THERE IS NO CONSCIOUSNESS,
BECAUSE THERE IS NO "I"
TO SAY IT IS ALL CONSCIOUSNESS.**

THE VEIL OF THE BODY

The perceiver appears through the abstracting process, and is part of the body. The body is perceived only as long as there is a perceiver. As mentioned in Section I, millions of stimuli are omitted, all but a fraction are selected out; that is why the perceiver sees a body. Once the body is seen by a perceiver, who knows how many "spiritual" and "psychological" ideas can emerge? Below is an enquiry into the nature of the body.

ENQUIRY INTO THE NATURE
OF THE CONCEPT OF THE BODY

Wolinsky: Where is this **consciousness** called "my" **consciousness**, which believes in the concept of the body?

Student: Here, in my head.

Wolinsky: How would this concept called "my" **consciousness** define the concept called the head?

Student: As pure energy and there are organs of perception and there are the organs of action and there are the instincts and there is a subtle body, causal body, and the body is made of blood and semen and light etc.

Wolinsky: So this concept called "my" **consciousness**, which believes in the concept of the body, the concept of an energy body made of the senses and the instincts and light and subtle body, causal body, etc. What assumptions has the concept called "my" **consciousness** made about all these other concepts?

Student: That without this body, without the organs of this body I would not be here. Thank God because of the body, **I am** sure that I will be here somewhere, because without the body concept then "kaput."

Wolinsky: Where is the concept called "my" "**consciousness**," which believes in the concept of a causal body so that the concept called a "you" has a place to belong, and where is the concept called "my" **consciousness** which believes in the causal body?

Student: In the heart around here.

Wolinsky: Now by the concept called "my" **consciousness,** which believes in the concept of a body, a subtle body, a causal body, an energy body, a body made of light believing in the senses and instincts—by that concept called "my" **consciousness** believing in all this what have been the consequences for the concept called "my" **consciousness?**

Student: Believing in eternal life."

Wolinsky: Now if this concept called "my" **consciousness,** the concept of the body, the concept of an energy body, the concept of instincts and senses, the concept of light body, the concept of a causal body in your heart that causes eternal life—if all of this including the know*er* and "awar*er*" of all of this were made of the same substance which had nothing to do with anything, then . . . ?

Student: Nothing . . . it feels like just a big question mark, like blank; so what now?

Wolinsky: And if the concept called *now* was not, and the concept of a past, the concept of a future, the concept of an I am, even the concept of doing, like I'm not doing what I have to do—if all of these concepts along with the know*er* and "awar*er*" of them, and they were all made of THE SAME SUBSTANCE, which have nothing to do with anything, then . . . ?

Student: Just *silence*, but there is also grief.

Wolinsky: By this concept called "my **consciousness,**" which believes in this concept called playing and doing, and I'm here and you're there, causal body and subtle body and hearts and eternal life. What has this concept called "my" consciousness done to itself?

Student: Preserved itself.

Wolinsky: So if the concept called "my" consciousness condensed down and created the concept of preserve or not preserve, the concept of **I am**, the concept of light body, the concept of instincts and senses, the concept of I'm here and you're there and let's play, concept of subtle body and causal body, which lives in the heart and the mind where there is eternal life—if all of these, along with the know_er_ and "awar_er_" of all these, were all made of the SAME underlying SUBSTANCE, which had nothing to do with anything, then . . . ?

Student: The chronic contraction, the knot will subside.

Wolinsky: Now if the concept called "my" consciousness, which believes in the concept of contraction and expansion, was made of the same substance as the know_er_ or "awar_er_" of them, then . . . ?

Student: It's just by itself.

Wolinsky: Now *if* the concept called "my" consciousness, which believes in all of these concepts: causal body, eternal life, light, concept of **I am**, believed all that, how could this, "my" consciousness, deceive another concept called "my" consciousness.

Student: By the concept of self, by saying **I am**.

Wolinsky: Now *if* the concept called **I am** came from the substance contracting, and it is all made of the same substance, which has nothing to do with anything, then . . . ?

Student: _____(Silence). There is a sensation in the head, like a vacuum cleaner that is absorbing everything, a nowhere, ... **NOTHING.**

Wolinsky: If this concept of a head, concept of a vacuum, concept of a **NOTHING,** including the know*er* of all of that, were all made of the same underlying **consciousness** then, ...?

Student: _____(Long silence).

Wolinsky: Now if the concept called "my" **consciousness,** which believes all of these concepts (of a) causal body in "is" and "not is" were all made of the same substance, which had nothing to do with anything, then ...?

Student: _____(Silence). This is like going back, ... much more comfortable.

Wolinsky: Now *if* the concept called "my" **consciousness** believed in the concept of **I am,** the concept of "is" and "not is," concept of light, body, instincts and senses, concept of subtle body, causal body, eternal life, a nothing that contracts, something from a thing called a head—if all of these ideas, concepts were made of the **SAME** underlying **SUBSTANCE** including the knower and the "awar*er*," then ...?

Student: _____(Silence).

Wolinsky: If this concept called "my" **consciousness,** which believes in the concept of head and the concept of subtle body, causal body, the concept of "is" and "not is" concept of **appearing,** disappearing, what must it now know?

Student: _____(Long silence)_____It's all bullshit.

Wolinsky: Why must this concept called "my" conscious-
              ness not know that all of this is bullshit?

Student: Because it doesn't want to go . . . then there's no
              . . . it's not.

Wolinsky: If the "awar*er*" and know*er* of all of this, includ-
              ing the concept of *it's all bullshit* itself—if all of
              that is made of the SAME underlying SUB-
              STANCE, which had nothing to do with any-
              thing, then . . . ?

Student: _____(Long silence)_____It is no more; it
              is not.

Wolinsky: If this concept called "my" consciousness, which
              believes in the concept of I am, the concept called
              "is" and "not is," the concept of a past, the con-
              cept of present, the concept of future, the con-
              cepts of light body, energy, the concepts of subtle
              body, causal body in your heart and mind, the
              concept of self, which has to have all these con-
              cepts to keep itself going, the concept of the
              body—if all of these concepts were made of the
              SAME underlying SUBSTANCE, including the
              "awar*er*" and know*er* of all of this, and it had
              nothing to do with anything, then . . . ?

Student: _____(Long silence)_____(silence).

CHAPTER 18

"States of Consciousness" Philosophical Concepts and the Virtue Trap

F ew people, if any, in "spiritual" circles could deny the implicit and often times explicit wish and promise to "attain," "get," "access," "resource," or in some way have a blissful state that contains not only the belief in a *permanent state*, which are deemed spiritual or as higher states possessing what they call "spiritual virtues or qualities" like love, peace, joy, etc. These virtues, which include love, compassion, forgiveness, kindness, and justice are certainly "admirable," "holy," and "virtuous" states. However, these questions remain unexamined: 1) Are these states really 'spiritual'? 2) Are they necessary to live a spiritual life? 3) Will this in some way lead me to *Nirvana* (here defined as heaven)? 4) Does it play any part in finding out who I am? 5) Does a *permanent* "state" exist? 6) What "I" is seeking this permanent state? and 7) Why does an "I" want to get or have this state?

The answer to all of these is *NO*. But before we throw too much water on "your" understanding, or burst the "spiritual" bubble, let us first define what we mean by "spiritual," and second, what we mean by a "state" or a "virtue" or a "quality."

If the goal of "spirituality" is to "reach" or "get" or "attain" *Nirvana* (as extinction), then nothing in the phenomenological world, (a world with bodies, which have senses and experiences) will do that. Why? Because *Nirvana* means extinction: YOU ARE NOT. Therefore, there is nothing that is "spiritual" or has anything to do with leading or having a "spiritual life (style)"; there is only an *illusion* of a spiritual life (style), which is part of the mirage and *is not*.

Next, where does this concept of a permanent state of consciousness, like a virtue or spiritual quality, come from? To appreciate this, it is paramount to go back to the western origins of the concept of virtue, and its roots.

More than a hundred years before Socrates and Plato, there was Pythagoras, the famous Greek mathematician. His Pythagorean theorem states that for any right triangle, the square of the length of the hypotenuse equals the sum of the squares of the lengths of the other two sides ($a^2 + b^2 = c^2$). Pythagoras believed that in *this world* (a world perceivable by the senses), it is not possible to draw a right triangle because it can *never* be exact, only an approximation. Hence, a "real" right triangle can never actually exist in the physical world. However, Pythagoras "believed" in the ideal—"somewhere" (in "another" more subtle world) there is a right triangle; *there is a truth*, a state of consciousness that is permanent and changeless in all situations. In other words, this "truth" exists as an "ideal" and the state of consciousness is *always true and permanent regardless of the situation*.

This underlying understanding of an *ideal, perfect, changeless, and permanent "truth"* was picked up by Socrates who, through his inquiry, asked, "What is a virtue?" Socrates was trying to capture a "virtue," a "state of consciousness," a *way of acting or being, or doing*, which was ideal, which is something to attain, aspire to or achieve, which was *permanent and always true*. Socrates believed that this *virtue* could or should, when focused upon, correct, transform, alter, and change for the better any vice or bad habit. Plato, a student of Socrates, followed this up with his concept of **forms**. Forms were prototypes, which, simply stated, were the "real" of which this world was merely an imitation or copy. Hence, for Plato, focusing on these forms and becoming them (even after death) was IT.

Plato, and later his student Aristotle, furthered this concept by looking for "virtues" or states of **consciousness** as midpoints between extremes, which he called the *Golden Mean* or *Middle Path*. Very simply stated,the "state between two extremes." Several famous ones are listed on the following page (the seven deadly sins, and their opposites), from which could arise, a Golden Mean—a "virtue," which was always was the "right" action, thought, behavior, feeling, etc., and was permanently IT. In other words, a standard, a reference point, by which actions could be both measured against and strived for.

In this way, for Aristotle, reaching for and developing midpoints that represent qualities or states of **consciousness**, or virtues that are permanent and "changeless," act as a reference point for changing vices (which were labeled as bad) into virtues (these ideal, changeless, reference point states). For example, overcoming passion with compassion, hate with love etc.[1] Unfortunately, these reference points or standard states then got fused with, and became, not only a determinant of behavior and spirituality, but also conceptual references point that the "I" could use to make judgments, measurements, inferences about, and comparisons with, to determine what should be done, experienced, or "the space you should come from" in life.

Now, these "idealistic" states, most people would agree, are kind of a wonderful thing to go for. *However, will it help you discover who you are? NO.* Why? Because they are *idealistic states* based on unexamined presuppositions and con-

---

[1] Here we are focusing on "Western" Philosophical traps.

Pride		Self-effacement
	Freedom	

Vanity		Timidity
	Honesty	

Avarice		Overly-generous
	Non-Attachment	

Gluttony		Overly-controlled
	Sobriety	

Lust		Prudence
	Innocence	

Sloth		Overly-industrious
	Right Action	

		Unbridled
Cowardliness		Reckless
	Courage	Action
		Heedlessness

cepts. *All concepts are states.* This raises the question, Is love a separate thing from hate, or is hate contained within love in a constant movement, as mentioned earlier with the *Gunas*? In other words, contained within Sattva is Raja, and contained within love is hate with the midpoint, which might be, let's say, acceptance, all in a constant motion or state. However, by looking for an idealistic, static, permanent, and changeless state we are deluding ourselves in several way; 1) That something made of **consciousness** can be changeless. *In Buddhism, the doctrine of impermanence is paramount.* 2) Is this not a trap, an attempt to control or bring on change or compensate one state (good) over another (bad state)? 3) Does it not imply that one state is better than another? 4) If all states are made of only **consciousness** (THE SAME SUBSTANCE), why go for a state? 5) Is love better than hate? 6) Should we temper a vice by developing a virtue?—and does such a technique and concept even work and 7) Is it not re-enforcing an "I" and increasing suffering when a *standard or reference point* is used to measure, compare, evaluate, and judge one's spiritual, psychological, or emotional health against something? These ideas are no doubt interesting; *however*, they are major traps in "getting" *Nirvana*; YOU ARE NOT. Why? Because *all are "states"; hence, impermanent, and there has to be an "I" there to experience these states.*

Why is all this so important, or why should we even bring up all of this?

Because the illusion of "spirituality" as it has been defined above is laden with traps. *Spirituality was seductively introduced to us, "taken on" by us, and unfortunately, somehow it makes sense.* In the above illustrations, there is an illusion that if an "I" focuses enough on the "good" (virtue) and pulls attention away from the "bad" (vice), the vice will lose its power and eventually it disappears, leaving a new *virtuous-"I."* This has manifested itself not only in "spiritual" circles, but also in the field of psychology, as "changing beliefs" to the Biblical concept of "conquering or overcoming evil with good."

These traps that form illusions and veils of **consciousness**, which pervade "our" **consciousness** are so strong, that they act as *seeds of illusions* ready to sprout with their enmeshing, entrapping fruit as they continue to be watered by "spiritual" or psychological theory. To cook those seeds of **consciousness**, we will offer the "understanding" of Nisargadatta Maharaj: **"You can't let go of something until you know what it is"** or Ramdas: **"You cannot get out of a jail until you know you're in one."** Offered below are the "101 Western Philosophical Traps" that act as seeds of **consciousness**, which bear the poisonous fruit of "psycho-spiritual" entrapment or entrapment in a *psychological mythology* or a *spiritual system.*

IF THERE IS NOT AN "AWAR*ER*," THEN THERE IS NO PHENOMENA.

Pure reason, which falls in the category of Sattva, and pure virtue, are similar to an archetype. Socrates asked (enquired) into this by asking people for definitions. So, for example, in one of his philosophical dialogues, Socrates enquired into the concept of justice. He enquired, "What do you mean by justice?" and before you knew it, the person realized he did not know what justice was; and that it was a concept to be discarded. Socrates also enquired into virtue, which "I" see as another seed of consciousness. To best illustrate seeds of consciousness let "me" give an example. Recently "I" was reading the famous German philosopher, Immanuel Kant. Very, very simply stated, Kant theorized that morality was linked to duty—doing one's duty was moral regardless of whether you liked it or not. In fact, one must do his or her duty as part of being moral in the "ultimate" sense.

This understanding is like a *seed made of consciousness.* Like a seed, this belief has to find fertile soil in which to take root and sprout. Now imagine this seed taking root in the California surf areas. It would not. It would be like trying to plant the seed of a mango tree in the middle of the desert; naturally, it would die. However, this seed of consciousness of the German philosoopher, Immanuel Kant, had no problem taking root in Germany, where, *as a huge generalization*, morality—doing one's duty, whether one liked it or not—is already part of the culture.

What I am trying to aim at in this discussion is 1) that the seed of philosophical understanding needs fertile soil to grow and thrive in, and 2) philosophies and philosophers did not discover something new, but rather they uncovered, as a *seed of consciousness*, that which was already present. In other words, the philosopher did not think up these things on his/her own. Rather, they uncovered an underlying unquestioned *seed of consciousness*, which lay dormant within the culture in seed form.

To review from before, the mathematician Pythagoras predates Socrates. Pythagoras came up with $A^2 + B^2 = C^2$ (later called the Pythagorean Theorem). Unfortunately there is no such thing as a right triangle, it exists, according to Plato, only as an "ideal" form, and hence, is hypothesized to exist in some "other" universe as the *perfect right triangle*. This would be the *ideal*. Plato began imagining and searching for the *ideal* of *virtue*. What is virtue? Socrates-Plato believed that *virtue* was "out there" in some "other world," and that no matter what the circumstances, it was always *TRUE*. There was *a right action* that existed in "another world," which under any circumstance (like the Pythagorean Theorem), was true. For Socrates-Plato, a *virtue* would be something that is true in all circumstances. Now, many people believe in this pure virtue and are looking for this *(pure virtue, pure reason, absolute purity*, something that is right *no matter what)* seed concept. This concept acts as a reference point that people use to *compare* actions, thoughts, emotions, etc., which forms a deep conceptual structure because in *comparing*, judging, and *measuring* actions or states against this ideal virtue, the "I" comes up short and suffers even more. And it is that search for something that is right no matter what, which obviously is just a concept that creates more pain and loss of pure **I amness**. It is this driving force towards something that is right no matter what, which is archetypical at one level, and a *seed of consciousness* at another. It is a very very deep seed within people: "If only I could find the true, right thing to do in the context of my daily life." That daily life could be my marriage, my business affairs, or my spirituality; then, ultimately, I would reach this *virtue* and be truly spiritual, healthy, and receive some reward. But what is important is that it is a concept. In therapy in the early 1980's, "I" called these unconscious standards, which organize psychological states and actions, *the book of rules*.

QUESTIONS AND ANSWERS

Student: Don't many people project that virtue onto God?

Wolinsky: All the time.

Student: That there is some right answer that we should ascribe to.

Wolinsky: Right; well, the Bible, A Course in Miracles: "Let's look it up and see what is right for us to do." Absolute virtue, or reason, whatever that virtue is. It is a concept you are searching for, the problem is that the concept called "you" is searching for a concept called virtue or reason or justice or right action or whatever. Hence, there is no satisfaction in it. People believe that if they get this virtuous thing each time, then everybody would say that someone did X, and everyone in the universe would be in some kind of agreement that it was great that he did that because it was a virtuous act. But, probably, a third of you would say it is great, a third of you would say it is shit, and a third of you would say you don't care.

Most people, "I" would say, in Western culture, have the idea that it (the ideal of virtue) exists. It is often their idea that there is a specific *right action* in every situation, which is *right* no matter what is happening in the universe.

ENQUIRY INTO THE NATURE
OF THE CONCEPT OF VIRTUE
OF PURE REASON, ALSO CALLED SATTVA

Wolinsky: So this concept called "my" **consciousness,** which believes in the concept of the virtue, called pure reason, this high kind of thing that is right in all situations—*where in the body is the concept called "my" consciousness?*

Student: It is out here, not in it.

Wolinsky: How would this concept called "my" **consciousness,** define this concept of the virtue of reason?

Student: It's there, but I can't experience it. I can't know it. It feels like a big umbrella that covers everything.

Wolinsky: So, it is an umbrella, you can't reach it. Those are all assumptions made about it. How would the concept called "my" **consciousness** define this concept called the virtue of reason?

Student: That there is an *ideal,* that it is the *truth.* That it is like an organizing principle. The number one organizing principle.

Wolinsky: Where in the body is this searching-seeking mechanism, which looks for this as a way to help it survive better?

Student: Yes, *Truth,* I think it is there all the time.

Wolinsky: Where would it be in relationship to your body or in your body?

Student: I think it moves through here (chest), but it goes through the head. A lot of it is concentrated up here.

Wolinsky: So this concept called "my" **consciousness** has this concept of the virtue of reason—like an umbrella. What other assumptions has the concept called "my" **consciousness** made about all these other concepts?

Student: It's there, but it is so subtle; it is not tangible, it is not obtainable. Very subtle; it seems like most activity is in relationship to it, even though there is not an awareness of that at all times.

Wolinsky: This thing called an organizer is like an umbrella, it organizes it but somehow there is not an awareness, there is not an awareness that is organizing it. So, where in the body do you have this structure that takes awareness away from recognizing the structure, as a structure?

Student: It is here (head).

Wolinsky: Okay, so that structure that has you unaware of itself and the structure of organization, tell me a technique that the structure uses to distract you from noticing all of this.

Student: I have to really sit with myself to get that.

Wolinsky: Okay. So, what happens if you try to get it?

Student: Well, there is confusion.

Wolinsky: Okay, so confusion is one technique "it" uses to hide itself.

Student: Yes, confusion and then it can't be figured out.

Wolinsky: So, the concept called confusion, the concept called figuring it out, the structure called it automatically has to figure it out, and the structure that tries to get out of it in some way, that is part of the way the structure operates, any other concepts that it uses to distract you from the awareness of how it works

Student: Yeah, it gets a lot of body sensations that start here in the chest and maybe move all over.

Wolinsky: Anything else that is part of the structure?

Student: Activity too, doing things, doing, I want to think about that for a bit.

Wolinsky: So, thinking about the structure is a way to distract itself from awareness of the structure of itself?

Student: Yes.

Wolinsky: We have a substructure that says you have to figure it out, or thinking, or confusion or some kind of activity, then there is a structure called awareness of it and unawareness of it. How big is that concept right now, called a structure that is aware of it and all the substructures.

Student: It is pretty big, but it is not the whole screen.

Wolinsky: Okay. So we have the concept called "my" **consciousness** and it is an umbrella concept for the concept of the virtue of reason, which is not quite reachable by your definition. Okay so it is a concept called not reachable, concept called aware, which runs through the body, a concept called unaware of it, which uses the techniques of confusion, figuring it out, actions as substructures to not find out the structure. If this concept called "my" **consciousness** believed in the concept of this big virtue out there, which is always organizing and an umbrella and substructures of confusion and the thing that runs through the body—if it believed all that, what would be the consequences for the concept called "my" consciousness?

Student: The consequences would be constant again, it is so, it diffuses so quickly, constant movement with a very subtle something behind it about purpose.

Wolinsky: Okay and what is its purpose by doing this whole structure and not structure substructure and organizing, what is the purpose?

Student: It is something to obtain and attain. Sense of coming home—I don't even know what that means.

Wolinsky: How are you doing now?

Student: Strange sensation. Things are running through my mind. Like I have never been really religious about anything or had any big belief and yet I am finding out how this still can run me. I could say I never really hooked into any real big thing, and you know, but it is there just the same.

Wolinsky: If the concept called "my" **consciousness**, which believed in the concept of the virtue of reason, which had the concept of an umbrella, had the concept called awareness of this thing running through your body, the concept of an awareness using the concept called figuring it out, the concept called confusion, the concept called "I'll never get it anyway," but still the striving for it— if all of these were concepts made of the SAME underlying SUBSTANCE including the one that is aware of it, and it all had nothing to do with anything, then . . . ?

Student: It is blank.

Wolinsky: This concept called "my" **consciousness**, which believes in the concept called **I am**, which believes in the concept called the virtue of reason, and a concept called an umbrella and a thing running through your body that is aware of how it organizes you and the whole way of being unaware of how it organizes you called the concept of confusion, the concept of figuring it out, also the concept called "I will never get it anyway, but I still have to attempt it, almost as a religious goal." If this concept called "my" **consciousness** were to believe that, what it could it do to another, either overtly or covertly?

Student: Well, it would be more covert I think. That the mere fact of that activity is somehow in relationship to this something, even though it may not be, there is no awareness of that, necessarily, at all times. Nonetheless it is communicated implicitly.

Wolinsky: Is there an implicit expectation that the other acts with some ideal "virtue"?

Student: Yes.

Wolinsky: And if they don't?—which of course, they can't.

Student: If they don't, they can go back into it figuring it out, perhaps confusion, the one who obtained that, so it goes this way, that way.

Wolinsky: If the person does not get this "virtue of reason," then, of course, "you" should have *the virtue of reason*, but of course you can't have that. Yet you should have it.

Student: Yes, absolutely.

Wolinsky: Good.

Note:
Notice how complex this archetypical *seed of conscious-ness* is on all levels. We have this concept called "my" **con-sciousness**, and the concept called "my" **consciousness** believes in this thing of *virtue or some right action or rea-son* of some sort, which, for all cases, it's right, it acts like an umbrella which covers you and organizes everything through your body and the "awar<u>er</u>'s" awareness of that. There is the concept called unawareness, counter con-cepts, like figuring it out, distractions like confusion. It also has the concept that other people should be acting in this kind of ideal virtuous way, but if they cannot, then *you should have the virtue of reason, right action, etc.,* to handle their lack of the virtue of reason.

Student: It is an assumption.

Wolinsky: An implicit assumption and, of course, if they can't either, which you aren't aware of, at least you expect them to, then it loops back into them. I should have the understanding of that virtue to handle the poor person's plight.

Now, if the concept called "my" **consciousness** and all these other concepts were all just concepts made of the SAME SUBSTANCE, including the one that was aware of it, and all had nothing to do with anything, then . . . ?

Student: There an idea that it doesn't matter.

Wolinsky: The concept called the idea doesn't matter or it matters, or I don't trust it, or I trust it—if all of these were still made of the SAME SUBSTANCE, including the one that is aware of it, and it had nothing to do with anything, then . . . ?

Student: Nothing_____Blank_____.

Wolinsky: If the concept called "my" **consciousness** were to believe in the concept called an ultimate ideal, a virtue and a concept called an umbrella, which runs through your body, organized around it but you shouldn't be aware of it, which is techniques that the counter techniques on this is going to be confusion and figuring it out in actions; the concept called I can never obtain this anyway, but I have to try, but I can't get it anyway, if the concept called, other people should have it, but if they don't have it, then I can understand it or I should be able to understand it, because I should have that virtue, but I will never get that anyway—if the concept called "my" **consciousness** believed all of that, what could it do to itself?

Student: Keep that whole loop going.

Wolinsky: This concept called "my" **consciousness**, which believes in the concept of incredible ideal virtue, which has kind of a concept of an umbrella, the concept of something running through it, that is aware of it, but also the counter concept called confusion, figuring it out and action, the concept called "I'll never get it anyway, but the other person should get it and I should get it, but of course I don't get it and I can never get it," and that whole looping, if it were to believe all of this, how could the concept of "my" **consciousness** deceive another concept called "my" **consciousness?**

Student: I think that even the whole way of communicating of even language, subtlety presupposes that there is deception just in communication, do you understand what I am saying?

Wolinsky: Yes, "I" do.

Student: In communication there is inevitably a point of reference, and if you take that point of reference and go with it, that is where it takes you. You have the two things but all things have to meet somewhere.

Wolinsky: If this concept called "two things have to meet somewhere" (We are getting into the seed of consciousness called Hegel's dialectic: Two opposing things will meet somewhere, and they create a third as a synthesis).

Student: There is this deep thing about that.

Wolinsky: Of course there is, you did not come up with that out of nothing.

Student: I did not know, where it came from.

Wolinsky: That is the whole thing. The *dialectic*. So, if there is a structure called "my" consciousness, which believes in the concept called this *ultimate virtue*, and which believes in the concept called an umbrella and the thing that runs through, and the concept called "you really can't get it," and the counter concepts called figuring out, confusion, and action, also that they should get it, but since they can't possibly get it, then I should be able to have the understanding and the virtue, but I can't possibly have that anyway, but then after all, with two points they do meet at a third angle up there. Now, if all of this were concepts made of the same consciousness of the concept called "my" consciousness, which had nothing to do with anything, including the one that is aware of it, then . . . ?

Student: Nothing_____(silence)_____

Wolinsky: Okay. Now if the concept called "my" **consciousness** believed in the concept called an umbrella and an *ultimate virtue* and a thing that runs through the body that is aware of it, and the counter concepts called confusion, figuring it out, and action and the concept called "I can't get it," the concept called "they should be able to have this ideal, but of course they can't get it, but I should be able to have that, but of course, I can't get it, but after all two points meet to join and form a new thing," then how could another concept called "my" **consciousness** deceive this concept called "my" **consciousness**?

Student: By trying to create even more of a structure.

Wolinsky: Any particular concept called "my" **consciousness** that might do that? Past, present or future?

Student: Sure. I don't know who because it so just there. It is not a who in particular, but there is a really. . . well, let's say the experience of *morality* for example, that gets communicated somehow that we take on. That this **consciousness** takes on and believes it is necessary for its functioning.

Wolinsky: So, this other concept called "my" **consciousness** had or has a *virtuous concept called morality*, which is now kind of a subtle expectation from "my" **consciousness** to this "other" **consciousness** that it has some kind of virtue of morality, correct? And how does this "my" **consciousness** respond to that?

Student: Yes!!!

Wolinsky: Okay, so it goes along with it. So you have this "my" **consciousness**, which believes in the *concept of a virtue*, and it has an umbrella and it has a thing running through the body, which is aware of it and how it organizes it, and there is a counter concept of confusion, figuring out, and action to keep it away from all of that, and it also has a concept called "can never get it anyway." It also has another here which is the expectation of the other act through this smaller virtuous way of course it can't possibly, but then again you should be able to understand their plight, but of course there is *two points, and two points always meet in the virtue of a "higher" third point anyway*, and there is this "other" **consciousness** which is now transmitted to this **consciousness** a whole thing about *morality*, which this "my" **consciousness** goes along with—now if all of this was made of the same underlying **consciousness**, the same substance, and had nothing to do with anything, along with the one who is aware of it, then . . . ?

Student: . ∴ . NOTHING_____(silence)_____

Wolinsky: And if this concept called "my" **consciousness** believed in this whole cosmology, everything from Hegel's dialectic all the way down to "I can't get it and you should get it," and the transmission of *morality*, the concept implicit that is the small and implicit going along with it, if all of this was believed by the concept called "my" **consciousness** how would this concept called "my" **consciousness** deceive itself?

Student: Again, it is really subtle but "*it is*" operating from all of that.

Wolinsky: So, does this concept deceive itself by thinking *it is*?

Student: Yeah, there is an ease in relationship to all that, all *that is that*.

Wolinsky: And it is real.

Student: Yes.

Wolinsky: If the concept *it is and not is* and *real and unreal* were all concepts that were all part of this including the one that is aware of it that had nothing to do with anything, then . . . ?

Student: Wow_____blank_____(silence).

Wolinsky: So, if this concept, called "my" **consciousness** believed in the concept called an umbrella and a *virtue* and running through the body and counter, it is aware of it, and also the counter concepts of figuring out and action, and confusion, concepts of the other person should be this *virtuous thing*, but it can't possibly because the concept of "it can't happen is there, therefore you should be able to have this, but of course you can't because you can't have it" concept is there, then you have the dialectic where *two points meet to form a "higher" third point*, now this other concept here that somehow transmits the virtue of morality, which this one goes along with, but doesn't know what it is really, Okay, and within this are all of the concepts called *is* and *not is* and the concept called *real* and *unreal*. If it believed all of this, what would the concept called "my" **consciousness** be unwilling to know?

Student: Wow what came up for me is there is nothing to know but that's assuming there is a definition called know.

Wolinsky: So, if the concept called "my" consciousness would believe in the concept called "there is nothing to know." Why would it believe in the concept called "there is nothing to know and not know," or even the concept of knowing.

Student: _____Blank_____(silence).

Wolinsky: If this concept called "my" consciousness believed . in the whole thing, including the whole dialectic—if this whole thing was believed by the concept of "my" consciousness, what can the concept called "my" consciousness not communicate about?

Student: It can't communicate that it doesn't exist.

Wolinsky: Tell me a concept that the concept called "my" consciousness cannot communicate about or should not communicate about?

Student: That it is all a lie.

Wolinsky: Why would the concept called "my" consciousness be unwilling to communicate that it is all a ·lie.

Student: Well, it believes that this whole structure would disintegrate then.

Wolinsky: If this concept called "my" consciousness achieved all this stuff, what must it not experience, or, what *can* it not experience?

Student: It must not experience a reference point without · direction.

Wolinsky: What does that mean?

Student: That *it is not*—

Wolinsky: It cannot experience that or it must not?

Student: It cannot—

Wolinsky: Why can it not? If it did, what would happen?

Student: I don't think anything would happen.

Wolinsky: Anything that it must not experience?

Student: _____(Silence)_____(long silence).

Wolinsky: And if all of this, all of it, were made of the same underlying **consciousness**, the same substance, including the one that is aware of it, and it all had nothing to do with anything, then . . . ?

Student: Then, **NOTHINGNESS**_____long silence.

Wolinsky: Prior to the emergence of the "my" **consciousness** which believed this entire structure, are you?

Student: Hmm_____(silence)_____(silence).

To Group: The dialectic of Hegel was a classic illustration of a *seed of consciousness* becoming manifest as an archetype. Now you see why some "great" philosophers lasted for so long. Hegel is tapping into some very very deep *seed of consciousness*, so a lot of people then say, "Wow, he is incredible to come up with all this," but actually, he is tapping into, or *uncovering*, a *seed of consciousness*, which is already there, but has not sprouted; in this case, very simply, two "opposing" points come together and form a "*synthesized*" third point.

Any philosophical theory, no matter what it is, is a *seed of consciousness*. Someone comes up with some understanding of something, and that becomes a school of thought, and then volumes would be written and taught at universities. This could last, and has lasted, thousands of years, or more than that. So you have a school that is teaching this stuff. *But what is this stuff?* This stuff is a construct, a seed sitting somewhere deep, deep down, in consciousness, which, if it is more universal and has fertile soil, will sprout as people say, "Oh god, that makes total sense. I will major in Aristotle, I will major in and study this "philosophy-mythology" as if it is true." *The "philosopher" did not actually sit there and think it up.* That is the illusion!! What happened is that it emerged and took root in fertile soil. And he or she wrote it down, imagining, "I thought of this"; and the reason people accept it is because it is a universal seed of understanding, which lies way way outside of awareness. *But it is still a concept, which, if believed in and acted upon, forms a spiritual-psychological-philosophical veil of consciousness.*

101 Western Philosophical Traps: The Seeds of Consciousness

Below is a list of Western Philosophic Traps (*seeds of consciousness*). Of course, the Eastern world overlaps, (like Plato's reincarnation and India's reincarnation)but it is imperative for "westerners" to look at the concepts that act as *seeds of consciousness,* which go unnoticed and unexamined, and which **appear** to be true.

Of course, the list below could go on and on, but as "you" go through them, you might be shocked to find several *seeds of consciousness* that undercut and undermine "your" "spiritual" understanding. All of these *seeds of consciousness* are *concepts,* and upon enquiry they dissolve.[2]

---

[2]If there is time in the future, "I" will devote a rather large volume to exploring, explaining, and dismantling all of these seeds of **consciousness**.

1) We are chosen.
2) I think therefore I am.
3) The mind moves the body.
4) The mind and consciousness are separate and independent, and cause external physical events.
5) The will of God is the cause of all things.
6) There are universal laws that are true in all cases.
7) The world, and life, are metaphors and symbols or copies for what is true.
8) We get into heaven not by our wits, but by the grace of God.
9) We come to know God by His words.
10) One should emulate or imitate the life of saints and teachers.
11) You should conduct your life in such a way as to attain salvation.
12) Everything you get is a gift, and you should be grateful to God.
13) The number of people that follow you around is equal to the amount of virtue you possess.
14) God created us in his image.
15) Man (the human race) is the center of the universe.
16) God or Source created us as a play (game).
17) "We have an obligation to know God ... It is our purpose, . . . the purpose of life."
18) Every time you realize causal connections, you make progress.
19) Disease arises because of your past sins.
20) There are reasons for the things that happen.
21) Reality is governed by law; law governs the cosmos.
22) Deny undisciplined emotions; never be controlled by passion.

23) There is total order, and you have a place in the universe.

24) Act within order.

25) There is a rational God who is present, and has a presence.

26) There is a constant participation of God that can and does influence the world.

27) God sends messengers to redeem and save man.

28) God has a reason and interest in you personally, and in the world.

29) You can make a covenant (a deal or pact) with God (i.e., you do these rituals [path] and God gives you protection, liberation, bliss).

30) There is a body that is separate from the Soul

31) The Soul is invisible, and is not a part of the body and goes somewhere after the body dies.

32) God is like an architect and organizer. He has a plan and an order.

33) God brings you out of darkness into the light.

34) The "vision" of God makes us happy.

35) The soul must turn away from darkness (the worldly) and focus on the light of the "other world."

36) Liberation is liberation from our bodily senses.

37) The soul existed before it came into the body.

38) If the soul has properly purified itself from its attachment to bodily things (this is called virtue), then after death it will no longer return into bodies but to "another world."

39) The soul doesn't belong here—it has fallen, it got attracted to bodies out of arrogance, curiosity, desire, power, etc.

40) Focus on God, don't rebel or resist; have a relationship with God.

41) God wounds in order to purify and heal.

42) There is a fatal flaw within us, call it whatever—original sin, etc.—that must be overcome.
43) By God crushing pride, that gives you the Grace of God.
44) It is spiritual and noble to see beyond life.
45) "Self-examination" inoculates you from misfortune and pain.
46) Worship of God saves you from pain and death.
47) This world is less important than the "other world."
48) Since all that happens to you is due to your past bad or good actions, etc., it's your fault if you get sick or if something bad happens; disease comes to someone because of an action.
49) If you become conscious of things, you can control things.
50) Truth leads to freedom.
51) There is a self or soul, which is connected to the divine.
52) You can overcome things and become a "superman" or perfected person and achieve perfection and virtue.
53) Misery and suffering is necessary for self-knowledge.
54) Hidden forces are behind events.
55) God creates everything perfectly.
56) "Somehow" you can work on yourself to perfect the body and make it immortal.
57) The substance is a space-less, mass-less, substance—consciousness exists as a stream or process; *that noumena is active and weaves experiences.*
58) If you play the game right, follow God's rules today, then tomorrow or the next life will be better.
59) Everything is possible.

60) If we all progress and do spiritual practice, it will lead to an enlightened world.
61) There is a guiding reason, a guiding light, or God.
62) There are universal rules and morals.
63) There are no accidents; everything has meanings, purposes, and lessons from God.
64) God speaks, acts, and does things, i.e., redeems, forgives, thinks, has wrath, grace, rules, redeems, rescues, etc.
65) Soul is separate and a purer form of you than the body.
66) Through outer rituals (the path), you get to know God.
67) Liberation is to be free of bodily senses.
68) There is a transmigration of souls.
69) After death, if the soul is purified of the bodily desires, it goes to the realm of perfect prototypes or forms.
70) Soul with body are returned, saved from death, and resurrected.
71) By believing in resurrected Christ, you share everlasting life.
72) (Guru) – God – Jesus takes us beyond suffering and death.
73) Since I am God and God created everything, then I create reality (i.e., If you have the wrong belief, then things go wrong.).
74) Confess and be absolved of sin (i.e., Tell your truth and you will be forgiven.).
75) If you are healed of sins, you can see God.
76) Once the flesh is purified, it becomes perfect and becomes God.
77) Human beings "enjoy divine protection in proportion to their (moral) perfection and religious piety."

78) God is in heaven "above" the world.

79) Everything is perfect; therefore, there must be a purpose, plan, or design.

80) God is the source.

81) Grace (from Greek, meaning favor) heals, overcomes disease, weakness, etc., so we can make good choices, and overcome sin.

82) Through grace you can see and understand God.

83) The soul has a spark, which is always with God.

84) We must *earn* grace.

85) Perseverance is grace.

86) Grace is achieved through a *conversion* experience.

87) Spiritual books and texts are the authority.

88) Everything has an order, coordinated in synchronicity in harmony with/by God, for a purpose.

89) In God's world, all is always for the best.

90) The source of evil is free will; *Thy will not my will, Oh Lord.*

91) Thinking something is almost the same as doing something: If you confess your sins, you will be forgiven and saved not damned to hell (more pain).

92) God allows evil so he can promote a greater good.

93) God uses evil to give us lessons and bring us closer to him.

94) There is a **source**, which has a location and origin.

95) Everything has a cause.

96) There is an ultimate **source point**, which causes everything, and it is above us.

97) God *tests* your faith in him through pain.

98) There is a good and evil.

99) Pain is compensated for; if you have faith, then you get an eternity of bliss.

100) Since even extreme pain is God's will—we should will it. Make God's will your will. Thy will be done.

101) The "love of God" is a hard love. It demands total self-surrender and disdain of our human personality.

WHEN SOMETHING DOES NOT FIT INTO THE "I's" REPRESENTATION OF THE WORLD OF SO-CALLED EXPERIENCE, THE "I" CREATES "ANOTHER WORLD," OR REALM, OR DIMENSION TO HOUSE AND/OR EXPLAIN IT.

THE EPILOGUE

THE POWER OF CONDENSATION

Maya could, metaphorically, be called the effect of the condensation process. This "condensation" carries with it the illusion of separation, and is part of the dream—**mirage**, and although it is made of the **SAME SUBSTANCE** as everything else, it exhibits, within **THAT ONE SUBSTANCE** the illusion of movement.

The great illusion is like a dream that **appears** when you sleep. What "makes the dream **appear?**" It is the same illusory **condensation** that makes the world and dreams **appear**—and disappear. *Between* waking and deep sleep is the Dream State. And it is this illusory "condensation" that forms what we call **consciousness**.

Because, as a flower must rise up toward the sun and live by the sun's rays as a force, so too, it is the imaginary force of "condensation," which animates, making "you" believe "you are."

"All this happens because of Maya [the condensation]. Maya is derived from the root 'ma' to measure out. That which makes experience measurable, i.e. limited, and severs the 'This' from 'I' and 'I' from 'This' and excludes things from one another . . . " (*Siva Sutras*, p. x)

Each veil or illusion of **consciousness** divides and "sees" itself as separate through or by the power of condensation and movement, which gives the illusion of separation, and of different substances. We can call this the power of condensation, or the power of contracting, or movement like the movement of the ocean—yet there is still only **THE SUBSTANCE**.

It is with this contraction, expansion, and movement that the concept of **consciousness** is formed. Once the contraction occurs, the **I am appears**, and makes you believe you are, yet **YOU ARE NOT**.

"Even innumerable means cannot reveal Siva [THE SUBSTANCE]. Can a jar reveal the Sun? Pondering thus, "one" gets absorbed immediately in Siva [THE SUB-STANCE]." (Singh, *Vijnanabhairava*, p. *21*)

No technique, which by its very nature must contain an "I" and an "awar<u>er</u>," can reveal or guarantee the realization of THAT. All paths, techniques, approaches, or processes must be done by an "I" and, without the proper enquiry and understanding, paths can lead only to more techniques, approaches, processes, paths, and explanations about why they do and do not work, all of which must be discarded.

Even "awareness," the product of an "awar<u>er</u>," also is only "condensed" consciousness. Knowing this alone, one is freed from the trap of an "awar<u>er</u>" gaining or imagining itself as the source or the origin of **consciousness**. If an "awar<u>er</u>" continues believing in itself or "another" as a source of **consciousness**, then it can also believe in not only the concept of source or **consciousness** playing a game to know itself (in Sanskrit, *leela*, or the Play of God), but may also believe in the deluded concept of an evolution of **consciousness**; or even a "person" who works on or with their own or another's **consciousness** by which they or "I" will get something. Obviously, this implies that there is an "I" and an "it" that is made of a **consciousness** that is separate and different from **consciousness** since **consciousness** does not evolve or expand; there is only an illusion that it does. It is only the veil or illusion of a separate substance called an "**awar<u>er</u>**"—awaring— awareness, which is part of the **mirage**, which deludes itself into believing in the concept of an evolution of **consciousness**, not *pure* **consciousness** (as THE SUBSTANCE). In this way the evolution or expansion of the awareness of **consciousness** can be understood as a concept or *veil* contained within the **mirage**, which is made of **consciousness**.

Some say that **consciousness** needs a vehicle. However, is not the vehicle also made only of the same **consciousness**? So, if there is only THAT ONE SUBSTANCE, what is there to perfect, change, transform or alter? "Imagine" **consciousness** as water, which when poured takes the form of a glass (the body), and realize that the body, also, is only made of the same **consciousness.**

In this way, why change a body, thought, emotion, or action, because it is only **consciousness**? Hence there is no **consciousness** and no separate doer (of psychological or spiritual practice) because in order to say, "It's all only **consciousness**," there would have to be another substance to say it is so. Moreover, ALL SPIRITUAL PATHS AND SPIRITUALITY ITSELF, ALONG WITH THE "I" OR "AWER_ER_" DOING IT, IS PART OF THE MIRAGE; THIS IS PART OF THE REALIZATION.

For this reason, we have these questions:

1) Who is doing the practice?
   Answer: **Consciousness** on one level, but nothing is doing the practice because there is no **consciousness.**

2) What does the "I" doing the practice want to attain, achieve, or become?
   Answer: The "I" that imagines it does spiritual practice wants to survive or preserve itself, which oftentimes is mislabeled as "enlightenment." However it is only **consciousness** on one level; and it is **nothing** or no **consciousness**, ultimately.

3) Why would an "I" want to achieve, get, or become, have a "state" of **consciousness**, which is *impermanent* at best and *not* at worst or vice versa?
   Answer: Because it doesn't know that *it is not*, and there is only **consciousness** on one level and **nothing** or no-**consciousness** on another.

When the great Sage Ramana Maharishi was on his death-bed, his disciples cried, "Don't leave," Maharishi said, "Where can 'I' go?" (If there is only **ONE SUBSTANCE**)

See you in Section III.

With Love
Your **mirage** brother,
Stephen

**LIKE A POLE VAULTER
WHO HAS TO LET GO OF THE POLE
TO GET TO THE OTHER SIDE,
TO DISCOVER "WHO YOU ARE"
OR
YOU ARE NOT – I AM THAT,
YOU MUST LET GO
OF YOUR "SPIRITUAL"
CONCEPTS, PATHS, AND RELIGION.**

PART III

The Veil of Enlightenment

BEYOND THE AWAR_ER_

"THERE IS NO SUCH CONDITION CALLED . . . ENLIGHTENMENT."

—*Buddha*
(Diamond Sutra)

"DO NOT THINK YOU WILL NECESSARILY BE AWARE OF YOUR OWN ENLIGHTENMENT"

—*Buddha*
(Dhammapada)

Enlightenment

This section brings us back not only to the origin and title of the book, YOU ARE NOT, but also to the roots of the human desire to seek pleasure (enlightenment), avoid pain (endarkenment) or, in a word, to **survive**.

Once we pierce the veils of solidified **consciousness**, which act as seeds and bring forth the delusions of personal enlightenment as the nervous system's desire to survive better, we can begin to understand enlightenment as quite the opposite.

The veil of personal enlightenment in today's "spiritual" circles are manifested as more teachers proposing their version of enlightenment; how to get "there," and I am (*Enlightened*). This has even brought forth schools with a wide range of technologies such as mantra, a relationship with an enlightened master, theories of living in the world (having it all) in some integrated way, schools that guarantee enlightenment (like a diploma or certificate if you finish the course) to get you there. All of these veils (theories) continue to change in order for these organizations to survive as the 20th century moves into the 21st century, and as the survival of the individual teacher becomes highlighted even more than ever. In this way, our "spiritual" institutions change to survive. In other words, if the purpose of the nervous system is to organize chaos and survive better, and if an organization is an extension of individuals, then the organization is also "hard-wired" for survival. This validates the statement in Laurence J. Peter's famous book of the 1970s, *The Peter Principle*: Peter's Second Principle—*At All Costs the Hierarchy Must be Preserved*. In this way the understanding of **Nirvana** and enlightenment was altered to fit the desire for survival of both organizations and people (teacher and students—guru and disciples) who use "spiritual" organizations to enhance survival. It is, therefore, no wonder that the *facts of the matter* remain not only undiscussed, but unaddressed as people's understanding of "spirituality" or religion gets mixed together with everything from community, to doing good deeds or service, to leading a spiritual looking life-style—in this way, avoiding the subject directly.

Once when "I" was with Nisargadatta Maharaj, he began screaming at me, "**Does Muktananda allow you to sit there and just ask these questions? Does he really *discuss the facts? NO*. He keeps everyone on the periphery of the wheel, and he stays in the center.**"

This unfortunate circumstance has lead to the misfortune of imagining "enlightenment" and **Nirvana** as some kind of self-help proposition. So, as we enter this last section, let us begin with three statements and two questions.

1. THERE IS NO-I WHO WILL GET ENLIGHTENED.
2. THERE IS NO PERSONAL
   INDIVIDUAL ENLIGHTENMENT.
3. NIRVANA MEANS EXTINCTION.

AND

1. HOW CAN A SELF THAT *IS NOT* GET SOME-
   THING THAT IS A DESCRIPTIONOF SOME-
   THING THAT IS NOT?
                    AND
2. PRIOR TO THE EMERGENCE OF THE
   AWAR*ER* . . .

ARE YOU?

THE SUBSTANCE

Prior to everything we see or know, including the s*eer* or know*er* or perceiv*er*, is **THAT SUBSTANCE.** The 10th century poet, Saint Janadeva, called **THAT SUBSTANCE** the *divine substance.* It is **THAT** of which, and by which, the universe seems to **appear.** We can use a metaphor to "describe" this **SUBSTANCE:** Imagine that everything is made of water, and that we had billions of differently shaped ice-cube trays, which formed differently shaped ice cubes. So too, this world is made of differently **appearing** substances or shapes and forms. Yet, all of them are made of only **THAT SUBSTANCE** or, in this metaphor, water.

To illustrate, "imagine" the ocean. At the surface of the ocean there are waves, bubbles, and drops of water, all crashing, water into water, with different currents going in different directions. Moreover, "imagine" that each wave, each bubble, each water droplet in the ocean has a different perspective, point of view, fantasized history, justification, and in a word, it *imagines* that *it is* separate from the rest of the ocean.

However, if "we" were in that ocean and began to *sink* slowly into deeper levels of the sea, the waves banging into one another, currents, etc., would have less impact upon us.

Sinking even deeper still, soon the ripples of the surface of the ocean would disappear, and there would be almost no movement. If we then could look up, we might "see" the waves, ripples, and bubbles from far away. However, from "down there," it would be easy to "see" that the bubbles, waves, etc., are all made of the same water (**SUBSTANCE**). Moreover, as we *sink* into or "*go back the way we came*," the "I" bubble at the surface of the ocean clearly is Not-me, and "we" realize that **I am not** the "I" "I" thought I was, but rather **THE SUBSTANCE** of which all the "I" bubbles and everything are made.

It is this *sinking* or "**going back the way you came**," which best exemplifies, as a metaphor, that there is **NO-I** and **YOU ARE NOT.**

Below the superficiality of the wave bubble, water droplet "I," there is **THE SUBSTANCE** from which and by which the waves, bubbles, droplets, and currents all *appear* to move and be made of different substances. However as **THE SUBSTANCE; YOU ARE NOT,** and even though the waves and drops ("I"'s) imagine they are separate, they are still **THE SUBSTANCE,** of which they are made, which never changes and always remains the same.

SINK.

LIBERATION: THE ULTIMATE GAME

Within the context of the **mirage**, there are so many games. And, "I" imagine that if you are reading this book, you are interested in the ultimate game.

Understand that it is all a **mirage**, and all is contained within the context of the **mirage**, including the concepts of bondage, death, enlightenment, awakening, spirituality, liberation, and spiritual paths.

Certainly, the **mirage** character imagines that, *they are* and *it is*; hence, it suffers and imagines that *it is* bound.

Spirituality, and over the last 150 years, psychology, aims to solve this problem. Spirituality uses prescribed rituals, called Mantras, Yantras, Tantras, or whatever. Psychology tries to solve the problem through work on your mother, your father, etc.

However, all is a **mirage**, and, as a **mirage**, there is no bondage, liberation, enlightenment, spirituality, or spiritual paths.

268 / *You Are Not*

The great illusion for a **mirage** character is to "say" it's all a dream, illusion, or **mirage**. Yet, somehow the "me" that "knows" or "views" the **mirage** illusion is not included as part of the **mirage**. *The one that says or "perceives" that it is all an illusion is part of the illusion*; HENCE, NOTHING IS REAL— ALL, INCLUDING SPIRITUAL PATHS, ARE PART OF THE ILLUSION.

This, and the "you" you call "yourself" exists only within the context of the **mirage**.

And, as long as you believe *YOU ARE*, and believe in the **mirage**, you will believe that spiritual or psychological games can save you, and the **mirage**, as the power of condensation will hold you like glue in the cycle of the game.

Of course, the *liberation game* or *spiritual game*, within the **mirage**, **appears** to be the way out; but soon, we see, we are more trapped than ever in this **mirage game**. We soon see that the spiritual-game-**mirage** only burdens the **mirage** character with more rules, regulations, hopes, fears, disappointments, and frustrations. When "I" first went to Nisargadatta Maharaj, I said, "Whatever Maharaj wants me to do, I will do." He looked at me as though I was crazy, and he said, **"Don't you understand? I don't play that game (spiritual, guru, disciple, etc.). If you want to do that, go somewhere else. If you want to stay—stay. If you want to leave—leave."** Please understand that I did not know "I" was a **mirage** or that "spirituality" and "spiritual paths" were part of the **mirage**; the shock of this was overwhelming.

In this way, understand that spirituality and spiritual paths are part of the illusion. Question and see through the falseness of the enlightenment "promise," and "see," in the words of the *Yoga Vashista*, **"Everything is made of consciousness, nothing exists outside of consciousness."**

Prior to consciousness, there is NOTHING, and as such, Nisargadatta Maharaj called this universe a "*pin prick*," a bubble universe floating in NOTHINGNESS. So, this cloud of cosmic dust forms the **mirage** character of **I am**. This **YOU ARE NOT; YOU ARE THAT VASTNESS** that this grain of sand universe in the middle of NOTHINGNESS floats in, realize the vastness beyond this grain of cosmic sand that "you" call "you" and the physical universe.

ALL SPIRITUALITY BEGINS WITH THE PRESUPPOSITION "I AM."

THE NEGATOR

One of the last things that "I" remember doing was looking to see who was doing all of these enquiries. When "I" (the "awar*er*") looked, there was nothing there, then the "awar*er*" was "seen" as just another structure or condensation of *THE SUBSTANCE.*

Maharaj Nisargadatta often called it the "*negator.*" You also could call it the "*enquirer.*" Both states of the awar*er* must also be dissolved.

ENQUIRY: BEYOND THE NEGATOR-ENQUIRER

Wolinsky: Where is the concept called "my" **consciousness,** which contains the concept called the negator or the enquirer, and how does this "my" **consciousness** define the concept of the negator/enquirer?

Student: The way or path to liberation, like opening up doors and looking through things.

Wolinsky: Now, regarding this **consciousness** called "my" **consciousness,** which believes in the concept of enquiry, I AM, and negation, which has the qualities of the concept of a path of liberation and

contains the concept of opening doors and seeing through—what assumptions has this concept
called "my" **consciousness** made about all these
other concepts?

Student: That the process of enquiring and negating is necessary, in order to be liberated and to reach this
endpoint.

Wolinsky: So this concept called "my" **consciousness**, which
believes in the concept of **I am**, the concept of an
enquir*er* and a negat*or*, which has a path to liberation and it is through this path to liberation
that you reach this concept of an endpoint. What
have been the consequences for this, "my" **consciousness**, in believing all of this?

Student: It helps to focus in on this process, as a path to
liberation, and trusting beyond reason.

Wolinsky: This concept called "my" **consciousness**, which
believes in a concept of **I am**, the concept of
enquirer and the concept of negation, the concept of trusting beyond reason, the concept of
focusing, the concept of a path to liberation with
an end— if all of this, along with the "awar*er*"
and know*er* of all of this, was made of the same
underlying substance, which had nothing to do
with anything, then . . . ?

Student: _____(Silence)_____Laughs.

Wolinsky: For this concept called "my" **consciousness**,
which believes in the enquirer/negator, the concept of **I AM**, the concept of a path of liberation
with an endpoint, which believes in a concept of
trusting beyond reason, what might this concept
called "my" **consciousness** do to itself?

Student: It would structure and filter its own experience so that it fits with the process of enquiry and negation.

Wolinsky: This structur*er*, where do you feel it in relationship to the body?

Student: Head.

Wolinsky: So if this concept called "my" **consciousness** were to believe in the concept of enquiry/enquir*er*/negator as a path to liberation with an endpoint, which could trust beyond reason, and also the structur*er* wants to structure the **consciousness** in such a way as to match this. Now if all of those concepts along with the "awar*er*" and know*er* of all those concepts were made of the same underlying substance, which had nothing to do with anything, then . . . ?

Student: Laughs_____(Silence).

Wolinsky: Now, for this concept called "my" **consciousness**, which believes in the concept of **I AM** and the concept of an enquirer/negator, and which believes in the concept of a "spiritual" path, or a path to liberation with an endpoint that also had a structur*er* to structure everything, which of course possesses a concept called "my" **consciousness**—if this concept called "my" **consciousness** believed all of that, how would it deceive itself?

Student: That it was guaranteed to work.

Wolinsky: So if this concept called "my" **consciousness**, which believes in the concept **I AM**, which believes in the concept of an enquiry process enquirer/negator that leads to the concept of a path to liberation with an endpoint, which is absolutely guaranteed to work and had a structurer that structured everything around this, and filtered everything through it, and truth beyond reason. If the "awarer" and knower of all of this was made of the same underlying substance then, ...?

Student: _____(Silence).

Wolinsky: If this concept called "my" **consciousness** believes in the concept of **I AM**, which believes in the concept of enquiry/enquirer/negator, which leads to a path of liberation with an endpoint that has a structurer that structures everything and also truth beyond reason. If the concept called "my" **consciousness** were to believe all of that, then what would this concept called "my" **consciousness** be unwilling to know?

Student: That it isn't, it disappears.

Wolinsky: Why would the concept called "my" **consciousness** be unwilling to know that?

Student: It isn't ... it would disappear.

Wolinsky: The concept called "my" **consciousness**, which believes in the concept called "**appear**" and concept called "disappear," the concept called **I AM**, the concept called enquiry/enquirer/negator process, which leads to a concept called a path to liberation and endpoint with guaranteed results, and the structurer, which filters and provides trust beyond reason. If all of these, including the "awarer" and knower of all of these, were made of the same underlying substance, which had nothing to do with anything, then ...?

Student: _____(Long silence).

Wolinsky: Considering this concept called "my" **consciousness**, which believes in the concept of enquiry/ enquirer/negator, path to liberation, endpoint, structurer, with the concept of guaranteed results and truth beyond reason—with all of these— what would the concept called "my" **consciousness** be unwilling to experience?

Student: The disappearing of these concepts.

Wolinsky: Why would the concept called "my" **consciousness** be unwilling to experience the disappearing of all of these?

Student: . . . nothing to hold, it wouldn't be_____ (Silence).

Wolinsky: This concept called "my" **consciousness**, which believes in the concept of being and not being, and believes in the concept of disappearance or the concept of **appearance**, the concept of **I AM**, the concept of enquiry/enquirer/negation process, which leads to the concept of an endpoint with a structurer, a filterer, and truth beyond reason, and if the knower of all of that and the "awarer" of all this were made of the underlying same substance as all of this, and it had nothing to do with anything, then . . . ?

Student: (Laughs) . . . (Silence)

THE "WHO AM I?" ILLUSION

**THERE IS A MISUNDERSTANDING THAT
YOU WILL DISCOVER *WHO YOU ARE.***

**THE CONCEPT OF "I" IMAGINES
IT WILL DISCOVER OR FIND OUT
AND THEN BE WHO OR WHAT IT IS.**

BUT, THERE IS NO *"I" THAT YOU ARE.*

**SO, AS EVERYTHING DISAPPEARS
UPON INVESTIGATION, SO TOO DOES
THE "I" THAT FEELS OR IMAGINES
ITSELF TO BE SOMETHING.**

**CONSCIOUSNESS IS WHAT AN AWARER
AND AWARENESS IS MADE OF.**

**PRE-CONSCIOUSNESS—THE *"REAL"*—
HAS NO AWAR*ER* OR AWARENESS.**

**ASK: "PRIOR TO THE EMERGENCE
OF THE AWARER—ARE YOU?"**

THAT SUBSTANCE IS PRIOR TO CONSCIOUSNESS.

**"GO BACK THE WAY YOU CAME"
IS TO GO PRIOR TO CONSCIOUSNESS ITSELF.**

**NISARGADATTA MAHARAJ ASKED,
"EIGHT DAYS PRIOR TO CONCEPTION,
WHO WERE YOU?"**

**IN THAT PRE-CONSCIOUSNESS "STATE"
OF UNAWARENESS, *YOU ARE NOT.***

THE MIRAGE

YOU ARE A MIRAGE,
WHICH DOES NOT KNOW IT IS A MIRAGE—
LIKE WATER APPEARING IN THE DESERT,
WHICH DOES NOT EXIST.
YOU ARE A MIRAGE,
WHICH DOES NOT KNOW IT IS A MIRAGE,
AND SO YOU BELIEVE THAT *YOU ARE.*

IT IS ONLY A CONDENSATION
OF CONSCIOUSNESS
THAT DEVELOPS WHAT IS CALLED
A NERVOUS SYSTEM,
WHICH CONSTRUCTS A WORLD
AND AN "I," WHICH IS NOT.

AND WHEN IT DOES THIS, IT BELIEVES
THAT IT HAS A PAST, A PRESENT, A FUTURE,
PAST LIVES, FUTURE LIVES, AND
IT BELIEVES THAT MAYBE
IT SHOULD BE DIFFERENT,
THERE IS A PLAN, THERE ARE LESSONS
TO LEARN, ETC.
THE STORY CAN GO ON FOREVER.

THE DREAM BODY

The body-mind made of **consciousness** is not bad or good. It is a reflection of or a condensation of THAT ONE SUB-STANCE. And, though through the "realization" YOU ARE NOT, the world **appears** like a cardboard character or a veil unraveling, floating in NOTHINGNESS; the cardboard character, also, is made of that same NOTHINGNESS.

It is the condensation that creates the illusion of a dream-body made of **consciousness** animated by the Life Force, which animates the perceptual apparatus.

In this way, we tend to not "see" or *apperceive* the nature of the dream body as THAT one UNDIFFERENTIATED SUBSTANCE.

Understand that all perceptions are animated by this imaginary division of THE SUBSTANCE, which becomes the concept called **consciousness**, even though it is still made of THAT SUBSTANCE. With "luck," the illusion of an individual entity vanishes like the darkness in a room when the light is turned on.

So, too, the dream world, body, and perceptual apparatus vanish, and then THAT VOID **appears** and reveals your nature AS VOID—DEVOIDS ITSELF (NOT-NOT)—and YOU ARE NOT.

THE SUBSTANCE APPEARS TO "BECOME"
CONSCIOUSNESS. THEREFORE, EVERYTHING
IN THE MIRAGE IS MADE ONLY
OF CONSCIOUSNESS, WHICH STILL IS
THAT SUBSTANCE. AND, JUST AS YOU CANNOT
SEPARATE THE RAYS OF THE SUN FROM THE SUN,
YOU CANNOT SEPARATE THE SUBSTANCE FROM
CONSCIOUSNESS OR THE RAYS OF THE SUN.
AND SO, THE COSMIC DUST OF THIS UNIVERSE
APPEARS IN AND ON THE SCREEN
OF NOTHINGNESS AS THE DREAM.
TO WAKE UP, IS TO DESTROY THE UNIVERSE,
TO STAY ASLEEP KEEPS THE MIRAGE DREAM
WITH ALL ITS CHARACTERS, ALIVE AND WELL.

**"THE SEARCH FOR REALITY
IS THE MOST DANGEROUS
OF ALL BECAUSE IT DESTROYS
THE WORLD IN WHICH YOU LIVE."**
—*Nisargadatta Maharaj*

AN I AM
IS A PORTAL OR GATEWAY.
STAY WITH I AM LONG ENOUGH
AND *MAYBE* IT TOO WILL EVAPORATE.

The most pivotal teaching of Nisargadatta Maharaj is this: The I AM, which is made of **consciousness**, when stayed with, discarding all else, leads to **consciousness**.

This leads to the *apperception* that everything is made of THAT ONE SUBSTANCE.

When the perceiver of THAT **one consciousness**, and the **consciousness** itself, are seen as the SAME SUBSTANCE, the NOTHING prior to consciousness is "realized" and all disappears.

THERE IS NO YOU
SEPARATE FROM THE EXPERIENCE
OF YOU.
NO SEPARATE "I"
THAT EXISTS SEPARATE FROM
THE EXPERIENC<u>ER</u> OF "I."

There appears to be a separate "I," which has both beliefs and experiences.

Actually, for the "I," its beliefs, experiences, knowing, memories, justification, cause-and-effect, past, present, future, and the belief I AM all arise together in "what is" commonly called an experience.

There is no "you" outside of the experience of a "you," which appears out of NOTHINGNESS.

THERE IS NO SELF
SEPARATE FROM THE LENS.

There is no separate self or "I," which has a frame of reference, or lens, or belief system that it has or looks through.

Rather, the lens or the frames of reference are also part of the self, which is looking. The self is not separate from the lens it views through; and the self is not separate from the world that is viewed.

When the self, the lens, and the world are "apperceived" as the SAME SUBSTANCE, then there is no-self or "I," and YOU ARE NOT.

EVEN THE VIEW*ER* OR AWAR*ER* OR WITNESS OF THE EMPTINESS OR VOID IS DEVOID OF ITSELF AND IS NOT.

THERE IS NO BEFORE (PAST) OR AFTER (FUTURE).

They all exist within the self-lens-world experience. This past-present-future concept justifies the I AM self, which is made of compacted **consciousness**, which also is NOT.

THERE IS NO SEPARATE "I" OR EXPERIENC_ER_ THAT EXISTS SEPARATE FROM THE EXPERIENCE.

IF THERE IS NO EXPERIENC*ER*,
THERE IS NO (YOU). THIS YOU
APPEARS-DISAPPEARS-
APPEARS-DISAPPEARS,
LIKE A GAP BETWEEN
THE FRAMES IN A FILM.

THERE IS NO "I" THAT YOU ARE.

THE "WHO AM I?" ILLUSION

IS THAT

YOU WILL DISCOVER WHO YOU ARE.

**THE ILLUSION CONTINUES
SO THAT THIS "YOU" *ILLUSIONS***

THAT "IT" WILL GO "BEYOND."

THERE IS NO BEYOND,

NOR AN "I" TO GO BEYOND.

With love
Your **mirage** brother,
Stephen

CHAPTER 19

There is No Beyond

The great illusion is that there is a Beyond, which is where a "You" goes. There is neither a "You," nor a "Beyond." The great illusion in "WHO AM I?" is that "You" will find out who "You" are, and then "You" will become something like "enlightened." Actually there is no "You."

ENQUIRY INTO THE CONCEPT OF BEYOND

Wolinsky: Concerning the concept called *beyond,* where, if anywhere, is that located?

Student: Here, all over my body.

Wolinsky: How would the concept called "my" **consciousness** define the concept of beyond?

Student: That beyond is you leaving everything and you go to another place, another location, and another space.

Wolinsky: What assumptions has the concept called "my" **consciousness** made about the concept of beyond, the concept of space, the concept of going to another location?

Student: That beyond is the place I want to go and I want to live there.

Wolinsky: This concept that **consciousness** has called beyond and location and a space, and I want to go there, what has been the consequences for "my" **consciousness** by having all of those concepts?

Student: It makes this **consciousness** not feel good to be here, it's trying to reach beyond, beyond, beyond—it's like beyond is a paradise, and you want to go there.

Wolinsky: Regarding the concept called "my" **consciousness** and the concept of beyond and the concept of going there, and it's a place, not here, it's over there and I want to go there and live, it's paradise—if all of those are just concepts, and all of those concepts are made of the same underlying substance, which has nothing to do with anything, then . . . ?

Student: Then everything collapses.

Wolinsky: For this concept called "my" **consciousness**, which believes in the concept of location and the concept called beyond, and a concept called a paradise, a place to go to get from here to there, different space, etc.—if "my" **consciousness** believed in this, what would or could the concept called "my" **consciousness** do to itself?

Student: It would try to *reach* something, to move to get something, to be something.

Wolinsky: *If* the concepts—beyond, location, paradise, space, movement, getting there, the concept of "I have to move to get there"—were all made of the same underlying substance, which had nothing to do with anything, then . . . ?

Student: . . . just blank.

Wolinsky: If "my" consciousness had this concept called beyond, location, space, place, location, I want to go there, movement, paradise, *if* a "my" consciousness believed all of that, how could the concept called "my" consciousness deceive itself?

Student: There exists something like a beyond, something like someplace I want to go.

Wolinsky: And if all of those concepts were made of the same underlying substance, which had nothing to do with anything, then . . . ?

Student: . . . just useless_____(Silence).

Wolinsky: For the concept called "my" consciousness, which has all the concepts of beyond, location, space, place, going there, movement, and techniques or paths to get there—regarding all of this, how could the concept called "my" consciousness be deceived?

Student: Speaking to another, this is so, so it must be, everything is made so, let's strive.

Wolinsky: And for the concept of "you strive hard enough, you get to this location," if all of these were concepts made of the same substance, which had nothing to do with anything, then . . . ?

Student: Just . . . (silence) . . . gone.

Wolinsky: Regarding this concept called "my" consciousness, which has the concept of beyond, location, space, place, striving, and paths and movements to get there—if the concept called "my" consciousness believed in all of that, what would the concept called "my" consciousness be unwilling communicate about?

Student: Everything is bullshit.

Wolinsky: Why would the concept called "my" **consciousness** be unwilling to communicate that all this is bullshit?

Student: Because even the concept of **consciousness** wouldn't *be* anymore if it realized that.

Wolinsky: And if the concepts of "be" and "not be" were made of the same substance, which had nothing to do with anything, then . . . ?

Student: Just concept_____blank_____(silence).

Wolinsky: If the concept called "my" **consciousness** believed in the concept of beyond and the concept of location and space, place, paradise, and paths, movements to get you to this place where you want to live, and "be" and "not be," what would the concept called "my" **consciousness** be unwilling to know about?

Student: That there's nothing to know.

Wolinsky: Why would "my" **consciousness** be unwilling to know that there's nothing to know?

Student: It wants to grasp something, it wants to have a point of condensation.

Wolinsky: And if all those concepts, which include it wants to grasp something, wants to have a point of condensation, if those were made of the same substance, which had nothing to do with anything, then . . . ?

Student: . . . just emptiness.

Wolinsky: And if the concept called "my" **consciousness** believed in the concept of beyond, location, space, concept of paradise, paths, striving to get there, movements, being, not being, condensing, not condensing—if the concept called "my" **consciousness** believed all of that—what would it be unwilling to experience?

Student: That it is all nonsense.

Wolinsky: And if all of these concepts, even the concept of nonsense and not nonsense, were all part of "my" **consciousness**, and even if the "I" that's hearing this and experiencing it also was made of the same substance, which had nothing to do with anything, then . . . ?

Student: . . . just emptiness _____ (silence) _____ (silence).

WE CAN USE THE WORD *BEYOND* TO DESCRIBE WHAT IS NOT.

"IT'S ALL AN ILLUSION" IS NOT A NEW STATEMENT; HOWEVER, IT LEAVES "ONE" IMAGINING THAT EVERYTHING "I" LOOK AT IS AN ILLUSION, NOT REALIZING THAT THE ONE WHO IS LOOKING IS PART OF THE ILLUSION.

NO GAIN, NO LOSS

A dear friend of mine, Karl Robinson, went to Nisargadatta Maharaj and asked him, "Should I go back to America or stay in India?" Maharaj replied,

WHETHER YOU STAY IN INDIA OR RETURN TO THE STATES, THERE WILL BE NO GAIN, THERE WILL BE NO LOSS.

This is pivotal: All "spiritual practice is done by an "I" to get something to reinforce its survival. If you are doing to get, it is *ego yoga*; if it just happens, it just happens.

Student: If I do spiritual practice, won't I get enlightened?

Wolinsky: You keep on talking about enlightenment like it is a thing, a state, something to be gained.

Student: Well, I don't like the state I'm in, and when I have a good meditation state, I want to keep it.

Wolinsky: You are beyond a state. States are by-products and reflections of I AM. They are not you. For this "I" you think you are there is a gain or getting a state and a loss like losing a state. Everything is ONE SUBSTANCE. How can something be gained or lost. What assumptions do you have about gain and loss?

Student: That it is what is?

Wolinsky: And if that was just a concept that had nothing to do with anything, then . . . ?

Student: _____(Silence)_____

ENQUIRE:

WHAT AWAR*ER* IS AWARING
THE AWAR*ED* OBJECT?
AND/OR
IF THE AWAR*ER* IS MADE
OF THE SAME SUBSTANCE
AS THE AWAR*ED* (OBJECT), THEN . . . ?

**THE BELIEF THAT "MY" CONSCIOUSNESS
CAN INFLUENCE ANOTHER'S CONSCIOUSNESS,
OR
HAS VOLITION OR CHOICE IS LIKE IMAGINING
THAT A DROPLET OF WATER IN THE OCEAN
CAN INFLUENCE THE MOVEMENT OF THE OCEAN,
OR
THAT A DROPLET OF WATER CAN CHOOSE
OR DOES CHOOSE, OR HAS A VOLITION (OR
MOVEMENT) THAT COULD BE DIFFERENT
FROM THE OCEAN.**

**IF CONSCIOUSNESS "GETS"
THAT EVERYTHING IS CONSCIOUSNESS,
THEN THERE IS NO CONSCIOUSNESS.
THAT WHICH IS PRIOR TO CONSCIOUSNESS
IS NOT.
THE KEY WORD IS *IS* BECAUSE
IT IMPLIES EXISTENCE,
JUST AS NOT-*IS* IMPLIES NONEXISTENCE.
THESE ARE CONCEPTS HELD TOGETHER
AND ASSOCIATED BY CONSCIOUSNESS;
BUT PRIOR TO THE EMERGENCE OF THE AWAR*ER,*
CONSCIOUSNESS IS NOT,
AND YOU ARE NOT.**

BEYOND THE AWARER

"Ultimate Reality is non-relational consciousness. It is the changeless principle of all changes. In it, there is no distinction of subject and object, of "I" and "This."" (*Siva Sutras*, p. v)

Thus everything is made of THAT ONE SUBSTANCE— call it God, **consciousness**, THE SUBSTANCE, or whatever. The illusion is that it **appears** "as if" it is made of separate and different substances; each veil (which is made of **consciousness**), **appears** to be different from itself. As each veil dissolves and is "seen" as **consciousness**, "YOU ARE NOT." *Once consciousness realizes there is only consciousness, then there is no longer consciousness because there is NO-YOU beyond consciousness, to say "this is consciousness": Hence, there is not ONE SUBSTANCE.*

CHAPTER 20

The Spanda

YOU THINK THAT YOU ARE;
BUT, ACTUALLY, THE CONCEPT OF YOU
APPEARS ONLY WITH THE THOUGHT I AM.
YOU ARE NOT. YOU APPEAR TO ARISE
AND APPEAR TO SUBSIDE; HOWEVER, PRIOR TO
THE EMERGENCE OF THE AWAR*ER*,
YOU ARE NOT.

YOU KNOW "I AM" ONLY WHEN THE "I AM"
ARISES AND THEN YOU IMAGINE YOU ARE;
THEN YOU *ASSUME* YOU ALWAYS WERE,
ARE, AND WILL BE. ACTUALLY, YOU APPEAR AND
DISAPPEAR, BUT "YOU" KNOW ONLY THE
APPEARANCE, NOT THE DISAPPEARANCE. IN THE
APPEARANCE PHASE, "YOU" DO NOT KNOW THAT
"YOU" CONTINUALLY DISAPPEAR. HOWEVER,
THERE IS NO APPEARANCE OR DISAPPEARANCE.
THIS, ALSO, IS AN ILLUSION OF "I."

THIS ILLUSION OF A PULSATION OR THROB
IS CALLED

SPANDA

THE ILLUSION OF SPANDA (THE THROB)

It is called the *spanda*, which is the throb or pulsation of appear-disappear-appear-disappear—the blink whereupon the "world" **appears** to arise and subside. **Appearing** and disappearing simultaneously, and ultimately not at all. The veil of I AM, makes us able to "know" only I AM, and unable to know or experience I AM NOT.

"The Universe is simply an opening out (unmesa) of the Supreme [THE SUBSTANCE]. The [rest] appears in the course of manifestation." (*Siva Sutras*, p. viii)

And as this is "realized" the illusion of cause-effect; the process whereby the nervous system or condensed **consciousness** imagines that the last "prior" event exists, has a past and has a cause or even the concept of *now* as part of the continuum of time, i.e. past, present and future dissolves into **Nothingness**. Between **appear** and disappear is **ksana** (Sanskrit for moment) which **appears**, according to Patanjali's Yoga Sutras, 10 times per second; according to other scientists, such as Itzhak Bentov, 17 times per second, **appears** "NOW" as condensed or contracted **consciousness** on the screen of itself, which witnesses an event that **appears** and disappears, along with the "I" which experiences and knows it. With the appearance of I AM is the veil of existence, past, time, space, etc.

"The whole universe appears and disappears alternately but the interval called a *ksana* is so small that it appears to be a continuous phenomena. We see a continuous glow in an electric bulb with an alternating current but we know that the glow is discontinuous and periods of illumination follow periods of darkness alternately at very short intervals. It is not only in *Samadhi*[1] that discontinuity enters in, it is present in all perceptions and thinking from

---

[1]The understanding that through the pulsation we are always going into and out of Samadhi was discussed in "my" earlier work, *The Tao of Chaos*.

the place of the level mind to the atomic plane. Wherever there is manifestation, there must be discontinuity or succession…" (Taimini, *The Science of Yoga*, pp. 299-300)

SPANDA AS THE ESSENTIAL NATURE OF THE SUBSTANCE

The first verse of this section describes Spanda-sakti represented by the unmesa (emergence) and nimesa (submergence) of the (primal energy) … and it also includes the individual is unmesa—nimesa.

"Unmesa and nimesa are only figuratively spoken of as occurring one after the other. As a matter of fact, they occur simultaneously." (*Spanda Karikas*, p. xviii)

To the linear mind, there is an appearance-disappearance-appearance-disappearance, and, it can be so described. However, appear-disappear occurs simultaneously as (IS – IS NOT) as one solid unit.

This is probably one of the most curious and difficult things to explain in language, but "I'll" try.

INTRINSIC OR CONTAINED WITHIN THE "I AM" IS THE "I AM NOT," WHICH APPEARS AS ONE SOLID UNIT. CONTAINED WITHIN THIS I AM – I AM NOT SEED IS BOTH "I AM" *AND* "I AM NOT" (OR NOT I AM).

Now, when *you are* (in) I AM, it is central (foreground), and NOT I AM is background. When you are in NOT I AM, then NOTHINGNESS and no "I" is (central) foreground and I AM is background. Prior to or between this appearance of I AM (presence)—I AM NOT (absence), YOU ARE NOT, and you are neither I AM nor I AM NOT nor NOT I AM. In other words, I AM (presence)/I AM NOT (absence) are one unit.

This is also true with the concept of *phenomena* and *nomena*. Both are intrinsic to, and contained within, the same seed along with an "I" that "knows" them.

Prior to, there is neither *nomena* nor *phenomena*, neither I AM nor I AM NOT, neither presence nor absence, and YOU ARE NOT.

Moreover, this is also true with the concepts of "inner" and "outer." It is clear that the "inner" inside me was made of THE SAME SUBSTANCE as the "outer" world, and when both were "seen" as the same, they disappeared. However, it is understood that, *a priori*, we have some kind of structure of belief, regardless of whether it is to believe in an "inner" and "outer" world that are separate, or to believe in a same-substance world (to be discussed later).

However, intrinsic to the "inner" world concept is the "outer" world concept, along with the understructure of "they are separate and they exist." Any attempt to rectify this situation implies that these concepts are true – rather than "inner" world and "outer" world appearing as one conceptual unit along with the "I" that knows them

For example, if you delude yourself into believing, as many New Agers do, that the "inner" creates the "outer," then the "inner" is central and the "outer" is background. If both are "seen" as appearing from the same seed—then the "inner" – "outer" conflict dissolves.

Hence, the very subtle illusion is that "you" or "I AM" appears and disappears in linear time. This is a "step" toward "understanding" *spanda*.

However, you and the world, and the disappearance of you and the world are contained within and are intrinsic to the same seed of consciousness—*prior to* YOU ARE NOT.

"In reality, nothing arises, and nothing subsides. It is only the divine Spandasakti which though free of succession, *appears* in different aspects *as if* flashing in view and *as if* subsiding. . . . The world is contained in the Spanda principle, and comes out of it. The world being contained in Spanda does not mean that the world is anything different. . . . Being contained in and coming out of, are only limitations of the human language." (*Spanda Karikas*, pp. xviii-xix)

In the same way, there is only ONE SUBSTANCE, giving the illusion of many substances. In this way, how can "you be," when that whole concept of *BE – NOT BE* IS NOT and can only arise as an idea to an "I" that believes it is made of a different substance than everything else, which IS NOT.

"Reality is neither psychological subject nor the psychophysical experience, nor is it mere void. Reality or Spanda is the underlying basis of the psychological subject . . . that can never be reduced to an object." (*Spanda Karikas*, p. xix)

It is the psychological subject ("I") that flashes forth, believing it IS, which is the great veil. To pierce *the veil of is-be/not is-not-be*, is to know THE SUBSTANCE that appears to flash forth, creating this dream world of Gods, Goddesses, houses, lives, and spiritual paths that cannot BE since all is ONE SUBSTANCE and hence is NOT.

"When the limited ego . . . of the individual is dissolved, he acquires the true characteristic of the Spanda principle." (*Spanda Karikas*, p. xx)

This is the essence of **Advaita (ONE-SUBSTANCE) Vedanta**. It is through the dissolving of I-dentity and ultimately the **I AM**, the primal I-dentity, which must occur for the ultimate "realization" of *spanda* to emerge.

"The experience of void does not prove that there is no Experient, for without the Experient, even the experience of void would not be possible. This Experient is the Spanda principle." (*Spanda Karikas*, p. xx)

Within the *spanda* principle also lies the witness. However, although it witnesses the principle, it is part of the principle. Although it **appears** as separate from the *spanda*, it is made of the same substance as the *spanda*. The realization of VOID is still an **appearance** or gap between I AM (presence) – NOT I AM (absence) and underlies the **mirage**. The Experient is condensed VOID "experiencing itself" without which there would be no VOID or experience or experient.

"Unmesa and nimesa denote succession. Succession means Time, but . . . [THE SUBSTANCE] is above Time. Therefore, unmesa and nimesa have not to be taken in the order of succession. They are simply two expressions of the Divine [THE SUBSTANCE]. . . It is only spanda which is *simultaneously* unmesa and nimesa." (*Spanda Karikas*, p. 21)

Both unmesa and nimesa (manifestation and absorption) simultaneously denote the "expression" of THE SUBSTANCE. They are not two mutually opposed principles. Whether the world is or is not—both are concepts intrinsic to one another and made of the SAME SUBSTANCE.

"When there is unmesa or revelation of the essential nature of the Divine, there is the . . . disappearance of the world. When there is nimesa or concealment of the essential nature of the Divine, there is the . . . appearance of the world." (*Spanda Karikas*, p. 23)

Once again, to best understand this, the concept of **disappearance** is contained within the concept of **appearance**, and the concept of **appearance** is contained within the concept of **disappearance**. Both are as one unit, and both are concepts, nothing more.

GAP THEORY

"The Yogi should be able to maintain the Niruddha state [gap] for a sufficiently long time to enable **consciousness** to pass through the "cloud" or void and emerge in the next plane." (Taimini, *The Science of Yoga*, p. 285)

Again, it should be noted that this "void" or emptiness is a subtle form of form, and contains the seeds of form.

Gap, A Blank Space, A Pause

The body is made of more than 90% water, and as the tides of the ocean arise and subside, so too, the "I" and the observer or knower of the "I" arises and subsides, and then there is a gap or space before the next observer or knower or "I" arises and subsides.

THAT SUBSTANCE of which and from which everything is made, when "sunken into" like waves, droplets arise and subside. Now, "from the point of view" of the wave-bubble or "I," IT IS.

However, when the knower of the "I" subsides, **they are not, it is not**, and *YOU ARE NOT*; *BUT*, you do not know that YOU ARE NOT. It is only when the knower of the "I" and the "I" arises that it postulates that it is, was, and will be; but when it subsides, **it is** *NOT* and *YOU ARE NOT*.

It this understanding, hopefully, that clarifies that there only **appears** to be a *spanda*, or pulsation, or an arising and subsiding. This leaves us with two crucial questions:

1) After the yogi has entered into Samadhi, upon his return into "I" **consciousness**, why does his or her psychological material reappear?

2) What is Samadhi, and why, in any eight-fold path of Eastern Buddhism or Hinduism Yoga, is Samadhi the last step?

To answer the first question: The illusion is that the void or big emptiness is what you want. However, carried within the void or emptiness are the subtle impressions in seed form of physical reality and the "I" thought. In short, to paraphrase the *Heart Sutra*, form (the thought or "I") is emptiness. Emptiness (the void) is form (the thought or "I") —they are one.

Samadhi with *NO* seeds, means No-me. This Samadhi occurs without concentration on an object (which has seeds) and burns the uncooked seeds. To explain further, Samadhi with seeds is "gotten" (fallen into) when an object is focused upon. However, Samadhi with seeds also carries the seeds of "I" consciousness.

"When" an "awar*er*" views the emptiness and realizes that it is made of the SAME SUBSTANCE as the emptiness, soon, *maybe*, the "awar*er*" sinks and disappears. However, this Samadhi (which some meditators mistake for sleep) is *seedless* Samadhi because the seed of the "awar*er*" and the seed contained within the emptiness, which is form, dissolve. However, Samadhi is the last step (state) on the eight-fold path because Samadhi is the last state we can discuss.

In short, even the void or Samadhi with seeds is a state and is part of the illusion and should not be taken for Nirvana.

When asked, "Are you in Samadhi?" Nisargadatta Maharaj replied, "No, Samadhi is a state, I am not in a state." This is one of the subtlest "points" of "realization."

"Beyond" this, "where" the "awar*er*" or the *spanda* is no more, is Nirvana, which is extinction.[2]

---

[2]Again, please note that the languaging at this point becomes nearly impossible.

304 / You Are Not

"BEYOND" THE VOID

"The sphere of the void also consists of the samskaras (impressions, dispositions) of the Citta [Mind], otherwise one who awakes (from the experience of the void) would not be able to follow one's duties." (Singh, *Pratyabhijnahrdayam*, p. 62)

The void, along with its knower, contains impression, concepts, habits, etc.

Since the void also is part of the mind because it requires and experienc*er* or know*er* to know it, the **VOID** contains the subtle seeds of experience, which is why when the gap—VOID—contracts we get its fruit (impressions) called, in yogaland, samskaras; or to psychology fans, patterns. Once Void-Not Void and the "awar*er*" are "seen" as the same, one is freed of the illusion of desiring **VOID**.

This is why Buddha said, "THOSE WHO SEEK NIRVANA ARE IGNORANT—THOSE WHO SEEK SAMSARA (the world) ARE IGNORANT." WHY? BECAUSE NIRVANA IS SAMSARA—SAMSARA IS NIRVANA.

CHAPTER 21

Neither This Nor That

"In reality nothing arises, and nothing subsides, only the Spanda which, though free of succession, *appears* in different aspects "as if" arising, and "as if" subsiding." (*Spanda Karikas*, p. 22)

"... nirvikalpa, i.e., it transcends the sphere of thought-constructs ... " (*Spanda Karikas*, p. 50)

Transcending thought constructs is sometimes referred to as Nirvikalpa Samadhi, by thought constructs where there is only the gap and even the "awar<u>er</u>" of the gap is "aware" that it is arising in, is not separate from, and is made of the same substance as, the gap, and hence, it too is NOT. In other words both the void that contains the seeds of thoughts and the thoughts are no more.

BEYOND BIRTH AND DEATH

"The world of life and death ceases to him who makes even the normal consciousness after trance similar to (Samadhi) (meditation) by a firm grip of the Spanda principle which is realized by unmesa Samadhi ... " (*Spanda Karikas*, p. 66)

This is pivotal: The concepts of birth and death, and the concept of what we call existence, act as *a trance*. Once these concepts are dispelled, the hallucination of death falls away. This means that even as the *void window* of death **appears**, to punch a hole and reveal itself in "this world," the yogi sees the *void*, not the hallucination of unprocessed beliefs appearing as this or that.

It is said in Tibetan Buddhism that all uncooked seeds **appear** at the moment of death 20 times stronger. No wonder there is such fear of death. However, *if* all that **appears** in the *void window* is seen as made of THE SAME SUBSTANCE, extinction or **Nirvana** occurs, like a lit candle's flame being extinguished. In this way, often it is said that at death you experience what you believe death to be. This is not quite accurate; you experience the full-blown fruit and trees (like a forest) of your uncooked seeds sprouting at the moment of death.

There is only the Spanda Principle, which arises as **consciousness** and/or not **consciousness** simultaneously—both of which are **NOT**. Thus visualizations and remembrances of experience are only memories and they require an "I" and they are only concluded, inferred, or drawn upon to subtlety prove **you are**—I am. They are self-reinforcing survival mechanisms designed to reinforce themselves.

"Whether it is word or thought or object, there is no state which is not . . . [made of THE SUBSTANCE]." (*Spanda Karikas*, p. 126)

THERE IS NO STATE WHICH IS NOT MADE OF CONSCIOUSNESS, INCLUDING THE "I" WHO EXPERIENCES THE STATE. THEREFORE, AS CONSCIOUSNESS NEITHER ARE AND THERE IS NO CONSCIOUSNESS.

SO TOO, WHEN "YOU"
GET THAT YOU ARE A MIRAGE,
THAT DOES NOT KNOW
IT IS A MIRAGE—
ALL DISAPPEARS;
THIS IS WAKING UP
(FROM THE DREAM).

CHAPTER 22

The One Substance

"Therefore the Absolute Reality [THE SUBSTANCE], whose own being is consciousness, who as . . . ever-present Reality appears as subject from God down to immovable entities, as objects like blue, pleasure, etc., which appear as if separate, though in essence they are not separate . . . [are] inseparable from [universal consciousness]." (Singh, *Pratyabhijnahrdayam*, p. 17)

All states from hate to bliss, from love to forgiveness, from fear to sadness, from VOID to Samadhi are only different aspects of **consciousness** or condensed mind-VOID. As you pierce all of those layers (veils) or illusion of states—even Samadhi—"you" are beyond the cloud universe and "I." There the location of a perceiver is dispersed and there are no longer states, layers, or veils.

"Every objective observable phenomenon (THE SUBSTANCE), whether external or internal **appears** as a form of . . . **consciousness**. . . . Sutra 17 says that . . . his Self is none else but Siva [THE SUBSTANCE], the Self the universe is made of." (*Siva Sutras*, p. xxii)

As the "awar_er_" and awareness itself are seen as **consciousness, YOU ARE NOT.** This world, is then "seen" as a cloud floating in the pure **nothing** called **consciousness,** which "you" are beyond, and it has nothing to do with anything.

Here the cloud universe is first "seen" as NOT-this, and the pure Nothingness of **consciousness** as "I." Later both the cloud and the Nothing are the same, and YOU ARE NOT.

CHAPTER 23

All Knowledge is Without Cause

"All knowledge is without cause, without base and deceptive. From the point of view of absolute Reality, this knowledge does not belong to any person. When one is given wholly to this contemplation, then, O dear one, one realizes [THE SUBSTANCE].... This is the device for entering the heart, i.e., the mystic center of reality." (*Vijnanabhairava* , pp. 90-91)

The heart is the Nothingness. It is **consciousness** that has the illusion and veil, which makes or imagines a cause and effect. It is the body that is perceived by a perceiver, which is an abstraction of the nervous system, which provides the cause-effect illusion. It is the nervous system and its perceiver that gives the illusion of cause and effect where there is none. There is only THAT ONE SUBSTANCE.

"ALL THAT HAPPENS IS THE CAUSE OF ALL THAT HAPPENS."

Nisargadatta Maharaj

DHARMAS SHOULD BE FORSAKEN.

(*Diamond Sutra*)

**DHARMAS, RULES, PATHS, AND
THE "SPIRITUAL" GAME AND LIFE(STYLE)
SHOULD BE FORSAKEN AND "SEEN" AS
A SEDUCTIVE VEIL OF CONSCIOUSNESS.**

**THERE ARE NEITHER BEINGS NOR NON-BEINGS
. . . BEINGS ARE NOT IN TRUTH BEINGS,
EVEN THOUGH HE HAS CALLED THEM BEINGS."**

(*Diamond Sutra*, p 25)

EPILOGUE

Enlightenment Is Not

How does one end a book called **YOU ARE NOT**?

Since *personal enlightenment is not*, perhaps the words of the Buddha would be apropos.
A questioner asked the Buddha, "Have you attained?" Buddha replied, "**I cannot claim that I have attained because I have attained.**" (*Diamond Sutra*)

This most crucial understanding also exists in the Guru Gita, namely "Those who claim to know me know me not.".
. . Nothing else but the SELF (THE SUBSTANCE) exists.

Why is there no personal enlightenment? Because *YOU. Are Not*, and since YOU ARE NOT, how can a "You," which *IS NOT*, possess, be, or have a thing or state—in this case, a personal enlightenment?
So how can one *claim* to attain when *They Are Not*?

EACH PARTI(CLE) OR I-DENTITY OBSERVER, AWAR*ER*, CONSCIOUSNESS, ETC., ARE POINTS OF VIEW WITHIN THE SUBSTANCE, AND ARE MADE OF THE SUBSTANCE. WHEN THEY DISSOLVE YOU ARE NOT.

I AM is like a particle of sand floating in the NOTHING-NESS, which, although it **appears** as different from the NOTH-INGNESS, it is the SAME SUBSTANCE and is pure NOTH-INGNESS. But even NOTHINGNESS means nothing because it, too, IS NOT. Why? Because it would require an "I" or an I am or an "awar*er*" to say that the NOTHINGNESS is or was. This would make the nothing into a something, which it is not. In this way, *not only the concept of I AM, but also the concept of a being, as well as the concept of Nirvana, is not.* The Buddha said:

"ALTHOUGH INNUMERABLE BEINGS HAVE THUS BEEN LED TO NIRVANA, NO BEING AT ALL HAS BEEN LED TO NIRVANA." (*Diamond Sutra*)

So to end this, I will recall a time when I was with Baba Prakashananda and I asked him about *liberation*. First he asked me what I meant by liberation. I said something like "bliss, oneness, merging," etc., which even as it left my lips, "I" knew they were concepts. He then said this to me:

"YOU DON'T WANT LIBERATION, BECAUSE IF YOU HAVE LIBERATION, YOU WON'T BE THERE TO APPRECIATE IT."

With Love
Your **mirage** brother,
Stephen

BY THE WAY.........

THERE IS NO CENTER OR NOT CENTER.
THERE IS NO ORIGIN OR NOT ORIGIN.
THERE IS NO ORIGINAL CAUSE
OR NOT ORIGINAL CAUSE.
THERE IS NO SOURCE OR NOT SOURCE.
THERE IS NO ORIGINAL BEING OR NOT BEING.

AND BY THE WAY, THERE IS NO
ONE SUBSTANCE
OR
MANY SUBSTANCES,

OR, AS THE BUDDHA SAID,
"THERE IS NO FUNDAMENTAL REALITY"
BECAUSE THERE WOULD HAVE TO BE AN "I"
THERE TO SAY IT WAS SO.
THEY ARE ALL JUST A PLAY OF CONCEPTS
AND
THEY ARE NOT
AND

YOU ARE NOT.

BYE-BYE

REFERENCES

* Means a must read.

American College Dictionary. (1963). New York: Random House.

Aranja, H. (1983). Yoga philosophy of Patanjali. Albany, NY: State University of New York Press.

Bahirjit, B.B. (1963). The Amritanubhava of Janadeva. Bombay: Sirun Press.

*Balsekar, R. (1982). Pointers from Nisargadatta Maharaj. Durham, NC: Acorn Press.

Bentov, I. (1977). Stalking the wild pendulum. Rochester, Vermont: Destiny Books.

Bohm, D. (1951). Quantum theory. London: Constable.

_____ (1980). Wholeness and the implicit order. London: Ark Paperbacks.

Bois, J. S. (1978). The art of awareness: A textbook on general semantics and epistemics (3rd ed.). Dubuque, IA: William C. Brown Co.

Bourland, Jr., D. D, & Johnston, P. D. (1991). To be or not: An e-prime anthology. San Francisco: International Society for General Semantics.

*Buddha. (1969). Diamond Sutra. (A. F. Price & M.-L. Wong, trans.).Boulder, CO: Shambhala.

*Buddhist Text Translation Society. (1980). The heart sutra and commentary. San Francisco: Buddhist Text Translation Society.

*Capra, F. (1976). The tao of physics. New York: Bantam Books.

*Chisholm, F. P. (1945). Introductory lectures on general semantics. Brooklyn, NY: Institute of General Semantics.

*Dunn, J. (Ed.). (1982). Seeds of consciousness. New York, NY: Grove Press.

* _____ (1985). Prior to consciousness. Durham, NC: Acorn Press.

* _____ (1994). Consciousness and the absolute. Durham, NC: Acorn Press.

Edinger, E. (1992). *Ego and the archetype: Individualization and the religious function of the archetype.* Boston, MA: Shambhala.

Encyclopedia of eastern philosophy and religion. (1989). Boston, MA: Shambala Press.

Gleick, J. (1987). *Chaos.* New York: Penguin Books.

*Godman, D. (1985). *The teaching of Ramana Maharishi.* London: Ankara.

Gregory, R. L. (1970). *The intelligent eye.* New York: McGraw-Hill.

Gregory, R. L. (1978). *Eye and brain: The psychology of seeing* (3rd ed.). New York: McGraw-Hill.

Hawking, S. (1988). *A brief history of time.* New York: Bantam Books.

Hayakawa, S. I. (1978). *Language in thought and action* (4th ed.). New York: Harcourt, Brace, Jovanovich.

Hua, T. (1980). *Surangama sutra.* San Francisco: Buddhist Text Translation Society.

*Ichazo, O. (1993). *The fourteen pillars of perfect recognition.* New York: The Arica Institute.

Isherwood, C., & Prhnavarla, S. (1953). *How to know God: The yoga of Patanjali.* CA: New American Library.

Iyer, R. (Ed.). (1983). *The diamond sutra.* New York: Concord Grove Press.

Janssen, G. E. (Ed.). (1962). *Selections from science and sanity.* Brooklyn, NY: Institute of General Semantics.

Jnaneshwar. (1969). *Jnaneshwari, a song-sermon on the Bhagavad Gita.* Bombay, India: Blackie & Sons Publishers.

Johnson, W. (1946). *People in quandaries: The semantics of personal adjustment.* New York: Harper.

Kaku, M. (1987). *Beyond Einstein: The cosmic quest for the theory of the universe.* New York: Bantam.

*_____ (1994). *Hyperspace.* New York: Anchor-Doubleday.

Korzybski, A. (1947). *Historical note on the structural differential* (audiocassette tape). Brooklyn, NY: Institute of General Semantics, 1947). The text of this audiotape appears in *Alfred Korzybski: Collected Writings—1920-1950* (M. Kendig, Ed.). Brooklyn, NY: Institute of General Semantics, 1990).

_____ (1950). *Manhood of humanity* (2nd ed.). Brooklyn, NY: Institute of General Semantics.

_____ (1993). *Science and sanity: An introduction to non-aristotelian systems and general semantics* (5th ed.). Brooklyn, NY: Institute of General Semantics.

Krishnamurti, U. G. (1984). *The mystique of enlightenment: The unrational ideas of a man called U.G.* New York: Coleman.

_____ (1997). *The courage to stand alone.* New York: Plover Press.

_____ (1988). *The mind is myth: Disquieting conversations with the man called U.G.* India: Dinesh Publications.

Mishra, R. S. (1968). *The textbook of yoga psychology of Patanjali's yoga sutras in all modern psychological disciplines.* New York: Julian Press/Crown Press.

Mookerjit, A. (1971). *Tantra asana. A way to self-realization.* Basel, Switzerland: Ravi Kumar.

Mueller, C. G. (1965). *Sensory psychology.* Englewood Cliffs, NJ: Prentice-Hall, Inc.

Muktananda, S. (1974). *Play of consciousness.* Ganeshpuri, India: Shree Gurudev Ashram.

_____ (1978). *I am that: The science of hamsa.* New York: S.Y.D.A. Foundation.

Natoli, J. (1997). *A primer to post modernity,* Malden, MA: Blackwell.

*Nisargadatta M. (1973). *I am that.* Durham, NC: Acorn Press.

Orage, A. R. (1974). *On love.* New York: Samuel Weiser.

*Osborne, A. (1960). *The collected works of Ramana Maharshi,* York Beach, ME: Samuel Weiser.

Ouspensky, P. D. (1949). *In search of the miraculous.* New York: Harcourt, Brace and World.

*Powell, R. (Ed.). (1987) *The nectar of the Lord's feet.* England: Element Books. (Published in 1997 as *The nectar of immortality.* San Diego, CA: Blue Dove Press.)

*_____ (1994). *The ultimate medicine.* San Diego, CA: Blue Dove Press.

*_____ (1996). *The experience of nothingness.* San Diego, CA: Blue Dove Press.

*Pula, R. P. (1979). *General Semantics Seminar.* San Diego, CA: Educational Cassettes, Inc., Album IV-D (A set of 6 audiotapes distributed by the Institute of General Semantics).

*Sawin, G. G. (1985/in press). The structural differential: Alfred Korzybski's general semantics diagram. In *Et cetera: A Review of General Semantics.* Concord, CA: International Society for General Semantics.

Shah, I. (1978). *Learning how to learn: Psychology and spirituality in the Sufi way.* San Francisco: Harper & Row.

*Singh, J. (1963). *Pratyabhijnahrdayam: The secret of self recognition.* Delhi, India: Motilal Banarsidass.

*———— (1979). *Siva Sutra: The yoga of supreme identity.* Delhi, India: Motilal Banarsidass.

*———— (1979). *Vijnanabhairava: Divine consciousness.* Delhi, India: Motilal Banarsidass.

*———— (1980). *Spanda karikas: Lessons in the divine pulsation,* Delhi, India: Motilal Banarsidass.

Suzuki, S. (1970). *Zen mind, beginner's mind.* New York: Weatherhill.

*Taimini, I. K. (1961). *The science of yoga.* Wheaton, IL: Theosophical Publishing House.

Talbot, M. (1987). *Beyond the quantum.* New York: Bantam Books.

Venkatesanawda, S. (1976). *The supreme yoga.* Melbourne, Australia: Chiltern Yoga Trust.

*Weinberg, H. L. (1959). *Levels of knowing and existence: Studies in general semantics.* Brooklyn, NY: Institute of General Semantics.

Weiss, T. M., Moran, E. V., & Cottle, E. (1975). *Education for adaptation and survival.* San Francisco: International Society for General Semantics.

Wolinsky, S. H. (1991). *Trances people live: Healing approaches to quantum psychology.* Norfolk, CT: Bramble Co.

*———— (1993). *Quantum consciousness.* Norfolk, CT: Bramble Books.

———— (1993). *The dark side of the inner child.* Norfolk, CT: Bramble Co.

———— (1994). *The tao of chaos: Quantum consciousness* (Vol. II). Norfolk, CT: Bramble Books.

———— (1995). *Hearts on fire: The tao of meditation.* Capitola, CA: Quantum Institute.

———— (1999). *The way of the human, Vol. I,* Capitola, CA: Quantum Institute.

———— (1999). *The way of the human, Vol. II,* Capitola, CA: Quantum Institute.

*———— (1999). *The way of the human, Vol. III,* Capitola, CA: Quantum Institute.

*———— (2000). *I am that I am: A tribute to Sri Nisargadatta Maharaj,* Capitola, CA: Quantum Institute.

BOOKS OF RELATED INTEREST

DANCING WITH THE VOID
The Innerstandings of a Rare-born Mystic
Sunyata
ISBN: 81-7822-134-9

TEN UPANISHADS OF FOUR VEDAS
Ram K. Piparaiya
ISBN: 81-7822-159-4

DIALOGUES ON REALITY
An Exploration into the Nature of Our Ultimate Identity
Robert Powell
ISBN: 81-7822-140-3

SATISFYING OUR INNATE DESIRE
Roy Eugene Davis
ISBN: 81-7822-198-5

COME, COME, YET AGAIN COME
Osho
ISBN: 81-7822-154-3

SILENCE SPEAKS
Baba Hari Dass
ISBN: 81-7822-172-1

I AM THAT I AM
A Tribute to Sri Nisargadatta Maharaj
Stephen Wolinsky,
ISBN: 81-7822-262-0

PATH WITHOUT FORM
A Journey into the Realm Beyond Thought
Robert Powell
ISBN: 81-7822-135-7

GETTING TO WHERE YOU ARE
The Life of Meditation
Steven Harrison
ISBN: 81-7822-202-7

KARMA AND CHAOS
New and Collected Essays on Vipassana Meditation
Paul R. Fleischman
ISBN: 81-7822-177-2

SUPERCONSCIOUSNESS
How to Benefit from Emerging Spiritual Trends
J. Donald Walters
ISBN: 81-7822-026-1

CAN YOU LISTEN TO A WOMAN
A Man's Journey to the Heart
David Forsee
ISBN: 81-7822-112-8

THE SCIENCE OF GOD-REALIZATION
Knowing Our True Nature and Our Relationship with the Infinite
Roy Eugene Davis
ISBN: 81-7822-082-2

THE SELF-REVEALED KNOWLEDGE THAT LIBERATES THE SPIRIT

Roy Eugene Davis
ISBN: 81-7822-050-4

BEYOND RELIGION
Meditations on Our True Nature
Robert Powell
ISBN: 81-7822-139-x

DISCOVERING THE REALM BEYOND APPEARANCE
Pointers to the Inexpressible
Robert Powell
ISBN: 81-7822-130-6

REBELLION, REVOLUTION AND RELIGIOUSNESS
Osho
ISBN: 81-7822-149-7

9 SECRETS OF SUCCESSFUL MEDITATION
Samprasad Vinod
ISBN: 81-7822-137-3

THE YOGA OF SELF-PERFECTION
Based on Sri Aurobindo's Synthesis of Yoga
M.P. Pandit
ISBN: 81-7822-077-6

SOUL QUEST
Journey from Death to Immortality
Anand Krishna
ISBN: 81-7822-234-5

THE YOGA OF WORKS
Based on Sri Aurobindo's Synthesis of Yoga
M.P. Pandit
ISBN: 81-7822-079-2

KUNDALINI YOGA
A Brief Study of Sir John Woodroffe's "The Serpent Power"
M.P. Pandit
ISBN: 81-7822-076-8

THE YOGA OF LOVE
Based on Sri Aurobindo's Synthesis of Yoga
M.P. Pandit
ISBN: 81-7822-057-1

THE YOGA OF KNOWLEDGE
Based on Sri Aurobindo's Synthesis of Yoga
M.P. Pandit
ISBN: 81-7822-078-4